MW01181812

August 30, 2021

April,

For someone who always goes beyond.. My friend! Thank You for everything

Your Friend

Kelly [illegible]

THE BOOK OF MATTHEW: FOR JESUS

KELLY KAYE AUKER

WestBow Press books may be ordered through booksellers or by contacting:

WestBow Press
A Division of Thomas Nelson & Zondervan
1663 Liberty Drive
Bloomington, IN 47403
www.westbowpress.com
844-714-3454

Interior Image Credit: Kelly Kaye Auker

Scripture taken from the King James Version of the Bible.

ISBN: 978-1-6642-2655-5 (sc)
ISBN: 978-1-6642-2656-2 (e)

Library of Congress Control Number: 2021904508

Print information available on the last page.

WestBow Press rev. date: 03/27/2021

THE BOOK OF

MATTHEW: FOR JESUS

KELLY KAYE AUKER

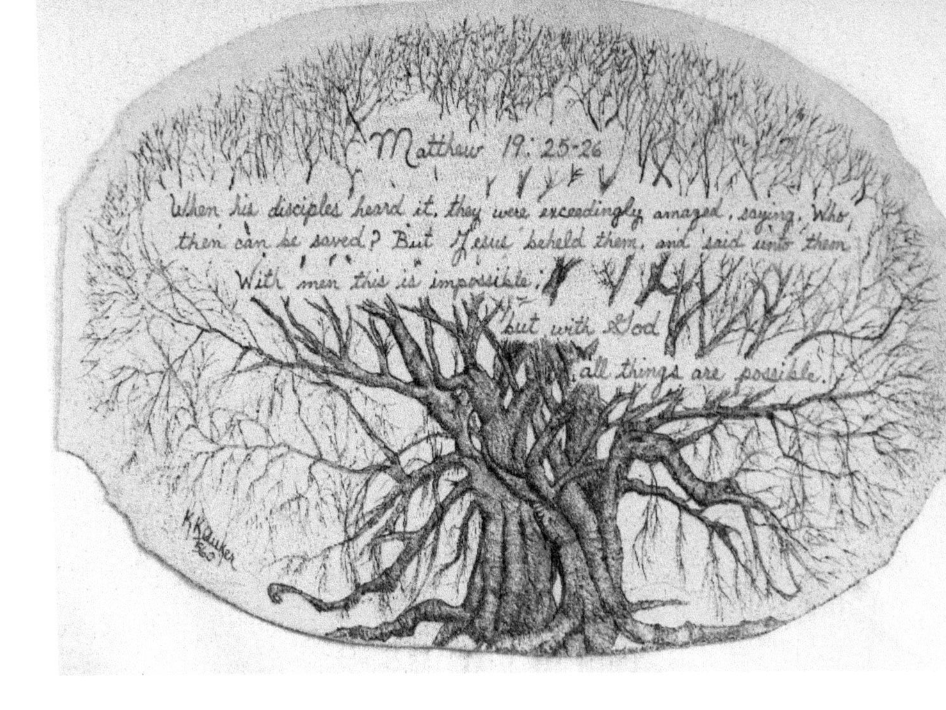
Matthew 19:25-26
When his disciples heard it, they were exceedingly amazed, saying, Who
then can be saved? But Jesus beheld them, and said unto them
With men this is impossible;
but with God
all things are possible.

Contents

PREFACE

My Father in heaven gave me many gifts, just like you, but at 55 I would receive a special gift. A gift no other had been given, at least to my knowledge. A gift like many receive, to be an artist. But my gift was specific. To transcribe and illustrate The Bible. The Holy Bible. After a few years of transcribing many pieces of work I was not really understanding the gift I was given. I questioned what I was doing. I had many pieces of scriptures, but I was lost at what to do with my gift. It was peaceful work, but it brought in only enough for supplies. One day in October of 2015 I gave the gift back to God. Done. I told him I tried, but it was too much. I had no direction and was not clear what to do with what I had done. Do I give it away? Do I hold onto it? I was confused. How long Lord, how long do I do this? When I had sought out help in the past from churches, Pastors told me I was confused. This was no job for one person. The current complaining session lasted a few hours before I left on an errand, only to return minutes later, sitting with the Holy Bible in front of me, like so many times. I closed my eyes, thumbed to a page, twirled my finger and pointed to a scripture that I would transcribe next. Only this time, it was different. I read it once and stopped. Was God talking to me? I read it again. This my vision, to write and put the bible on tablets. I felt amazed as he told me specifically what I was to do with my gift. And again, he would speak to me as I wait impatiently for him because I am human, and he says to me:

Habakkuk 2:1-3

The very next morning when I awoke, I knew I was to transcribe the entire Book of Matthew. It was as clear as my name is to me.

A gift to the world to explain Jesus Christ, the Savior, the Son of man. Who, what and why his Son walked the earth in a collection of art and words. A gift for Jesus, 2000 years after his birth. A gift to anyone who cares to look upon the possible. To read it in pieces, a little at a time, or all at once.

Dedication

The Book of Matthew is ultimately a work that I did for Jesus Christ our Savior. It is he who brought with him divinity, grace, hope, faith, joy and love. It is he whom God is well pleased. For that, I shall follow. His road is my road. Sometimes the high road is the most difficult, but the high road gives you rewards every day of your life. And an inside peace of knowing why you are.

Also, to my family, who stood beside me watching and helping me go through this journey. Through the confusion of what I was doing, to the finish, my husband Patrick was always there believing in me and my calling. Encouraging me when I would procrastinate. My family and their blind faith, never faltering as I had my visions to rely on. They relied on me and my faith. I thank them all for the courage and inspiration necessary to complete this task given to me from the Lord above. I would not have completed it without you. You are the instruments in my orchestra. I love you all so very much. Patrick, Patrisha, Jay, Brandy, Todd, LeRoy, Lindsay, Chrystell, Jeremy, Mindy, Kayedance, Jaymasen, Cody, Austin, Pearly, Trina, Dominic, Hazel, Joni, Bailey and Coy. It is you who inspire me to do my best. For you are my precious rewards of this world. You were here watching, touching, reading and feeling each piece with me as they slowly came together for this book. It is a great honor to call you my own.

Matthew 1:1-3 The book of the generation of Jesus Christ, the son of David, the son of Abraham. Abraham begat Isaac; and Isaac begat Jacob; and Jacob begat Judas and his brethren; And Judas begat Phares and Zara of Thamar; and Phares begat Esrom; and Esrom begat Aram;

KKAnker
539

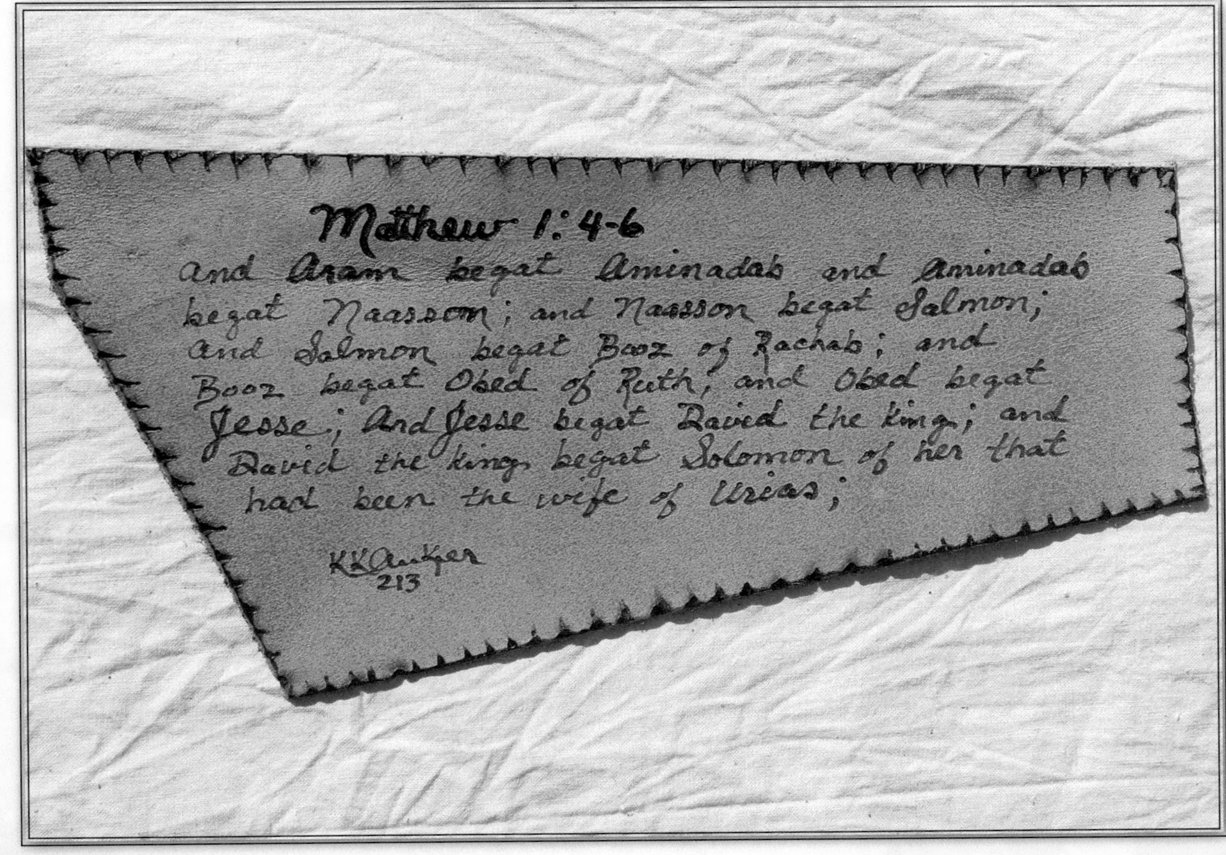

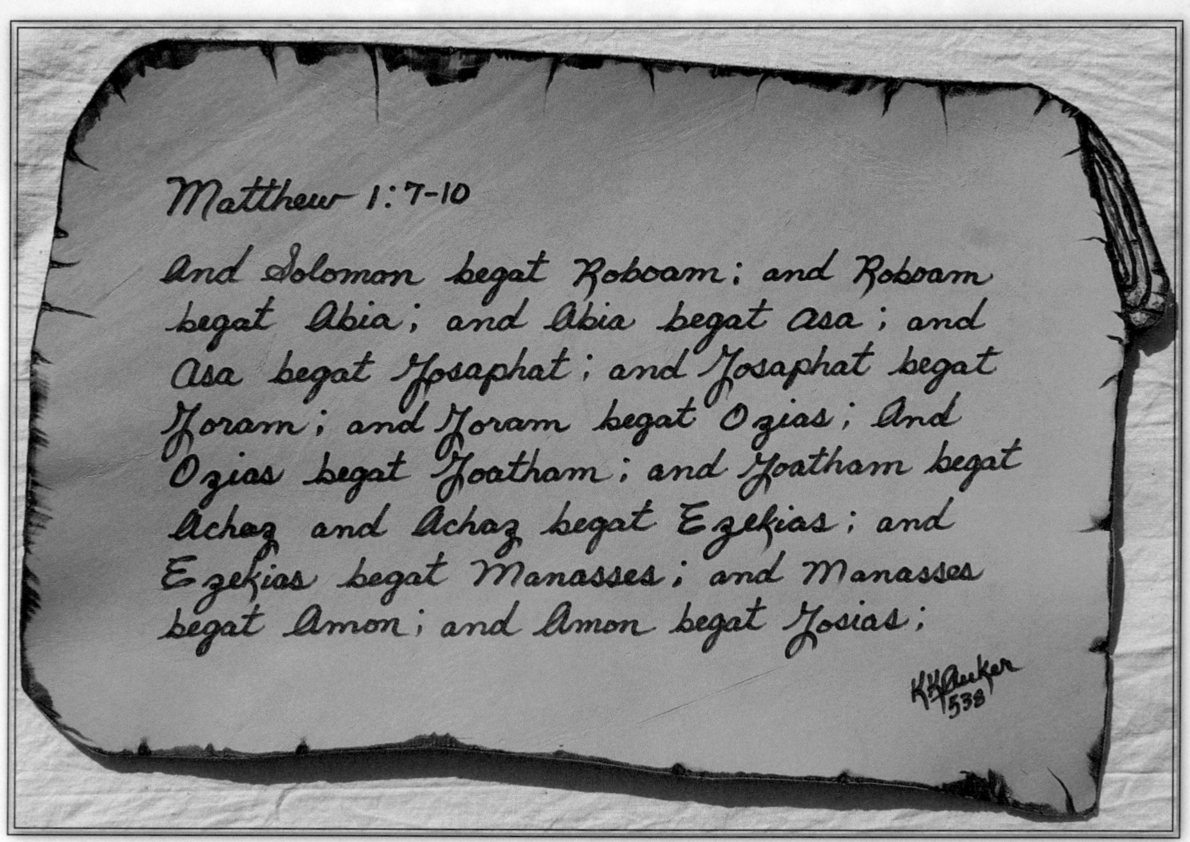

Matthew 1:11
And Josias begat
Jechonias and his
brethren, about the
time they were
carried away
to Babylon;

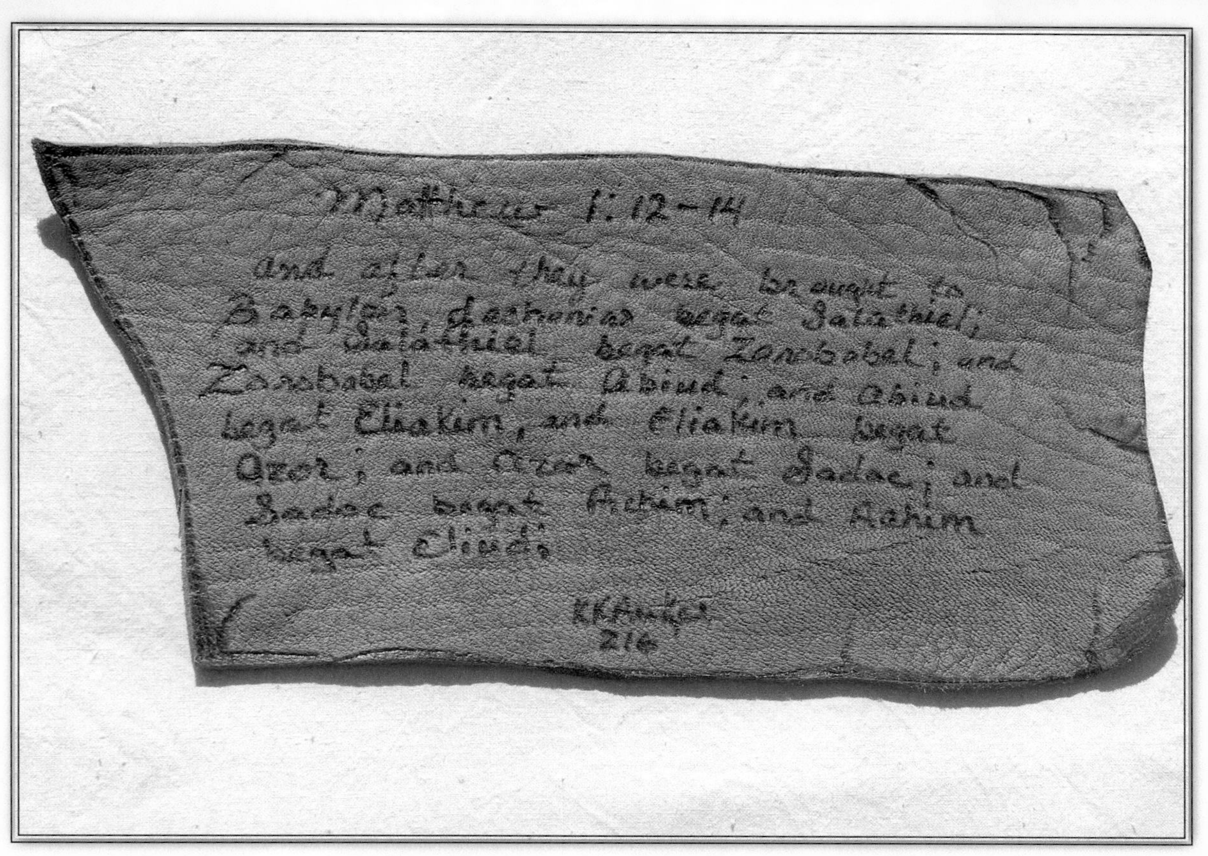
Matthew 1:12-14
And after they were brought to
Babylon, Jechonias begat Salathiel;
and Salathiel begat Zorobabel; and
Zorobabel begat Abiud; and Abiud
begat Eliakim; and Eliakim begat
Azor; and Azor begat Sadoc; and
Sadoc begat Achim; and Achim
begat Eliud;
KKAuker
216

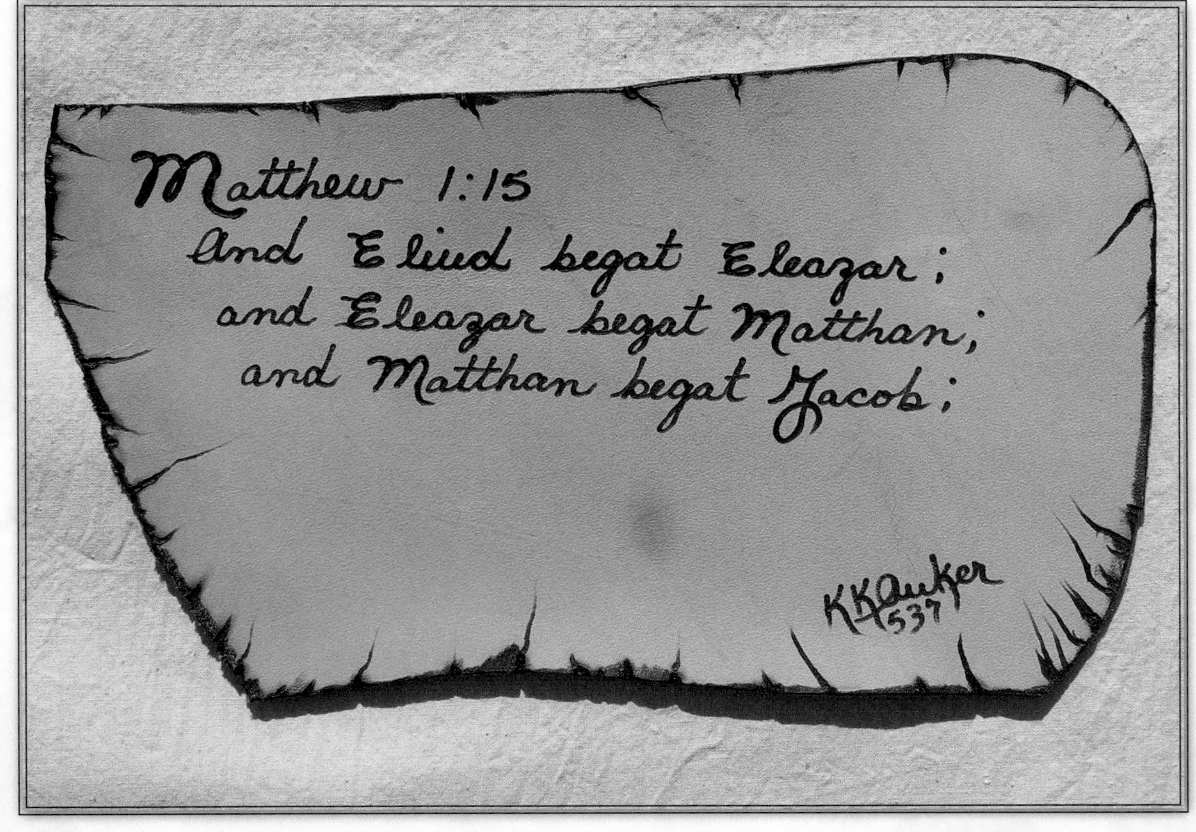
Matthew 1:15
And Eliud begat Eleazar;
and Eleazar begat Matthan;
and Matthan begat Jacob;
KKAuker
537

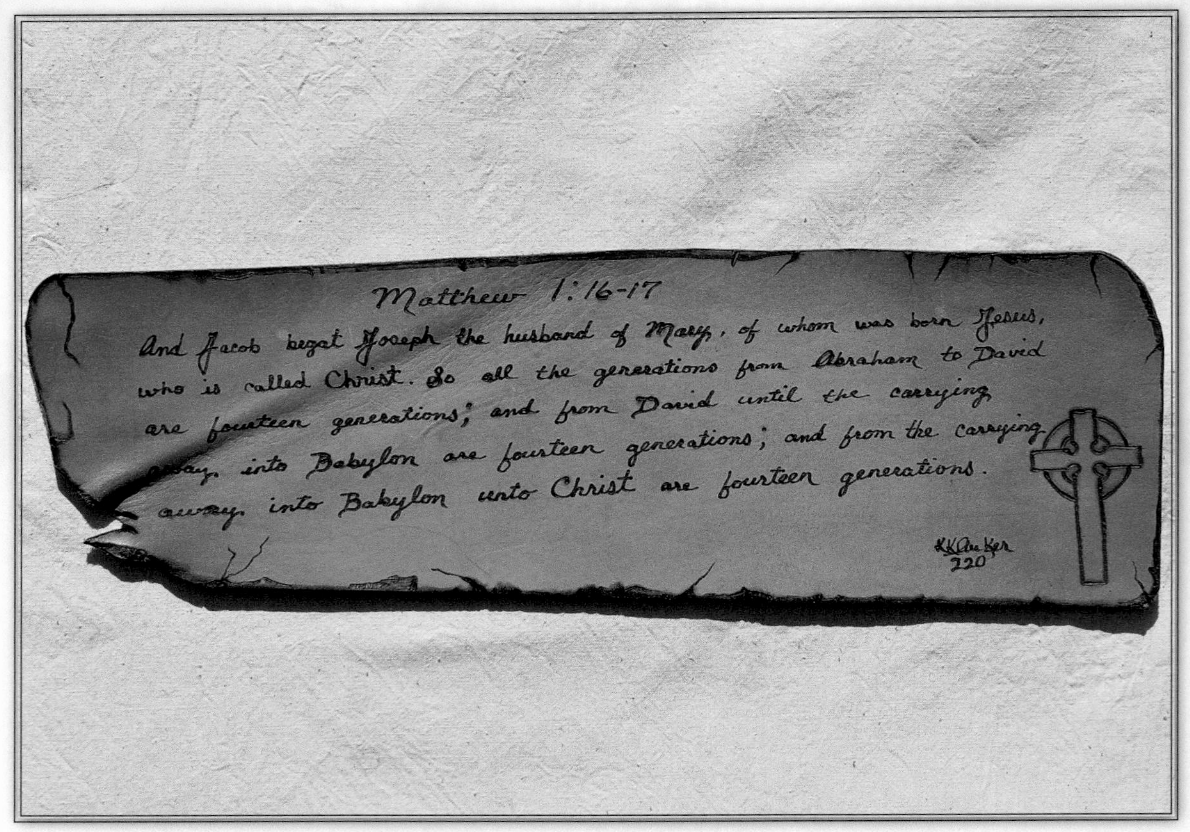
Matthew 1:16-17
And Jacob begat Joseph the husband of Mary, of whom was born Jesus,
who is called Christ. So all the generations from Abraham to David
are fourteen generations; and from David until the carrying
away into Babylon are fourteen generations; and from the carrying
away into Babylon unto Christ are fourteen generations.
KKAnker
220

Matthew 1:18
Now the birth of Jesus Christ was on this wise:
When as his mother Mary was espoused to Joseph,
before they came together she was found with
child of the Holy Ghost.

Matthew 1:19

Then Joseph her husband, being a just man, and not willing to make her a publick example, was minded to put her away privily.

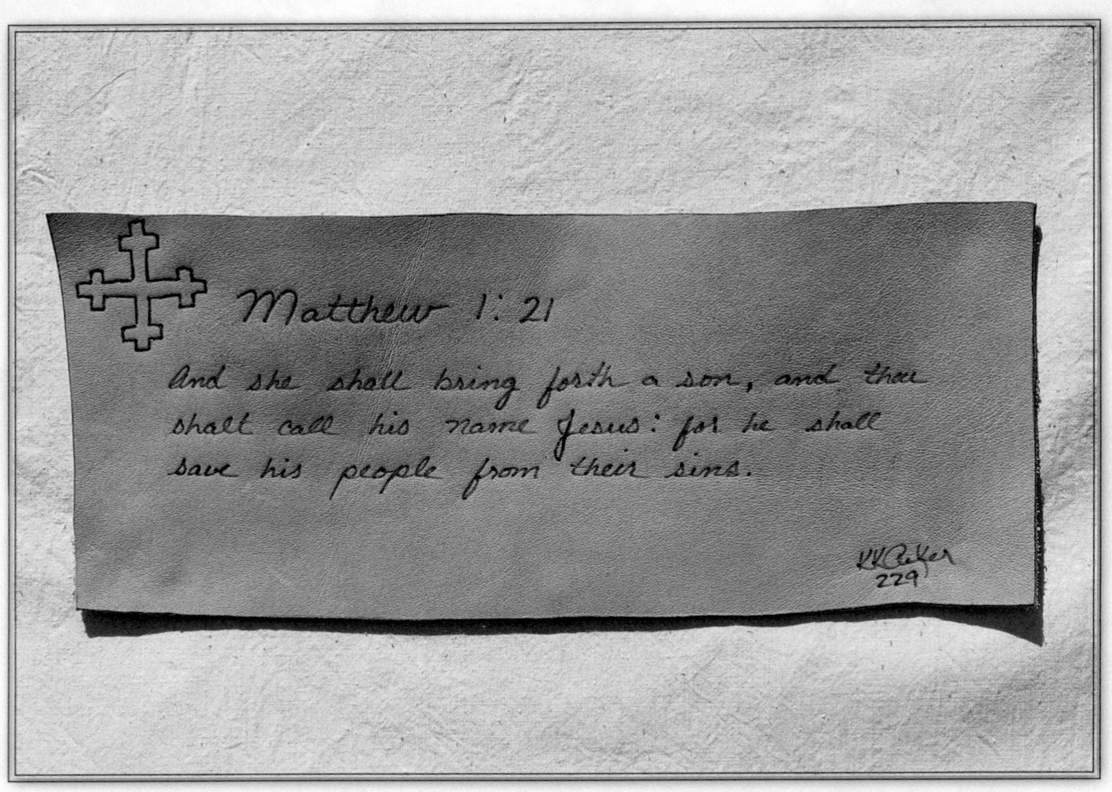
Matthew 1:21
And she shall bring forth a son, and thou
shall call his name Jesus: for he shall
save his people from their sins.
KKClucker
229

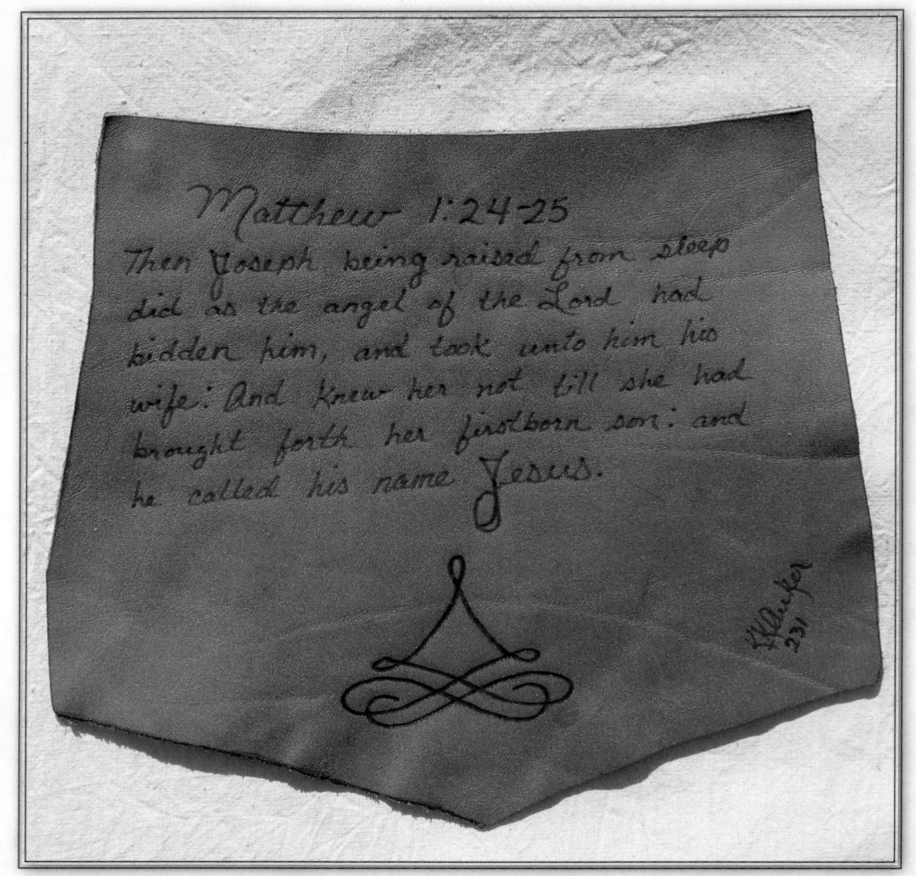
Matthew 1:24-25
Then Joseph being raised from sleep
did as the angel of the Lord had
bidden him, and took unto him his
wife: And knew her not till she had
brought forth her firstborn son: and
he called his name Jesus.
KKClucker
231

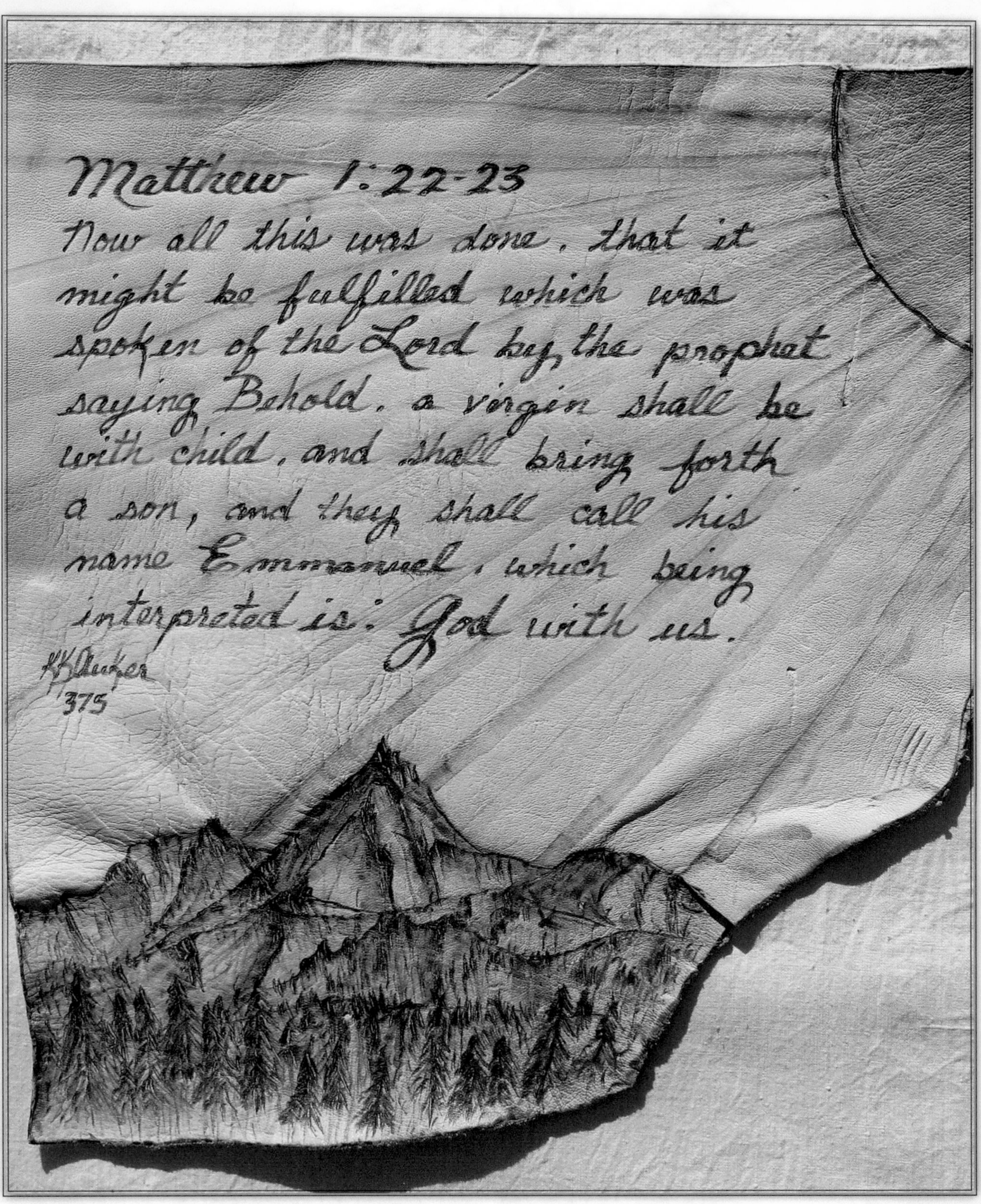
Matthew 1:22-23
Now all this was done, that it
might be fulfilled which was
spoken of the Lord by, the prophet
saying Behold, a virgin shall be
with child, and shall bring forth
a son, and they shall call his
name Emmanuel, which being
interpreted is: God with us.
'375

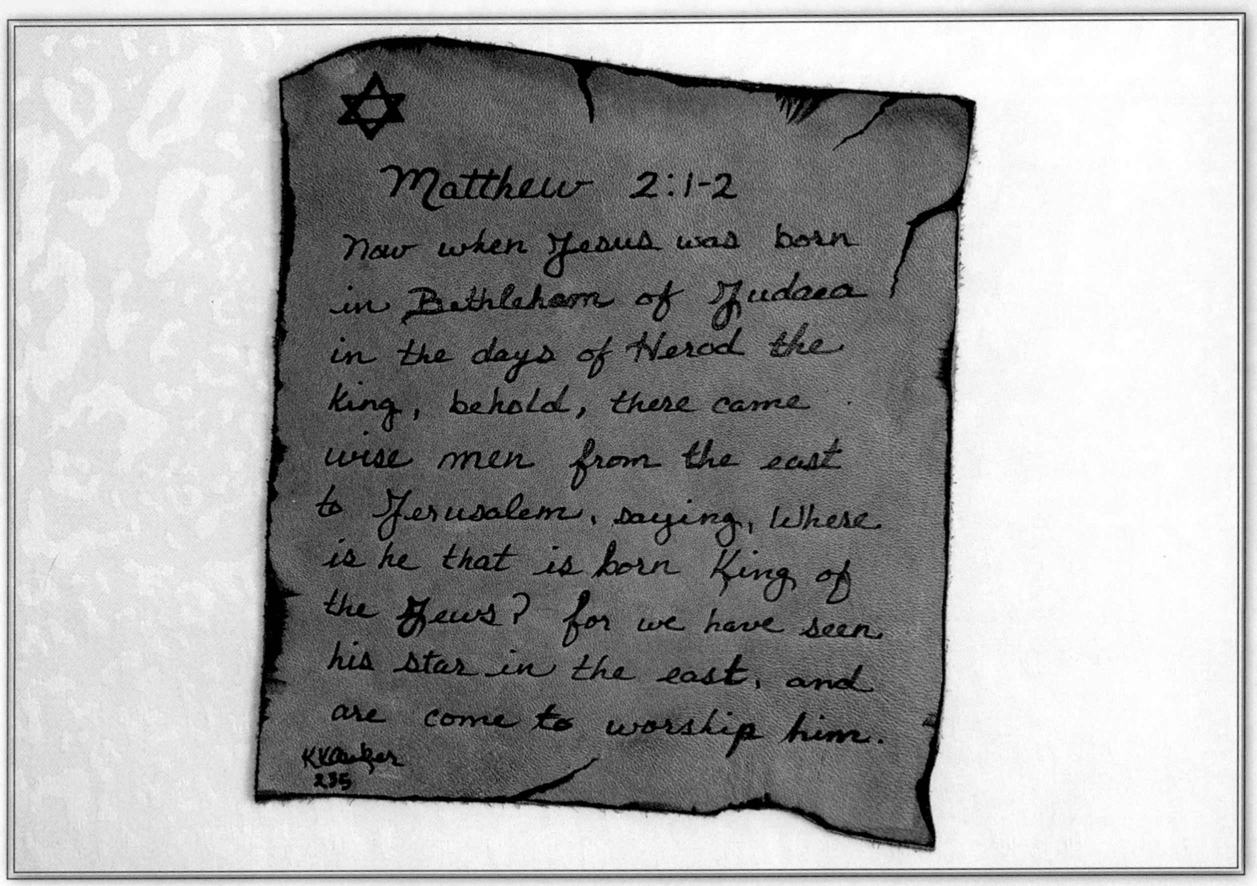
Matthew 2:1-2
Now when Jesus was born
in Bethlehem of Judaea
in the days of Herod the
king, behold, there came
wise men from the east
to Jerusalem, saying, Where
is he that is born King of
the Jews? for we have seen
his star in the east, and
are come to worship him.
KVAnker
235

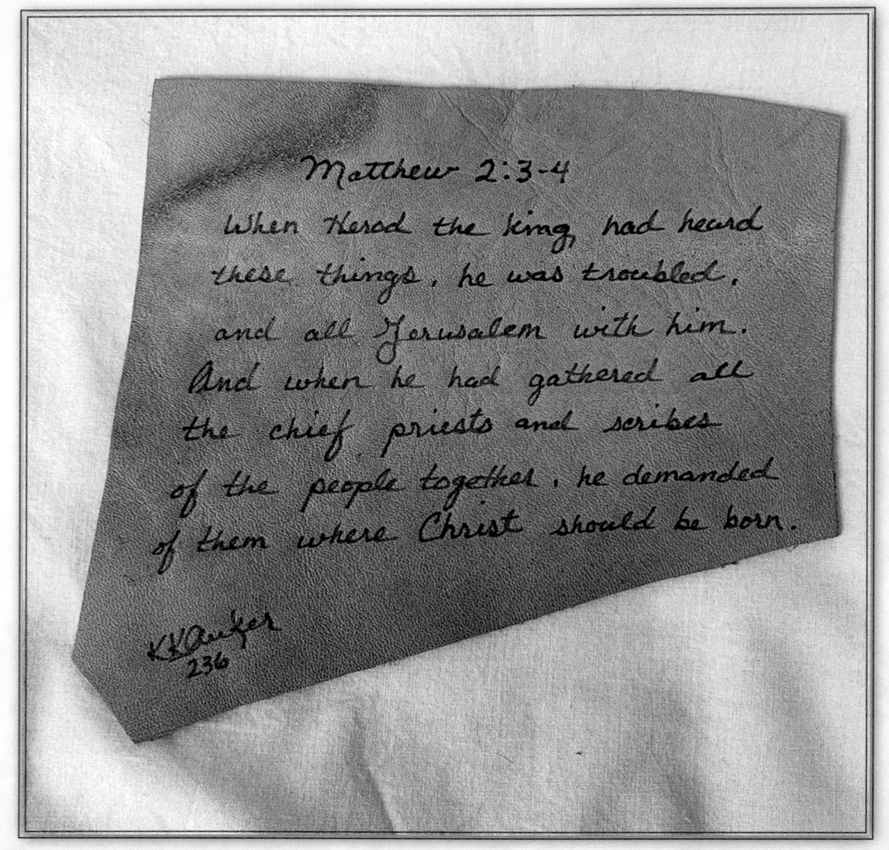
Matthew 2:3-4
When Herod the king had heard
these things, he was troubled,
and all Jerusalem with him.
And when he had gathered all
the chief priests and scribes
of the people together, he demanded
of them where Christ should be born.
KVAnker
236

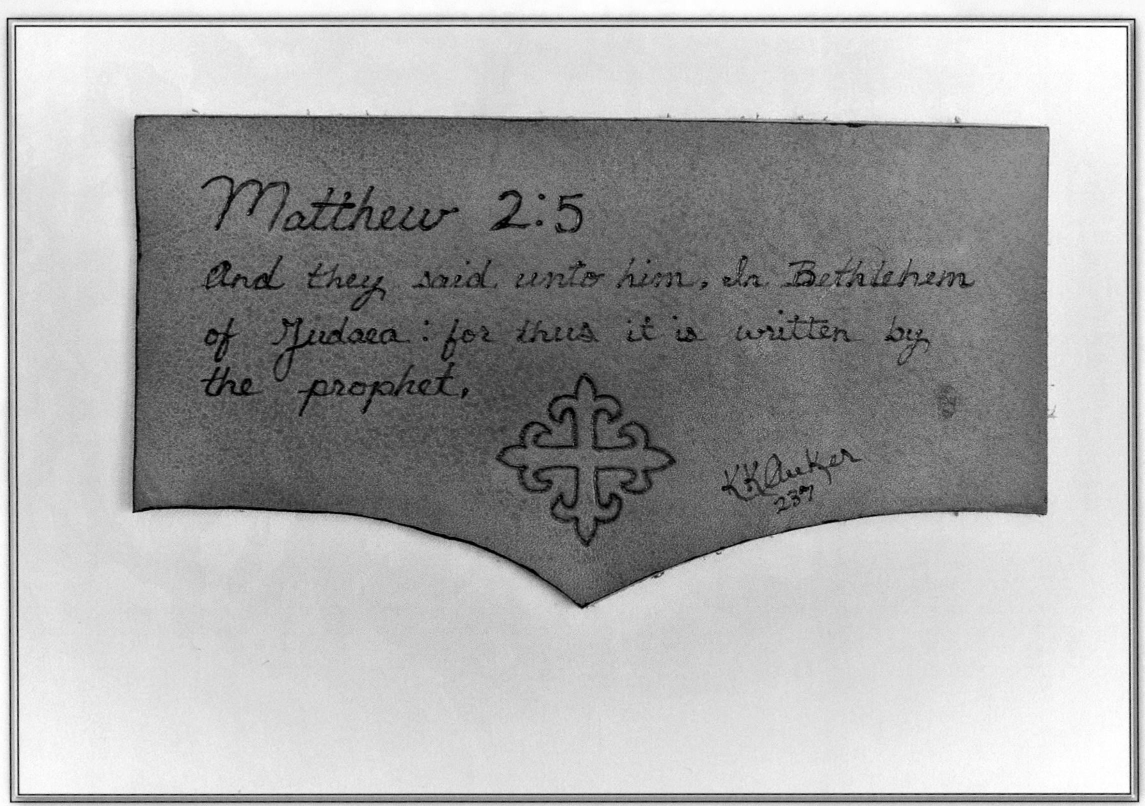
Matthew 2:5
And they said unto him, In Bethlehem of Judaea: for thus it is written by the prophet,
K.Kluker
237

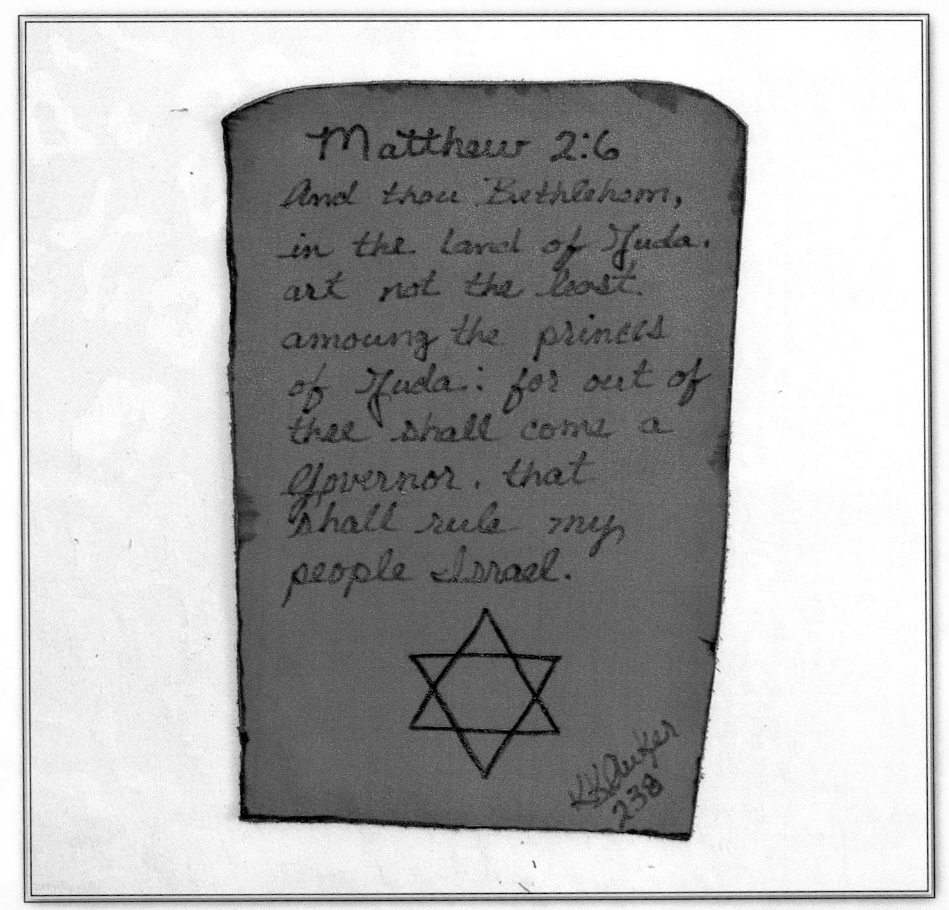
Matthew 2:6
And thou Bethlehem,
in the land of Juda,
art not the least
amoung the princes
of Juda: for out of
thee shall come a
Governor, that
shall rule my
people Israel.
K.Kluker
238

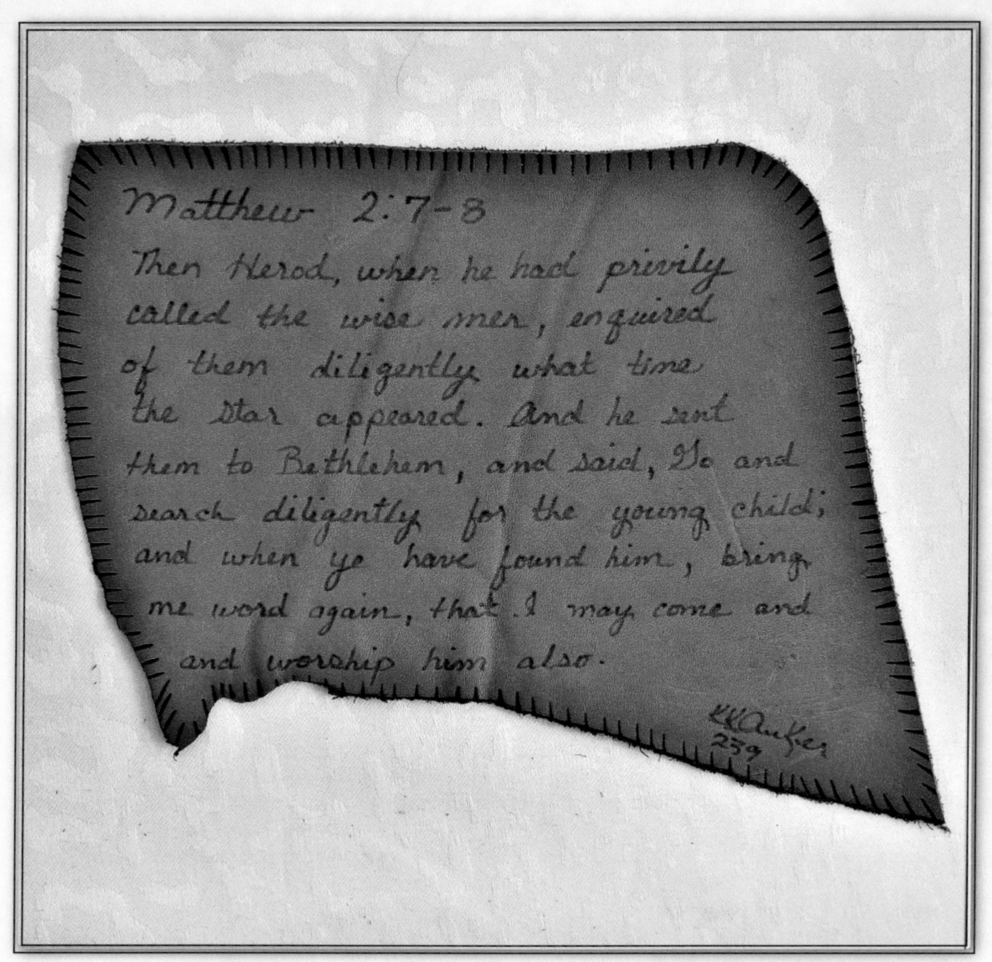
Matthew 2:7-8
Then Herod, when he had privily
called the wise men, enquired
of them diligently what time
the star appeared. And he sent
them to Bethlehem, and said, Go and
search diligently for the young child;
and when ye have found him, bring
me word again, that I may come and
and worship him also.
KKAnker
259

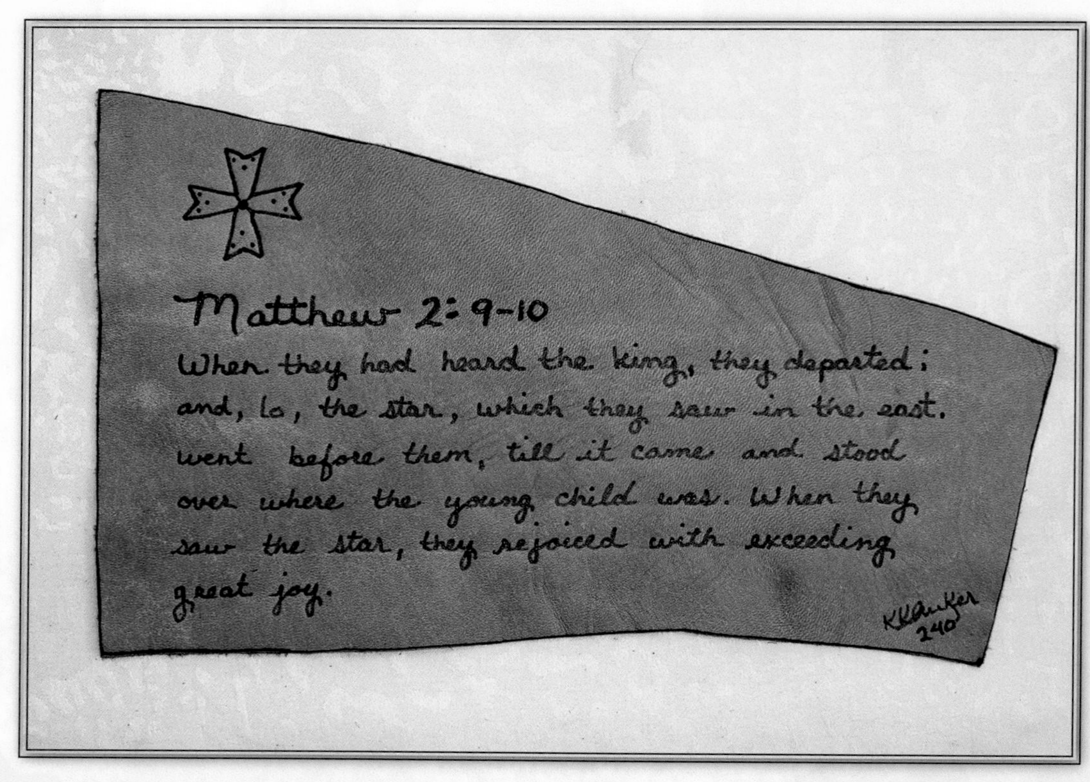
Matthew 2:9-10
When they had heard the king, they departed;
and, lo, the star, which they saw in the east,
went before them, till it came and stood
over where the young child was. When they
saw the star, they rejoiced with exceeding
great joy.
KKAnker
240

Matthew 2:11 And when they were come into the
house, they saw the young child with Mary his
mother, and fell down, and worshipped him: and
when they had opened their treasures, they presented
unto him gifts; gold, and frankincense, and myrrh.

Matthew 2:12

And being warned of God in a dream
that they should not return to Herod,
they departed into their own country another way.

Matthew 2:13-14 And when they were departed, behold, the angel of the Lord appeareth to Joseph in a dream, saying, Arise, and take the young child and his mother, and flee into Egypt, and be thou there until I bring thee word: for Herod will seek the young child to destroy him. When he arose, he took the young child and his mother by night and departed into Egypt.

243

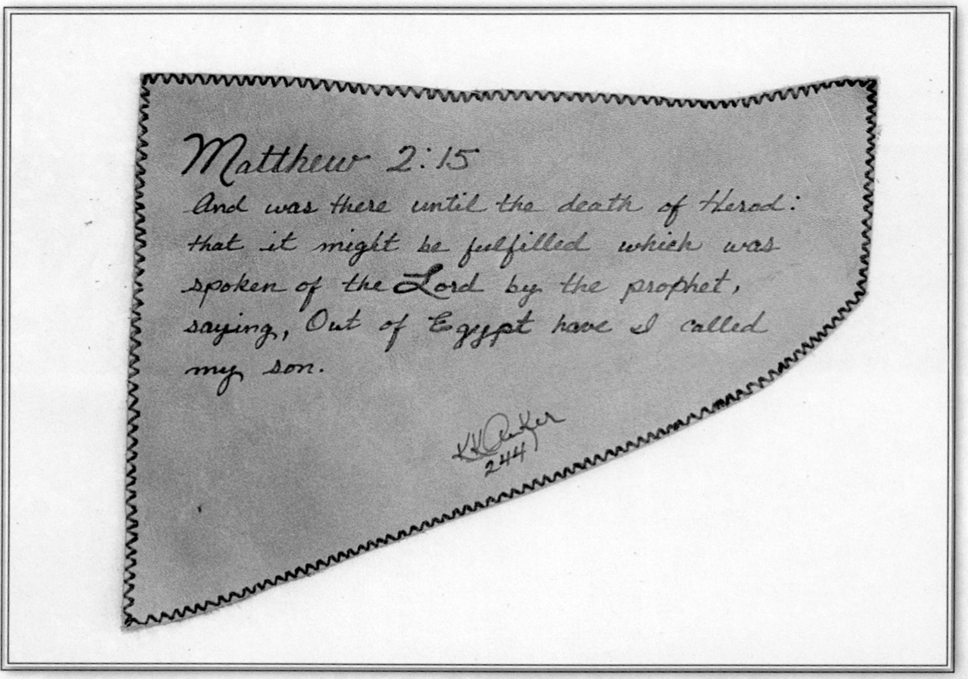

Matthew 2:15

And was there until the death of Herod: that it might be fulfilled which was spoken of the Lord by the prophet, saying, Out of Egypt have I called my son.

244

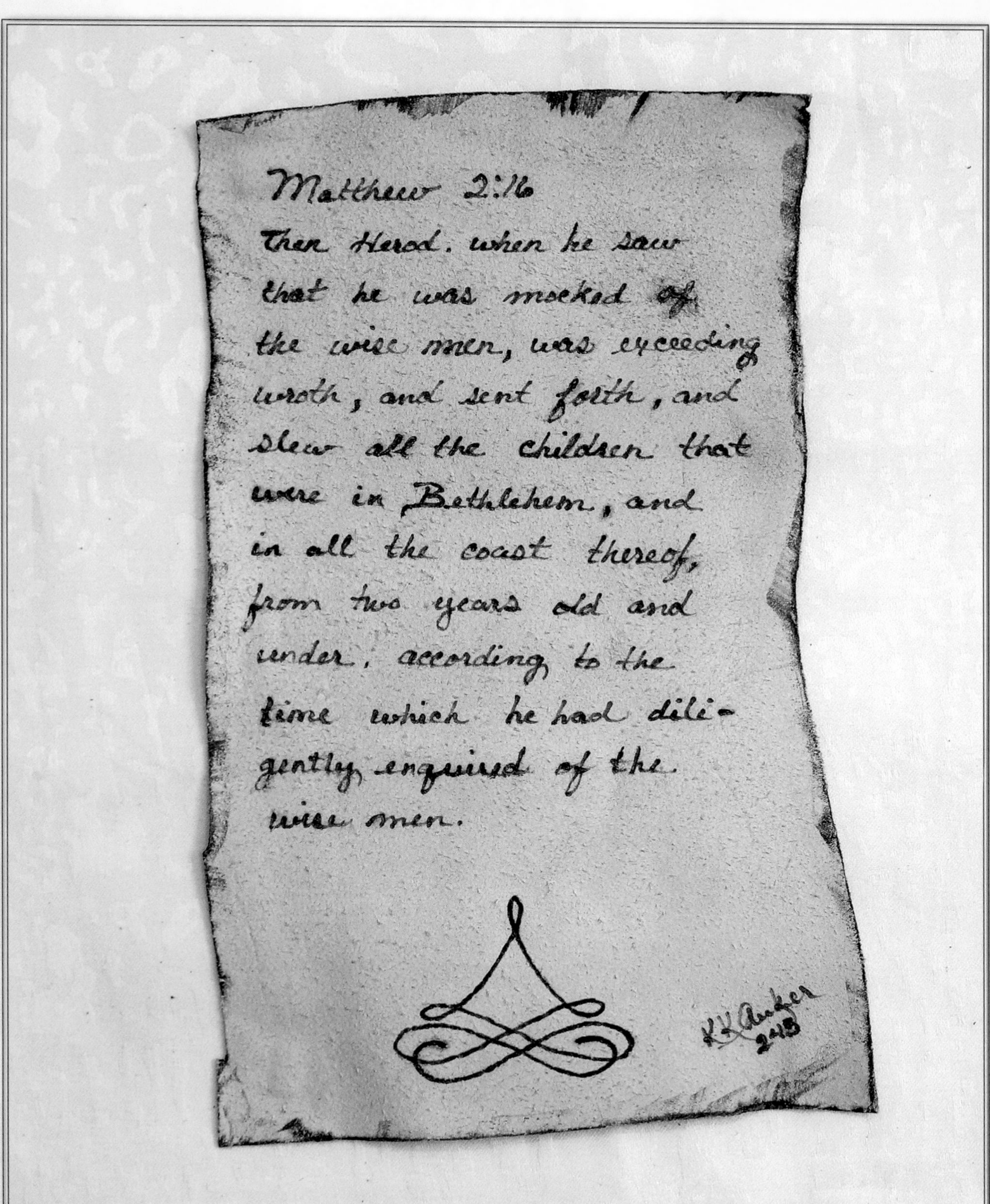

Matthew 2:16

Then Herod, when he saw
that he was mocked of
the wise men, was exceeding
wroth, and sent forth, and
slew all the children that
were in Bethlehem, and
in all the coast thereof,
from two years old and
under, according to the
time which he had dili-
gently enquired of the
wise men.

Matthew 2:17-18

Then was fulfilled that which was spoken by Jeremy the prophet, saying. In Rama was there a voice heard, lamentation, and weeping, and great mourning, Rachel weeping for her children, and would not be comforted, because they are not.

KKAuker
246

Matthew 2:19-23 But when Herod was dead, behold, an angel of the Lord appeareth in a dream to Joseph in Egypt, Saying, Arise, and take the young child and his mother, and go into the land of Israel: for they are dead which sought the young child's life. And he arose, and took the young child and his mother, and came into the land of Israel. But when he heard that Archelaus did reign in Judaea in the room of his father Herod, he was afraid to go thither: notwithstanding, being warned of God in a dream, he turned aside into the parts of Galilee: And he came and dwelt in a city called Nazareth: that it might be fulfilled which was spoken by the prophets, He shall be called a Nazarene.

KKAuker
542

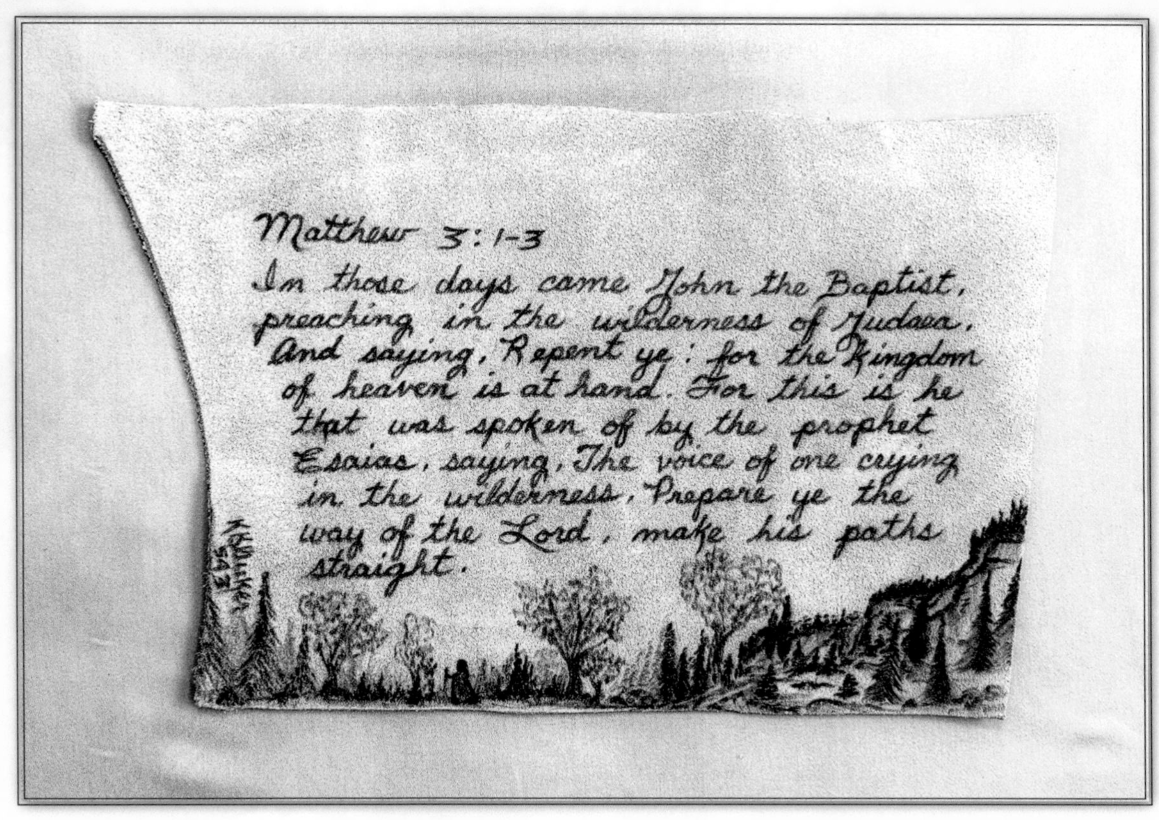
Matthew 3:1-3
In those days came John the Baptist, preaching in the wilderness of Judaea, And saying, Repent ye: for the Kingdom of heaven is at hand. For this is he that was spoken of by the prophet Esaias, saying, The voice of one crying in the wilderness, Prepare ye the way of the Lord, make his paths straight.

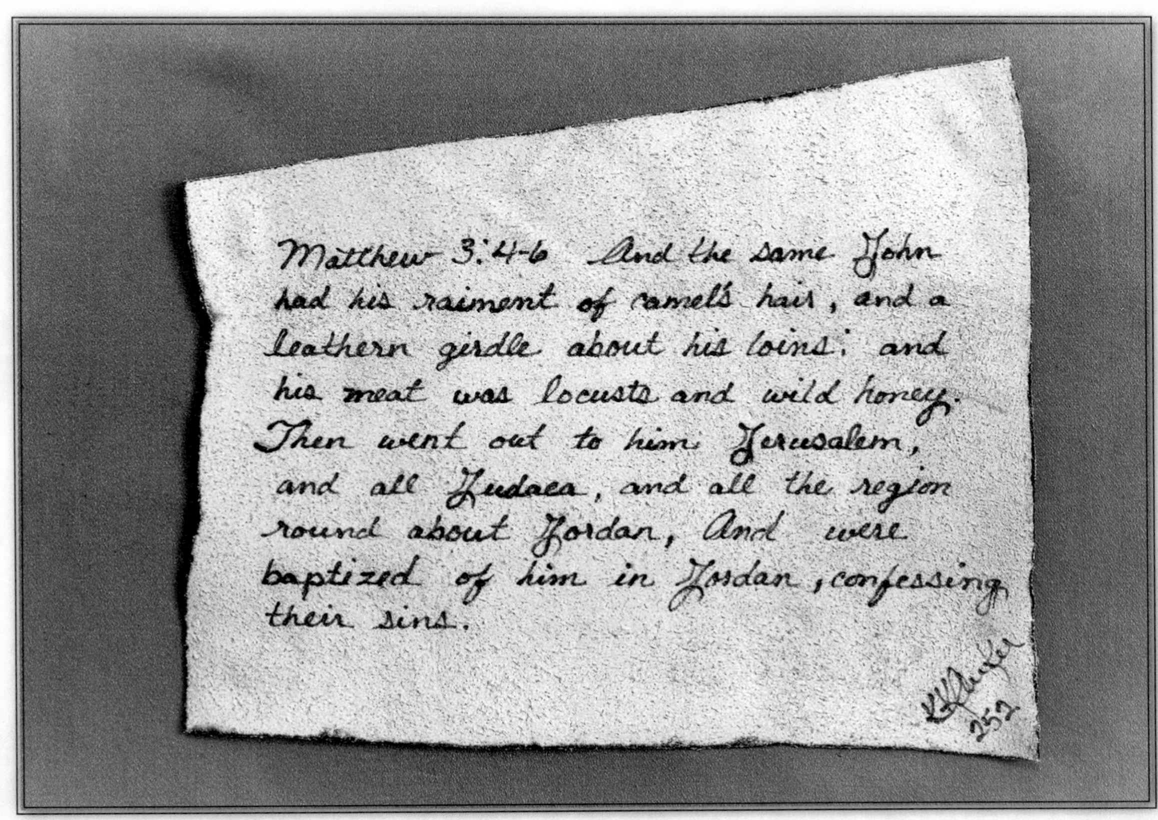
Matthew 3:4-6 And the same John had his raiment of camel's hair, and a leathern girdle about his loins; and his meat was locusts and wild honey. Then went out to him Jerusalem, and all Judaea, and all the region round about Jordan, And were baptized of him in Jordan, confessing their sins.

Matthew 3:7 But when he saw many of the Pharisees and Saducees come to his baptism, he said unto them, O generation of vipers, who hath warned you to flee from the wrath to come?

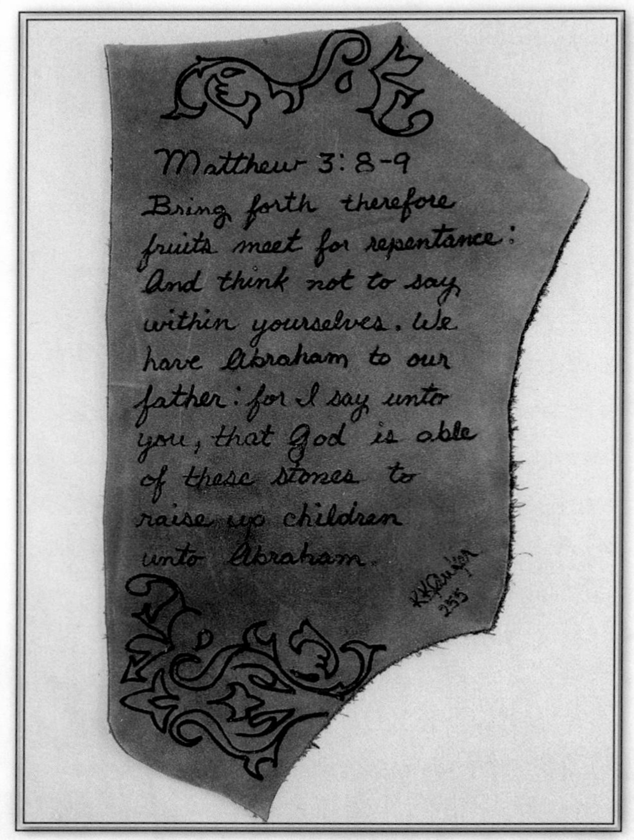

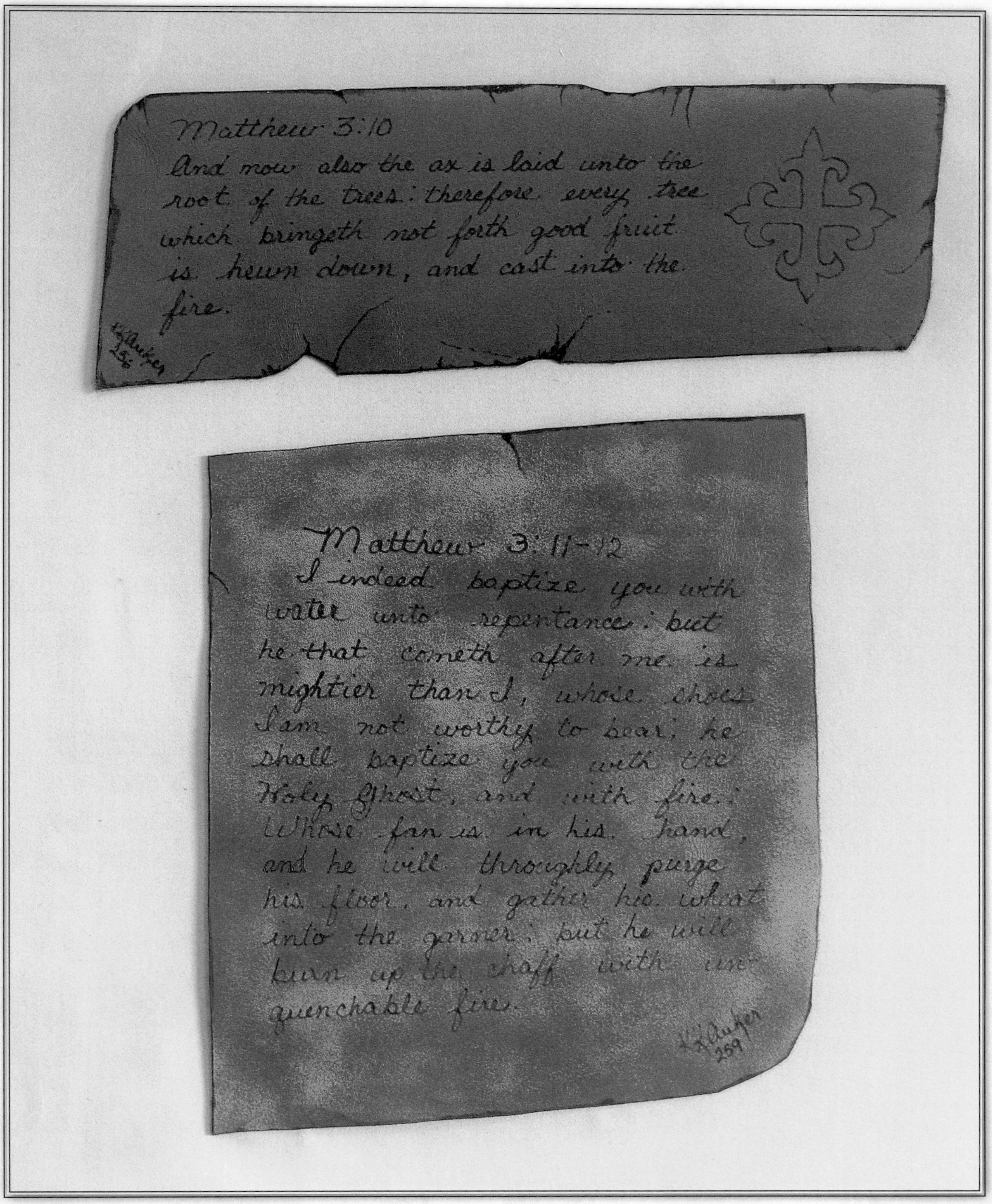

Matthew 3:10
And now also the ax is laid unto the root of the trees: therefore every tree which bringeth not forth good fruit is hewn down, and cast into the fire.

K. Auker
256

Matthew 3:11-12
I indeed baptize you with water unto repentance: but he that cometh after me is mightier than I, whose shoes I am not worthy to bear: he shall baptize you with the Holy Ghost, and with fire: Whose fan is in his hand, and he will throughly purge his floor, and gather his wheat into the garner; but he will burn up the chaff with unquenchable fire.

K. Auker
259

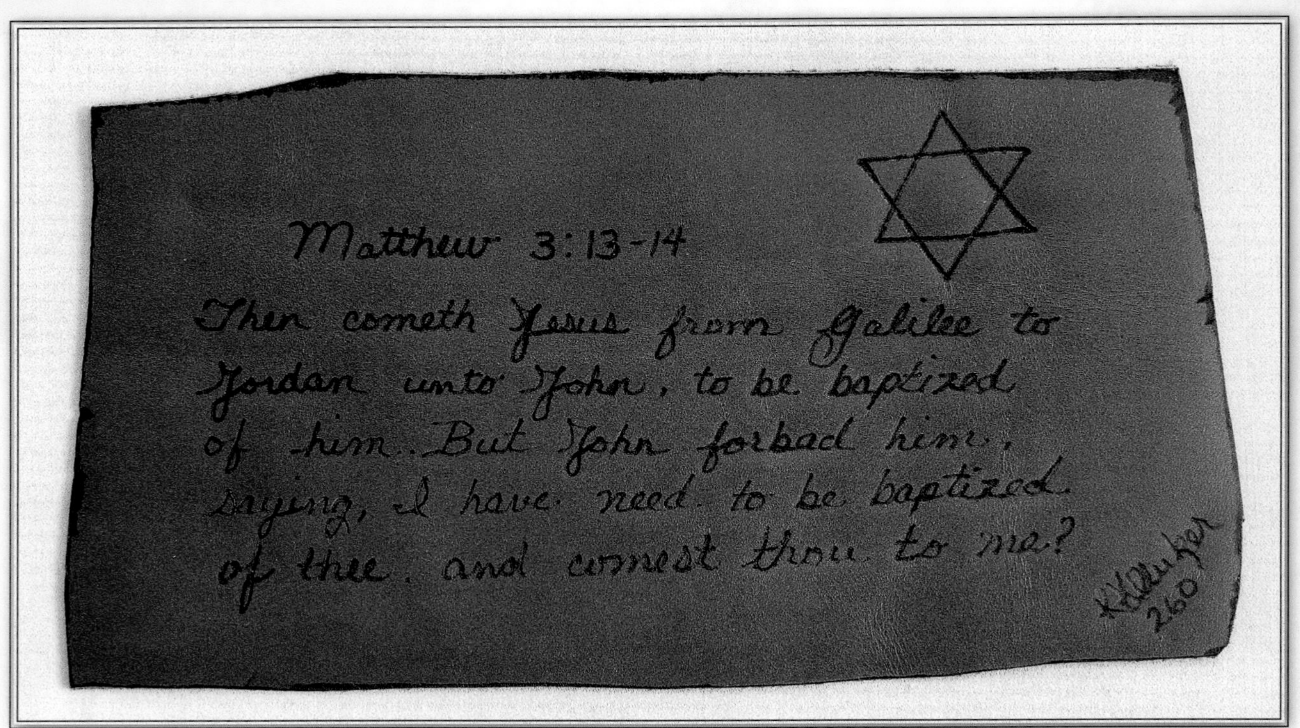
Matthew 3:13-14
Then cometh Jesus from Galilee to
Jordan unto John, to be baptized
of him. But John forbad him,
saying, I have need to be baptized
of thee, and comest thou to me?
260

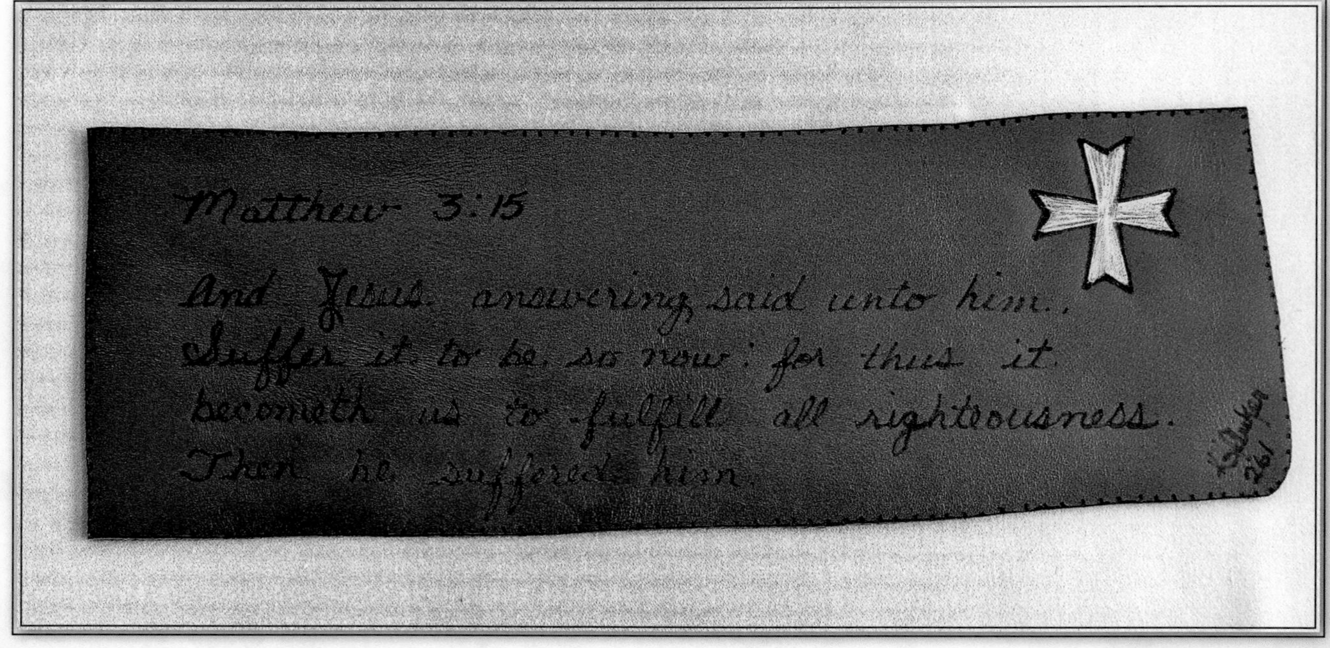
Matthew 3:15
And Jesus answering said unto him,
Suffer it to be so now: for thus it
becometh us to fulfill all righteousness.
Then he suffered him
261

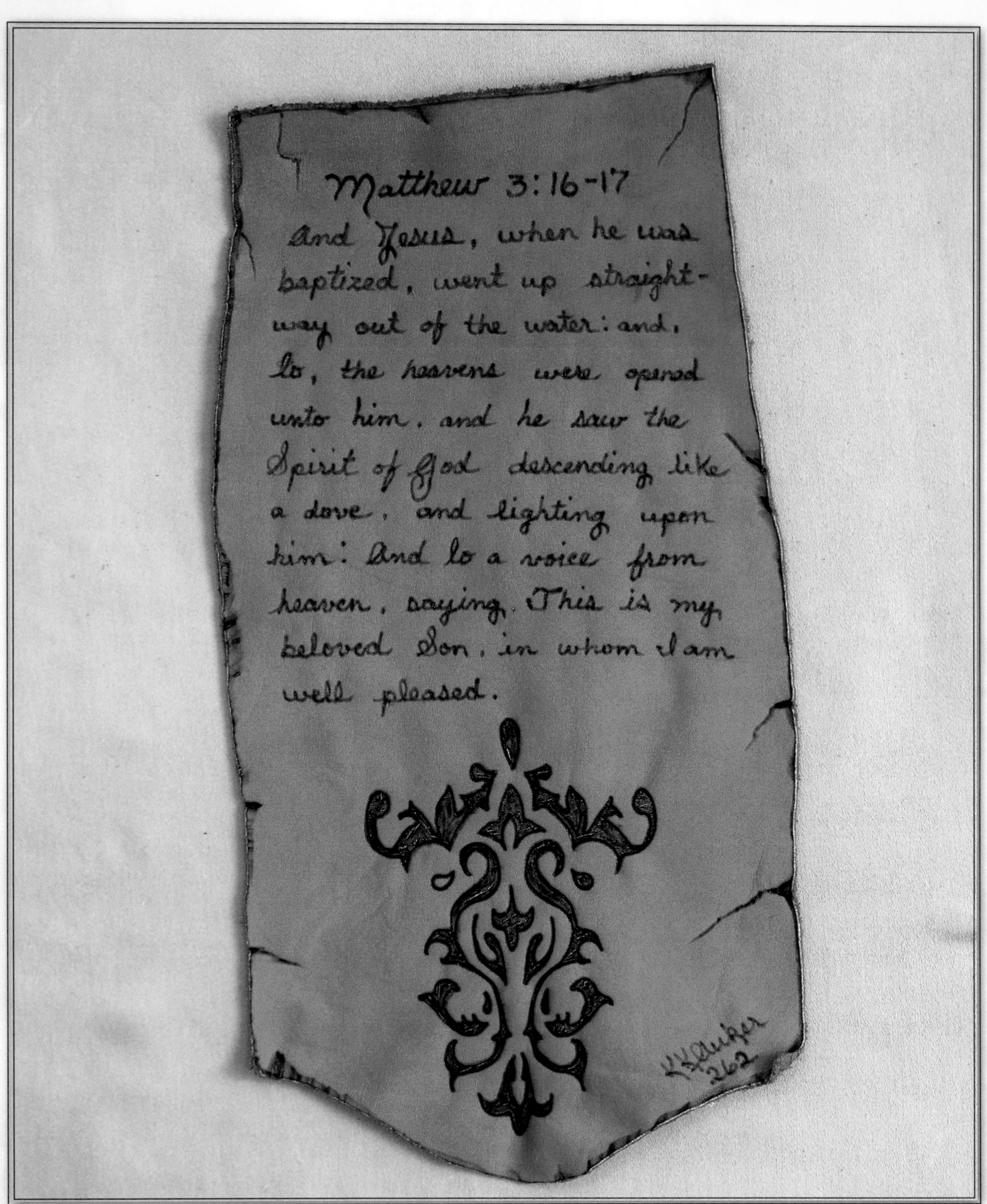
Matthew 3:16-17
And Jesus, when he was
baptized, went up straightway out of the water: and,
lo, the heavens were opened
unto him, and he saw the
Spirit of God descending like
a dove, and lighting upon
him: And lo a voice from
heaven, saying, This is my
beloved Son, in whom I am
well pleased.

Matthew 4:1
Then was Jesus led up of the Spirit into the wilderness to be tempted of the devil.

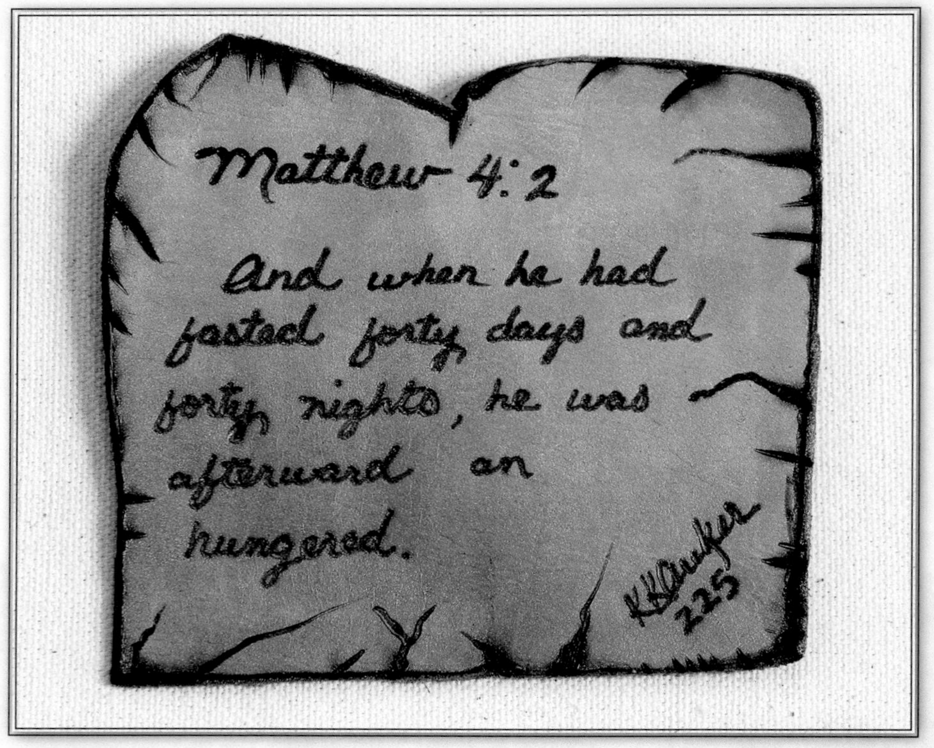
Matthew 4:2
And when he had fasted forty days and forty nights, he was afterward an hungered.
KBanker
225

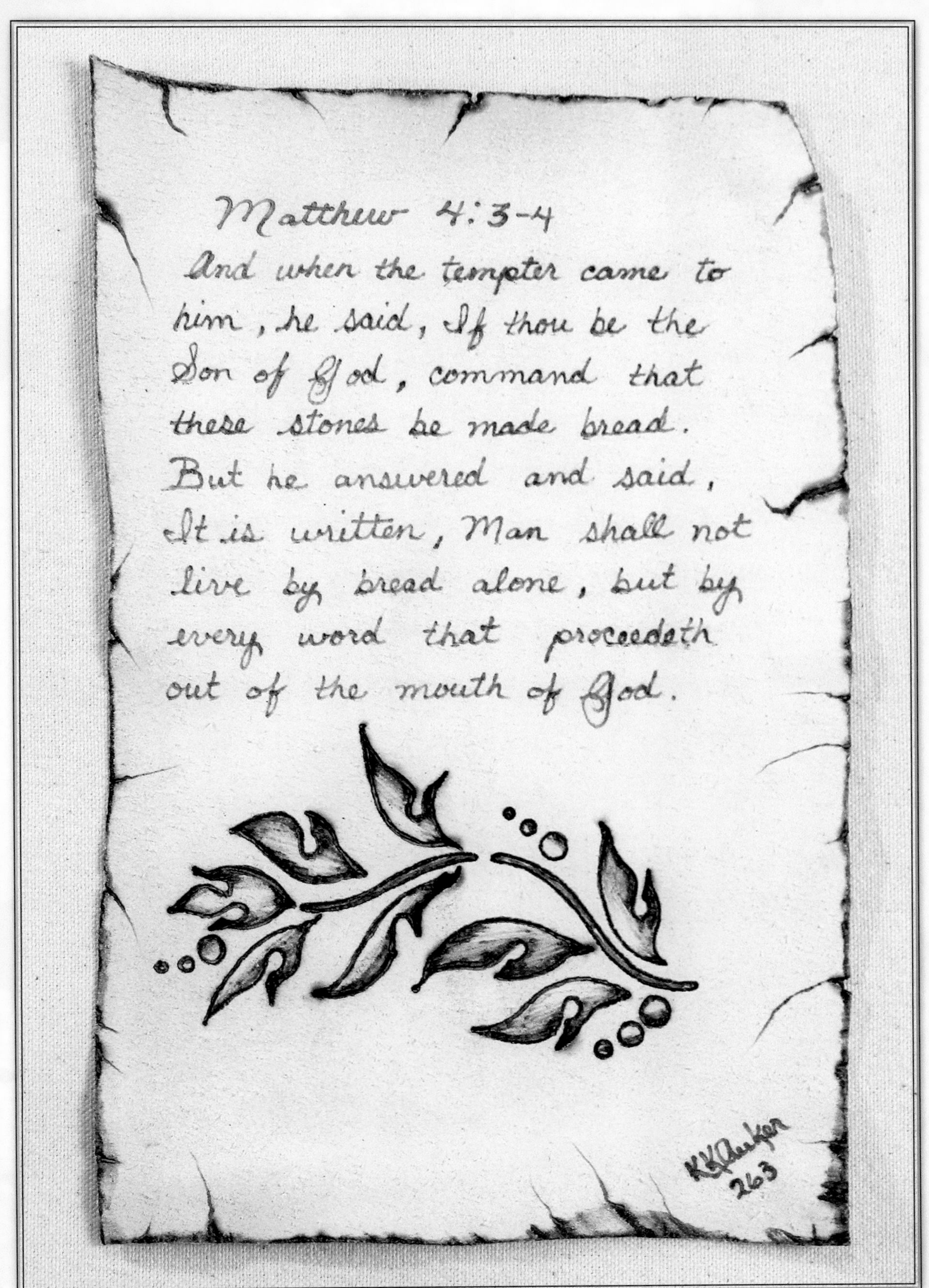
Matthew 4:3-4
And when the tempter came to
him, he said, If thou be the
Son of God, command that
these stones be made bread.
But he answered and said,
It is written, Man shall not
live by bread alone, but by
every word that proceedeth
out of the mouth of God.
KKParker
263

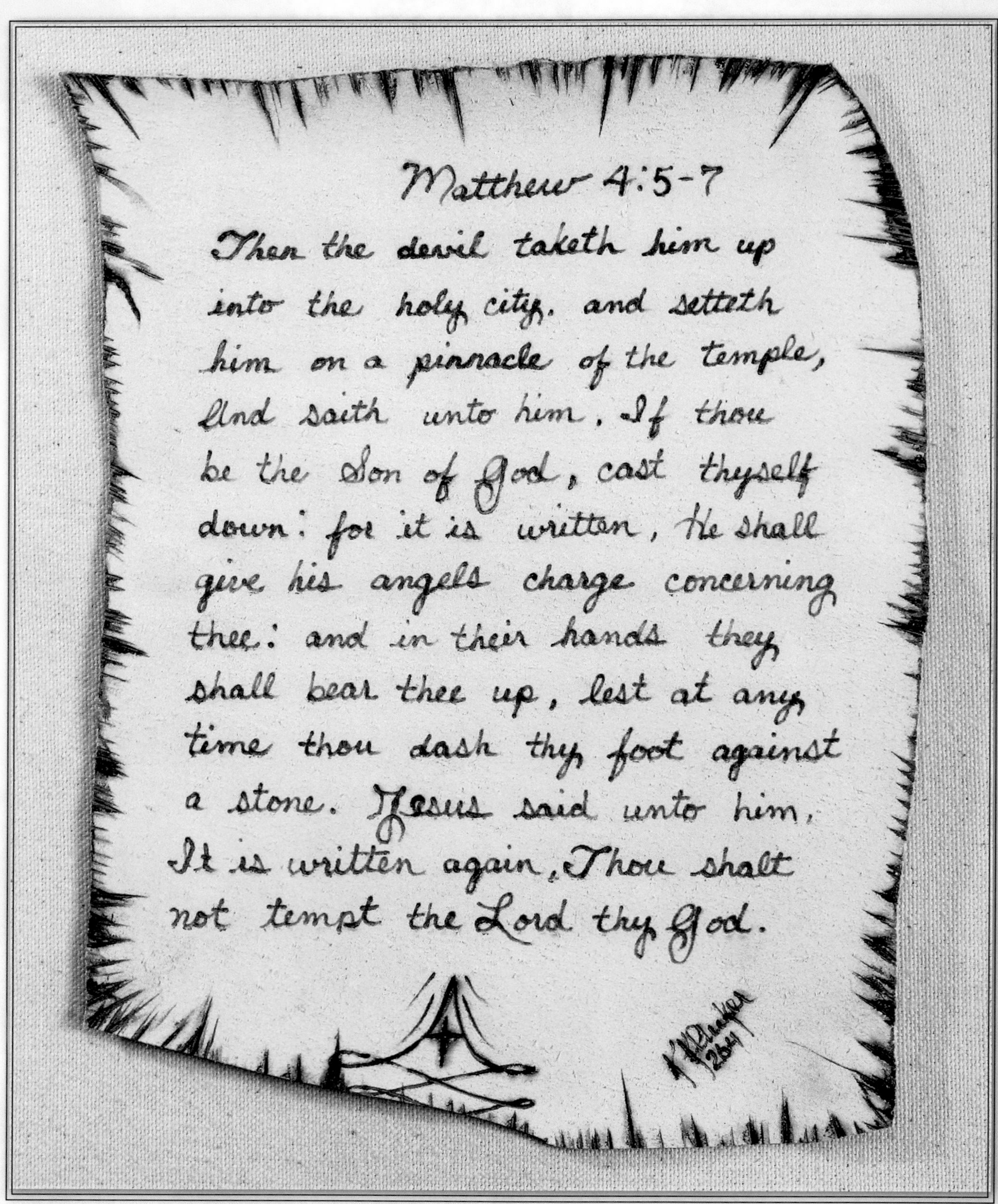
Matthew 4:5-7
Then the devil taketh him up
into the holy city, and setteth
him on a pinnacle of the temple,
And saith unto him, If thou
be the Son of God, cast thyself
down: for it is written, He shall
give his angels charge concerning
thee: and in their hands they
shall bear thee up, lest at any
time thou dash thy foot against
a stone. Jesus said unto him,
It is written again, Thou shalt
not tempt the Lord thy God.

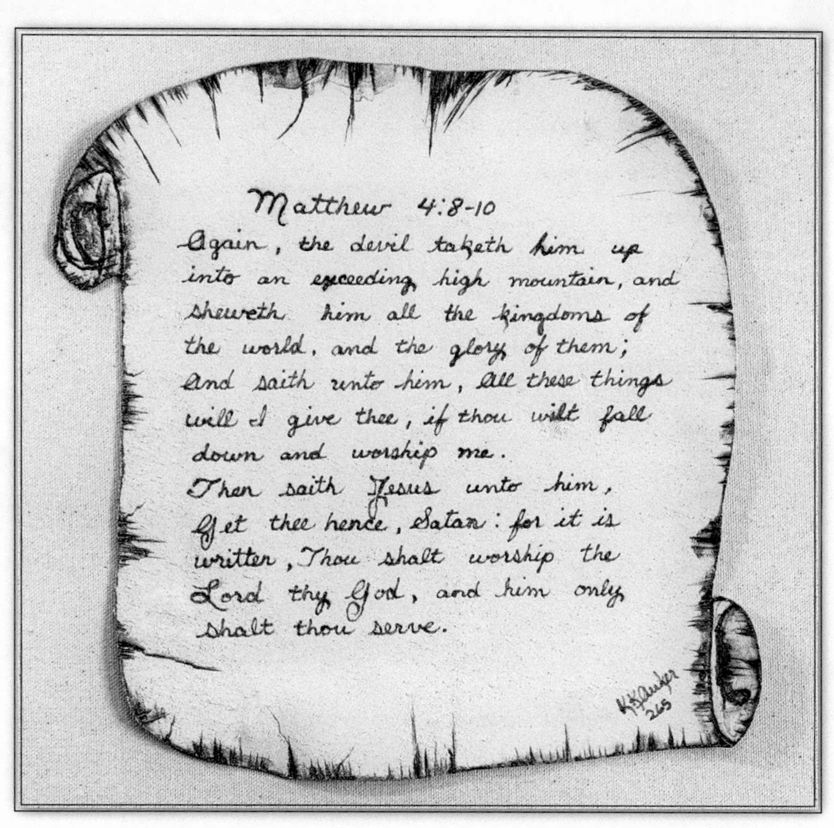
Matthew 4:8-10
Again, the devil taketh him up into an exceeding high mountain, and sheweth him all the kingdoms of the world, and the glory of them;
And saith unto him, All these things will I give thee, if thou wilt fall down and worship me.
Then saith Jesus unto him, Get thee hence, Satan: for it is written, Thou shalt worship the Lord thy God, and him only shalt thou serve.
KKauker
265

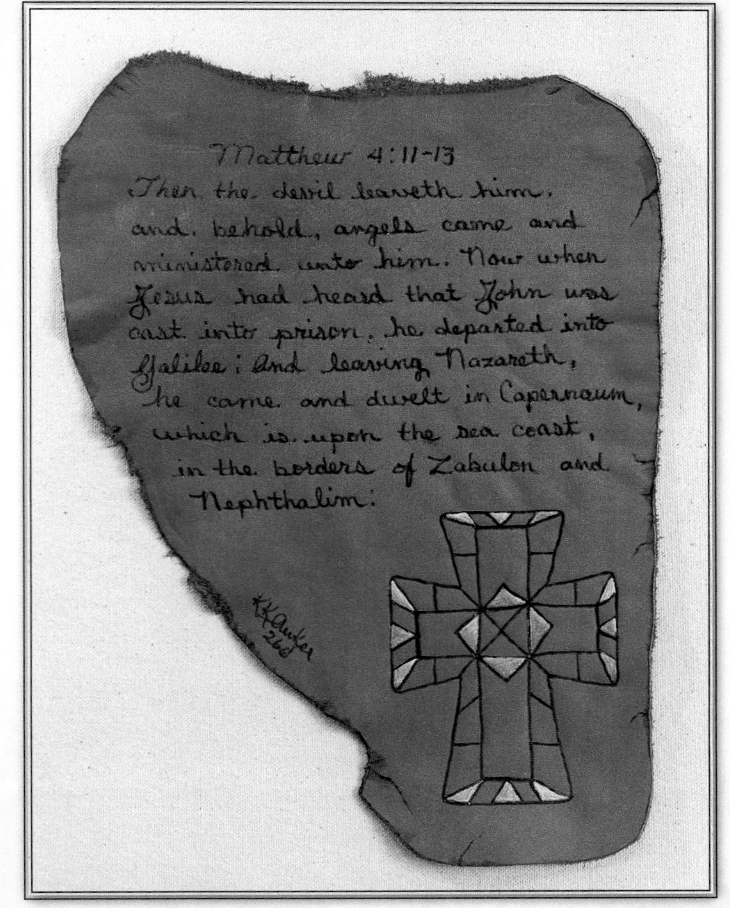
Matthew 4:11-13
Then the devil leaveth him, and, behold, angels came and ministered unto him. Now when Jesus had heard that John was cast into prison, he departed into Galilee; And leaving Nazareth, he came and dwelt in Capernaum, which is upon the sea coast, in the borders of Zabulon and Nephthalim:
KKauker
266

Matthew 4:14-16 That it might be fulfilled which was spoken by Esaias the prophet, saying, The land of Zabulon, and the land of Nephthalim by the way of the sea, beyond Jordan, Galilee of the Gentiles: The people which sat in darkness saw great light; and to them which sat in the region and shadow of death light is sprung up.

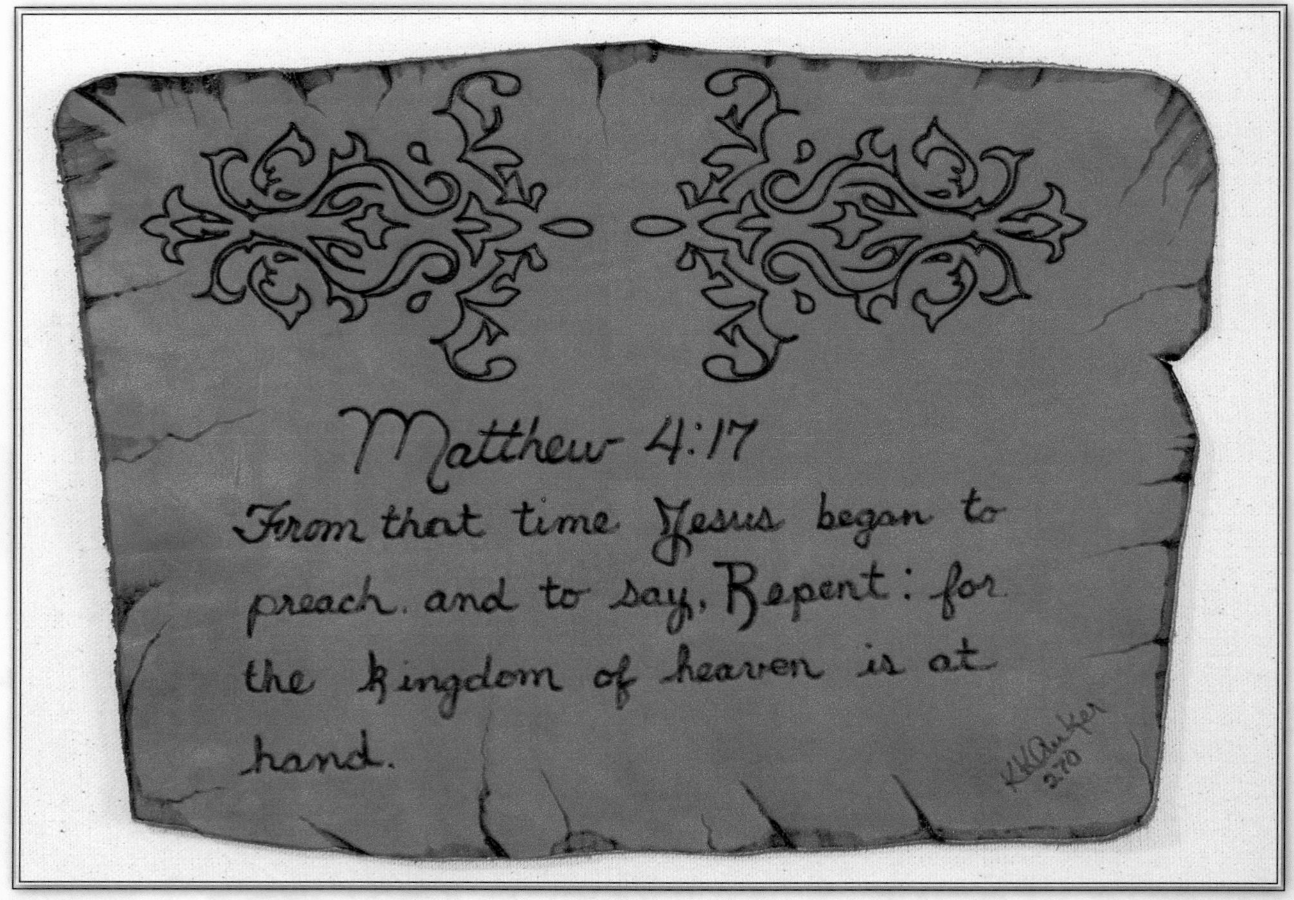

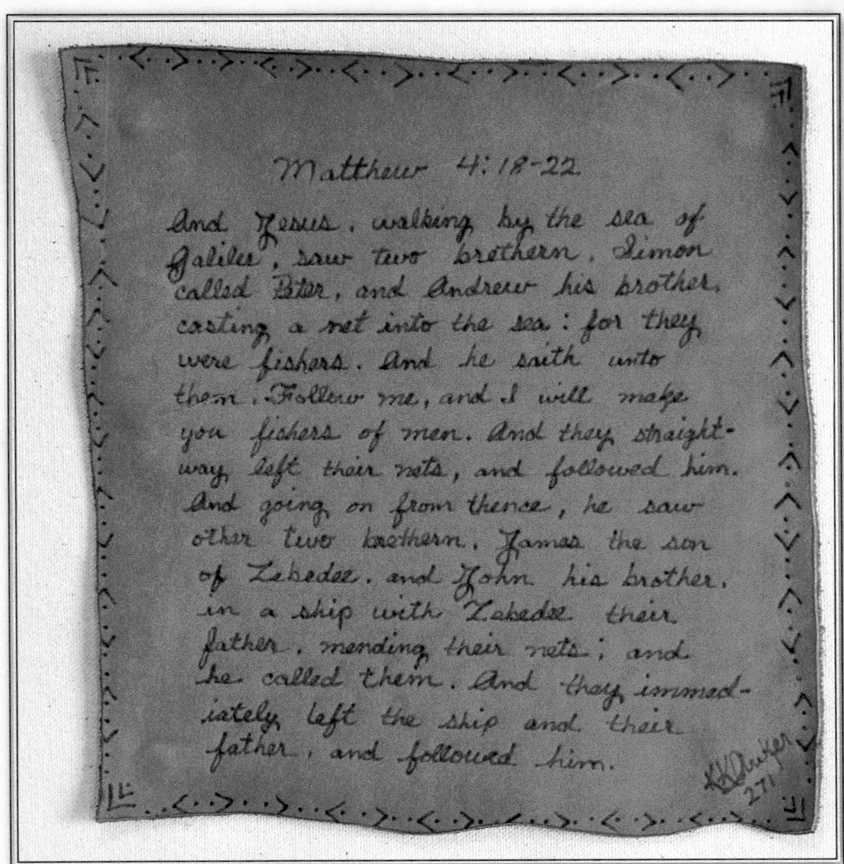
Matthew 4:18-22
And Jesus, walking by the sea of
Galilee, saw two brethern, Simon
called Peter, and Andrew his brother,
casting a net into the sea: for they
were fishers. And he saith unto
them, Follow me, and I will make
you fishers of men. And they straightway left their nets, and followed him.
And going on from thence, he saw
other two brethern, James the son
of Zebedee, and John his brother,
in a ship with Zebedee their
father, mending their nets; and
he called them. And they immediately left the ship and their
father, and followed him.

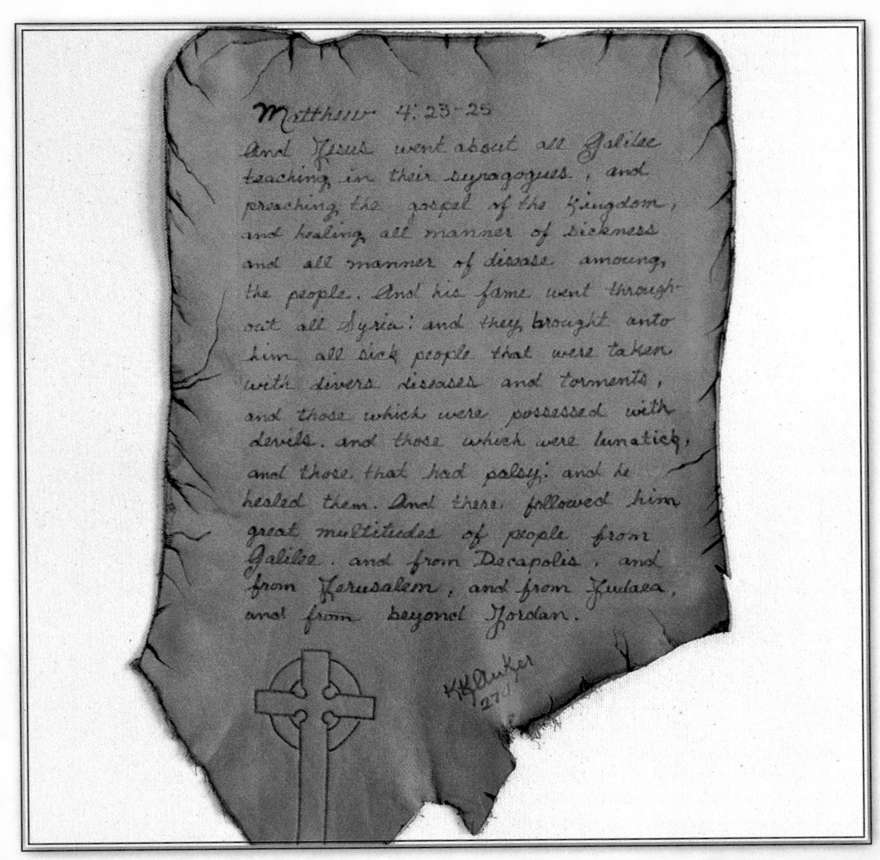
Matthew 4:23-25
And Jesus went about all Galilee
teaching in their synagogues, and
preaching the gospel of the kingdom,
and healing all manner of sickness
and all manner of disease amoung
the people. And his fame went through-
out all Syria: and they brought unto
him all sick people that were taken
with divers diseases and torments,
and those which were possessed with
devils, and those which were lunatick,
and those that had palsy; and he
healed them. And there followed him
great multitudes of people from
Galilee, and from Decapolis, and
from Jerusalem, and from Judaea,
and from beyond Jordan.

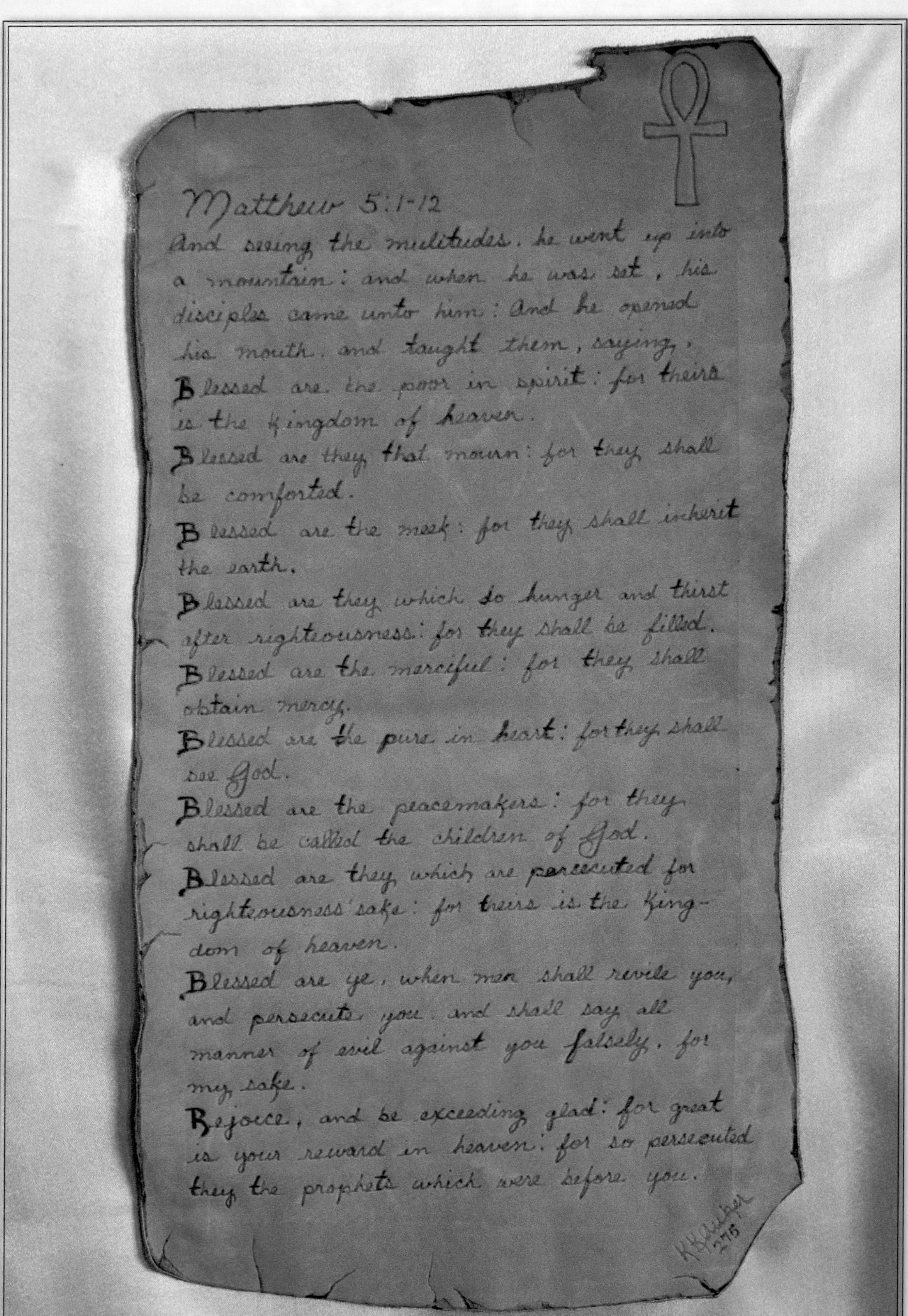

Matthew 5:1-12

And seeing the mulitudes, he went up into a mountain: and when he was set, his disciples came unto him: And he opened his mouth, and taught them, saying,

Blessed are the poor in spirit: for theirs is the kingdom of heaven.

Blessed are they that mourn: for they shall be comforted.

Blessed are the meek: for they shall inherit the earth.

Blessed are they which do hunger and thirst after righteousness: for they shall be filled.

Blessed are the merciful: for they shall obtain mercy.

Blessed are the pure in heart: for they shall see God.

Blessed are the peacemakers: for they shall be called the children of God.

Blessed are they which are persecuted for righteousness' sake: for theirs is the kingdom of heaven.

Blessed are ye, when men shall revile you, and persecute you, and shall say all manner of evil against you falsely, for my sake.

Rejoice, and be exceeding glad: for great is your reward in heaven: for so persecuted they the prophets which were before you.

Matthew 5:13
Ye are the salt of the earth:
but if the salt have lost
his savour, wherewith
shall it be salted? it is
thenceforth good for
nothing, but to be cast
out, and to be trodden
under foot of men.
276

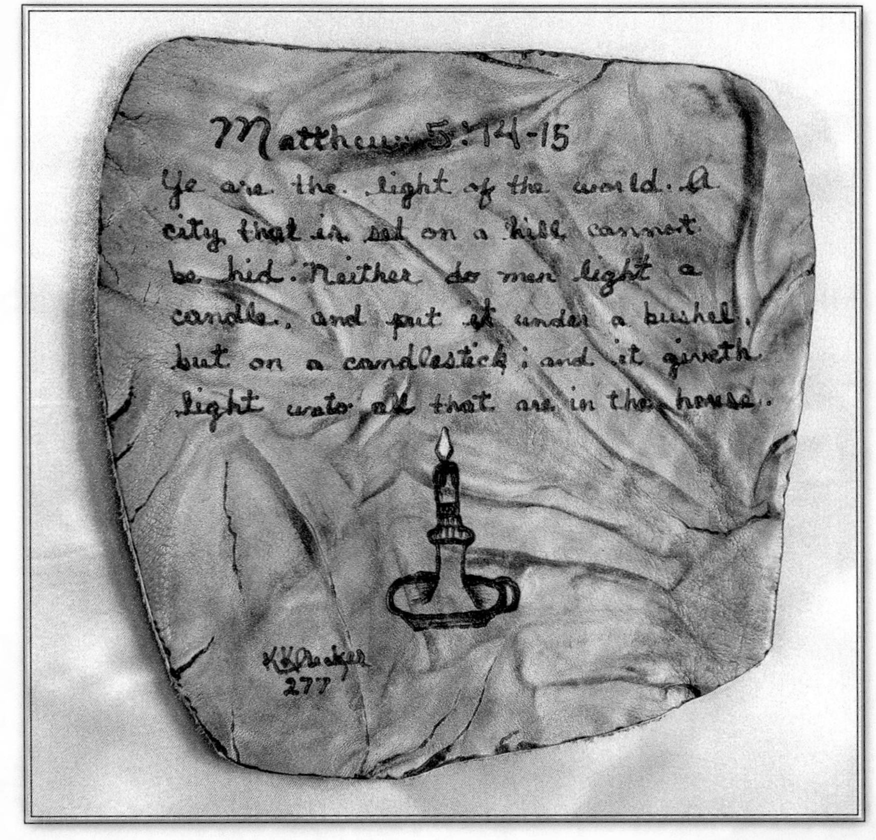
Matthew 5:14-15
Ye are the light of the world. A
city that is set on a hill cannot
be hid. Neither do men light a
candle, and put it under a bushel,
but on a candlestick; and it giveth
light unto all that are in the house.
277

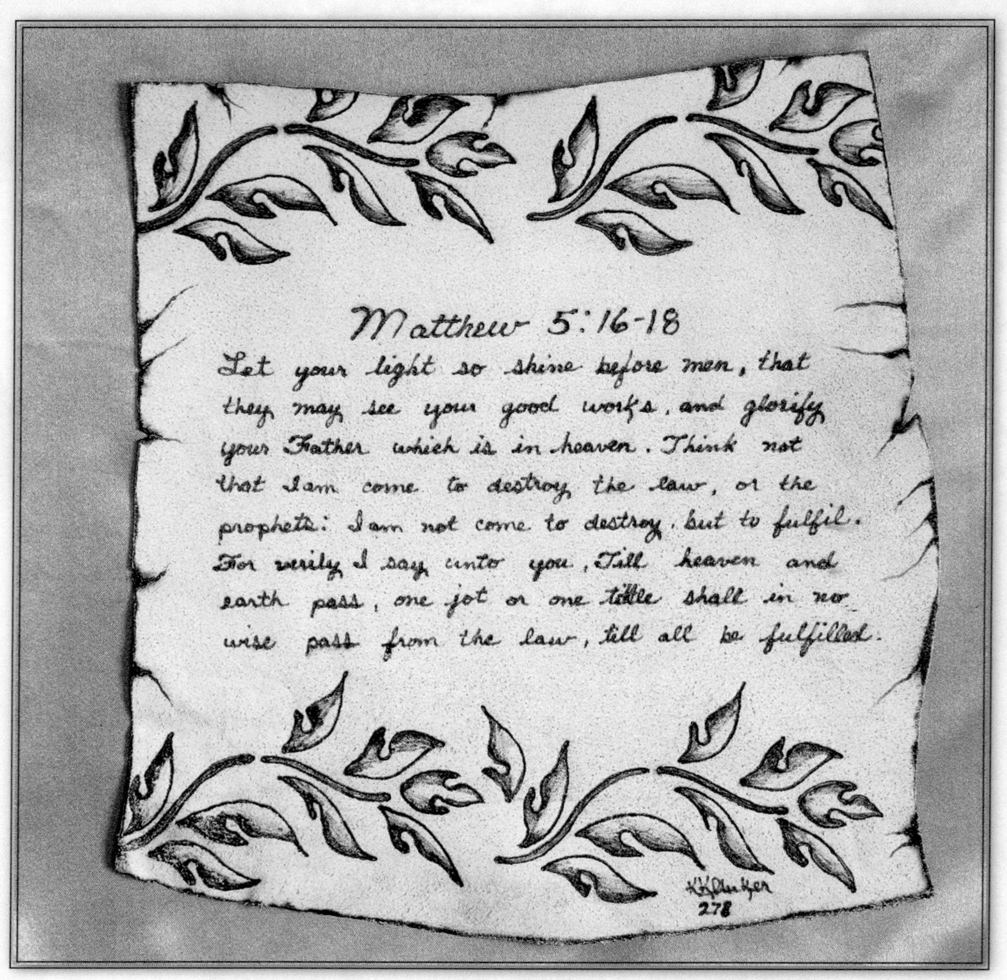
Matthew 5:16-18
Let your light so shine before men, that
they may see your good works, and glorify
your Father which is in heaven. Think not
that I am come to destroy the law, or the
prophets: I am not come to destroy, but to fulfil.
For verily I say unto you, Till heaven and
earth pass, one jot or one tittle shall in no
wise pass from the law, till all be fulfilled.
278

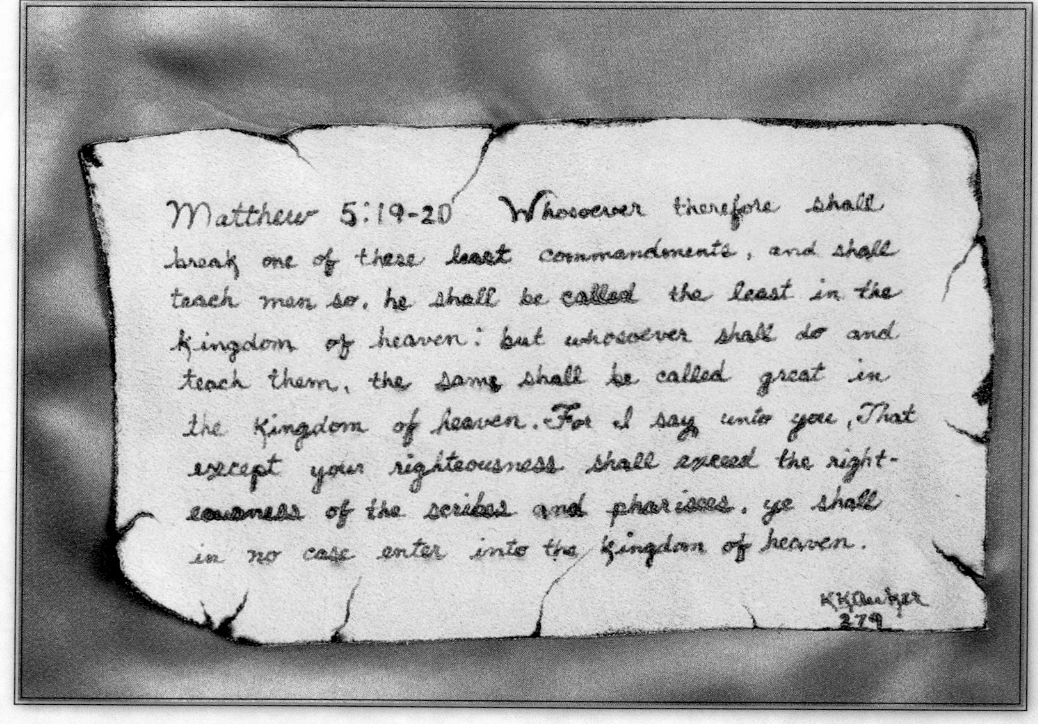
Matthew 5:19-20 Whosoever therefore shall
break one of these least commandments, and shall
teach men so, he shall be called the least in the
kingdom of heaven: but whosoever shall do and
teach them, the same shall be called great in
the kingdom of heaven. For I say unto you, That
except your righteousness shall exceed the righteousness of the scribes and pharisees, ye shall
in no case enter into the kingdom of heaven.
279

Matthew 5:21
Ye have heard that it was said
by them of old time, Thou shalt
not kill; and whosoever shall
kill shall be in danger of
the judgment.

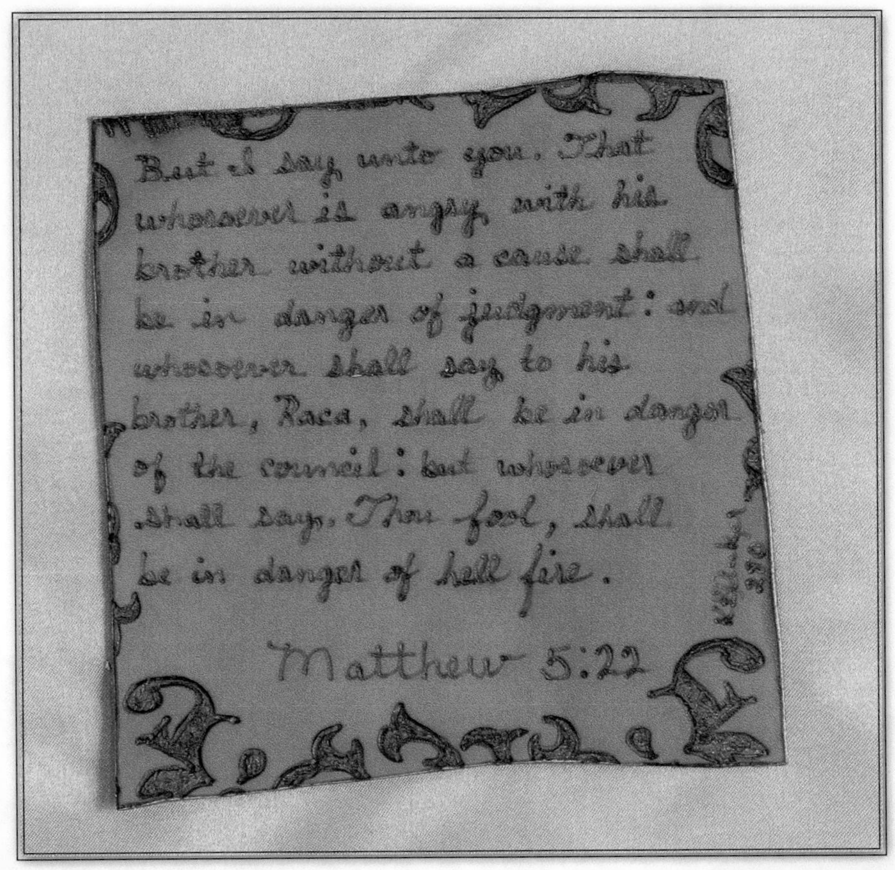
But I say unto you, That
whosoever is angry with his
brother without a cause shall
be in danger of judgment: and
whosoever shall say to his
brother, Raca, shall be in danger
of the council: but whosoever
shall say, Thou fool, shall
be in danger of hell fire.
Matthew 5:22

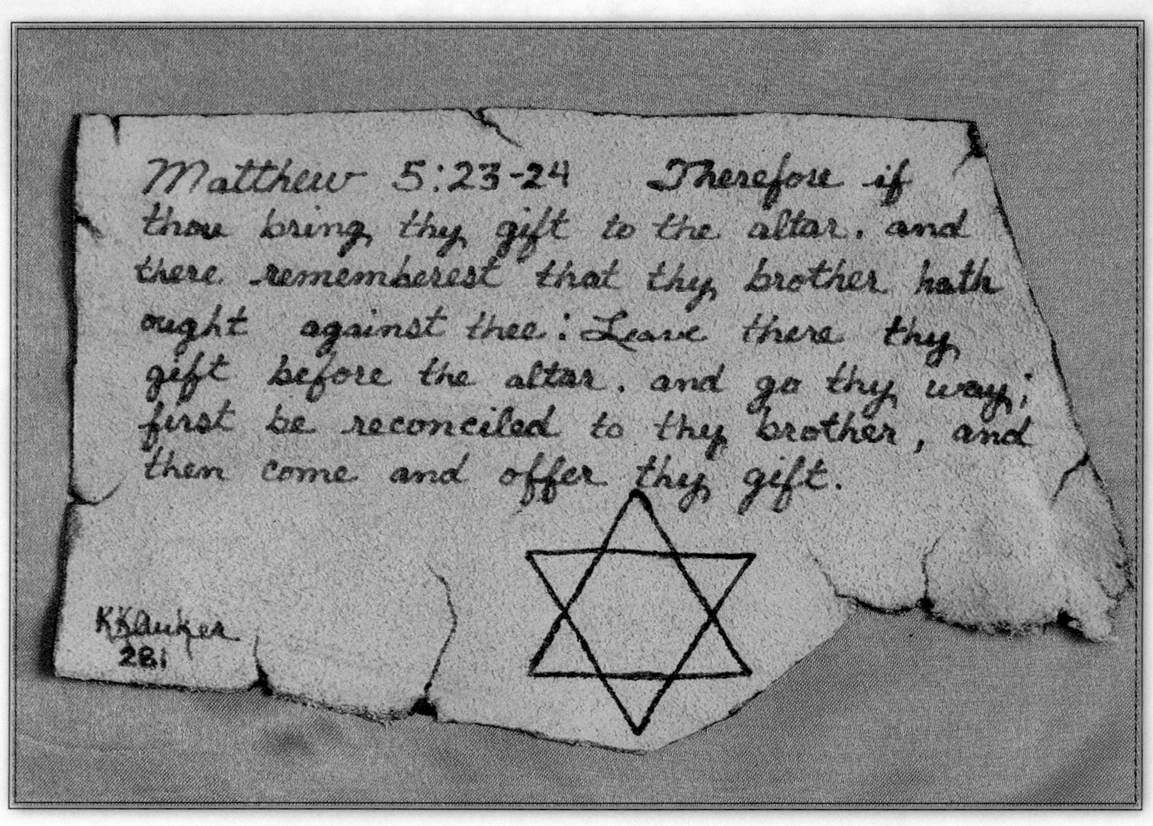
Matthew 5:23-24 Therefore if
thou bring thy gift to the altar, and
there rememberest that thy brother hath
ought against thee: Leave there thy
gift before the altar, and go thy way;
first be reconciled to thy brother, and
then come and offer thy gift.
KKlauker
281

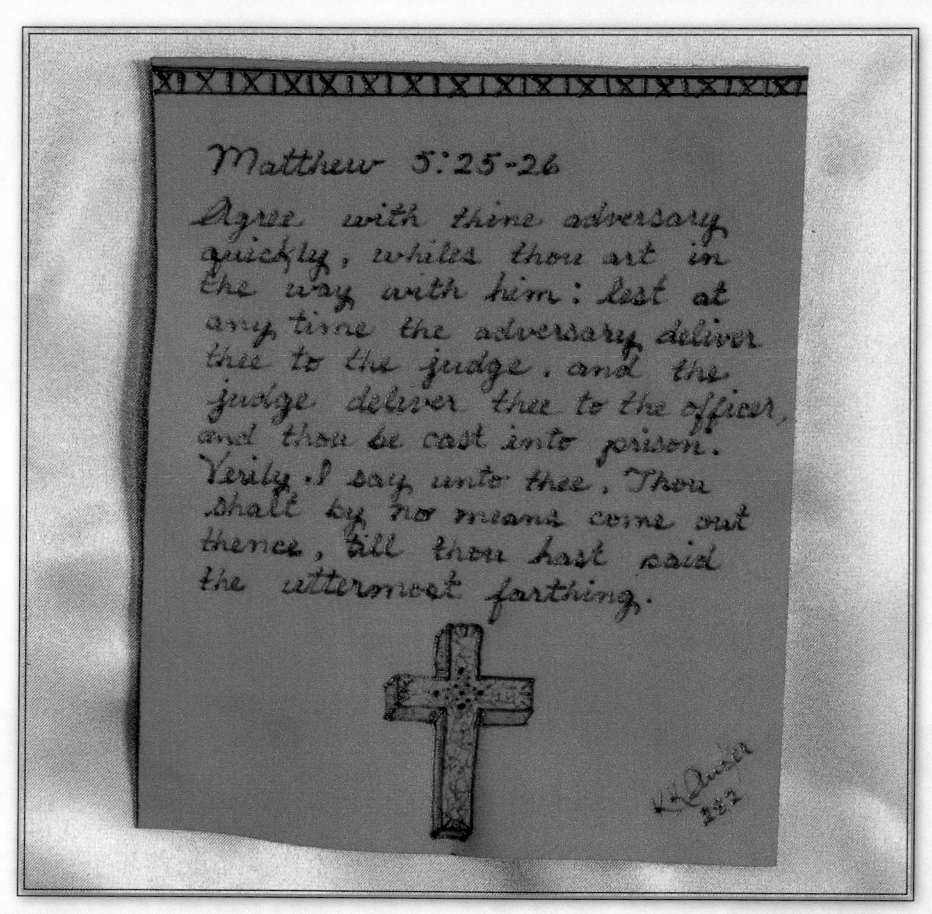
Matthew 5:25-26
Agree with thine adversary
quickly, whiles thou art in
the way with him: lest at
any time the adversary deliver
thee to the judge, and the
judge deliver thee to the officer,
and thou be cast into prison.
Verily I say unto thee, Thou
shalt by no means come out
thence, till thou hast paid
the uttermost farthing.
282

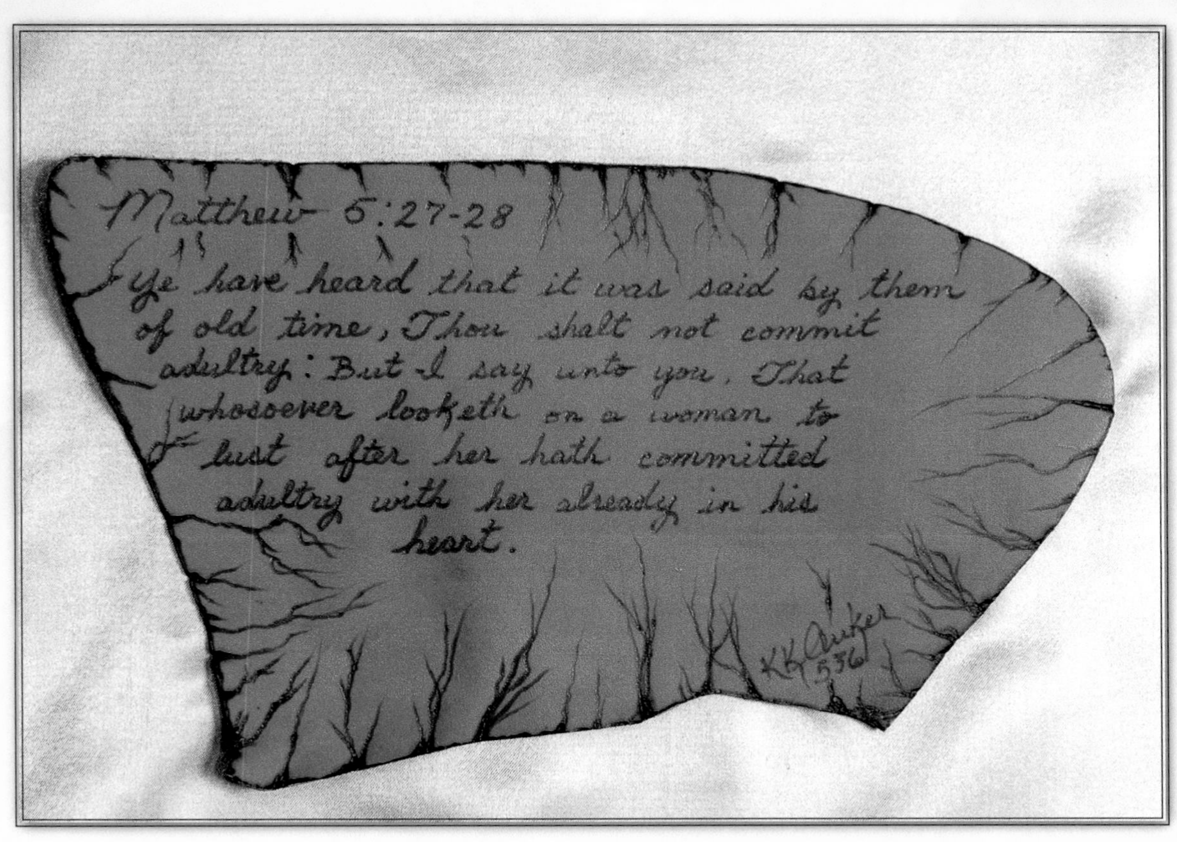
Matthew 5:27-28
Ye have heard that it was said by them of old time, Thou shalt not commit adultry: But I say unto you, That whosoever looketh on a woman to lust after her hath committed adultry with her already in his heart.
KKAnker
536

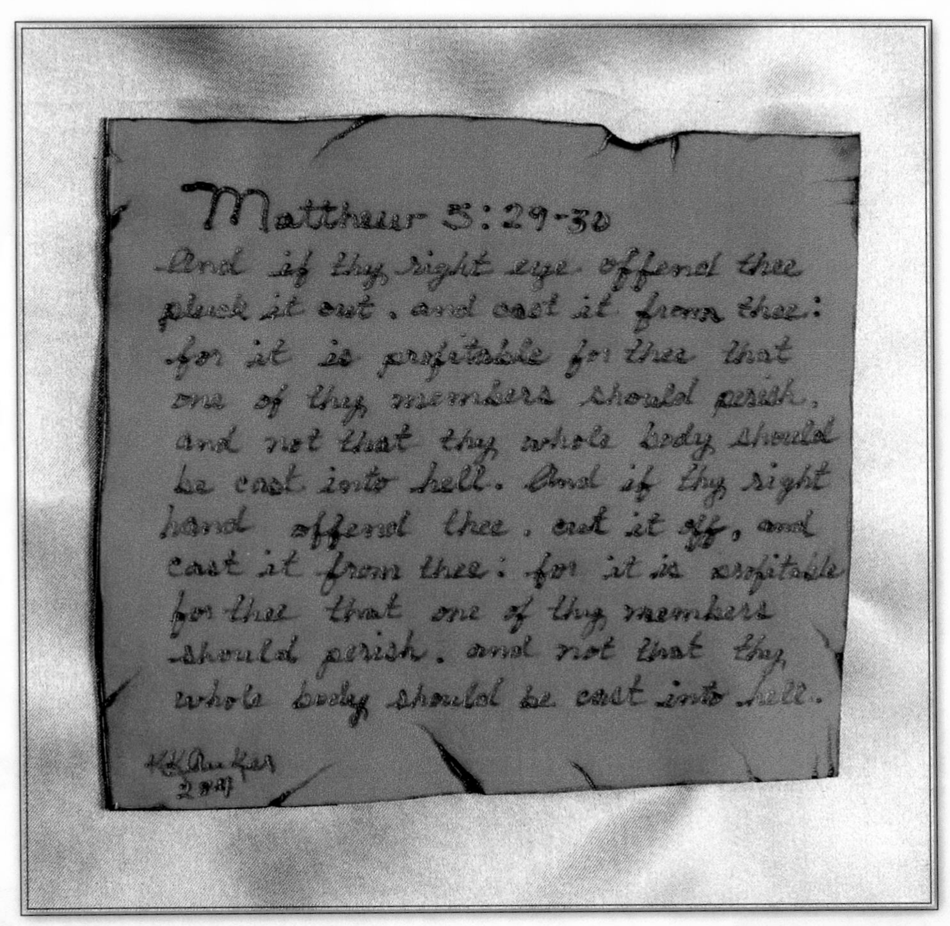
Matthew 5:29-30
And if thy right eye offend thee pluck it out, and cast it from thee: for it is profitable for thee that one of thy members should perish, and not that thy whole body should be cast into hell. And if thy right hand offend thee, cut it off, and cast it from thee: for it is profitable for thee that one of thy members should perish, and not that thy whole body should be cast into hell.
KKAnker

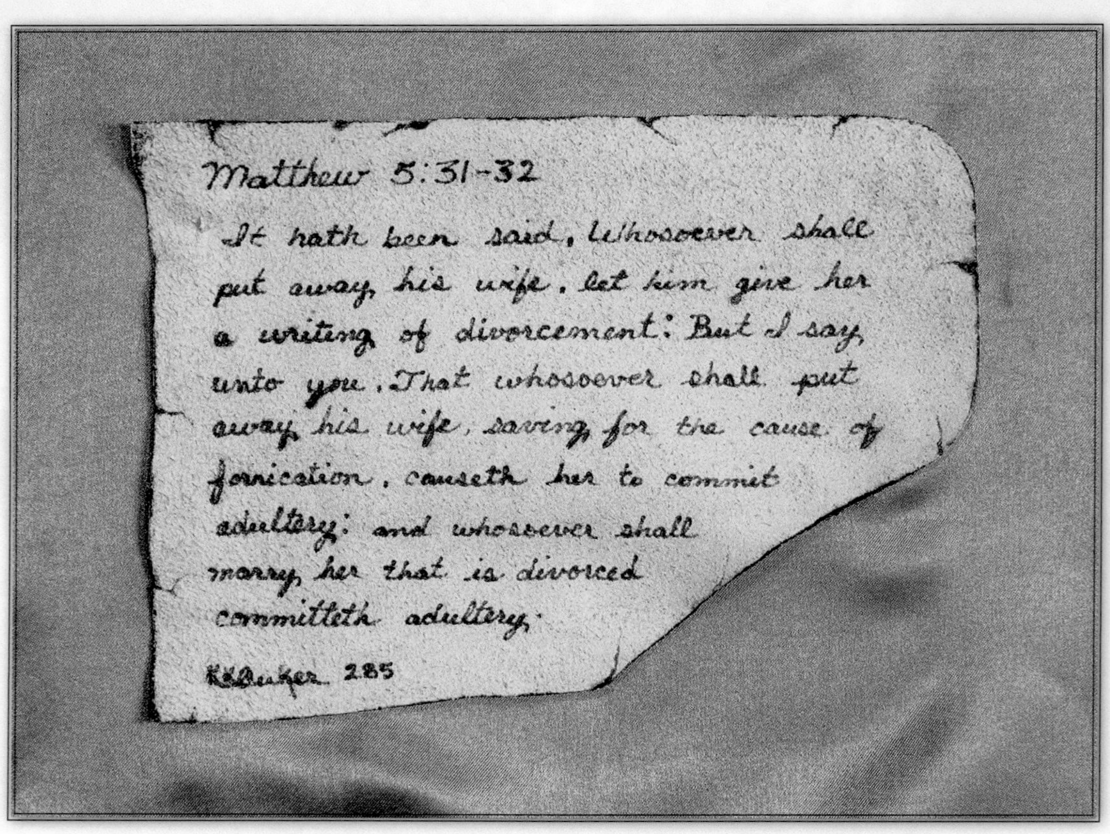

Matthew 5:31-32

It hath been said, Whosoever shall put away his wife, let him give her a writing of divorcement: But I say unto you, That whosoever shall put away his wife, saving for the cause of fornication, causeth her to commit adultery: and whosoever shall marry her that is divorced committeth adultery.

KKAuker 285

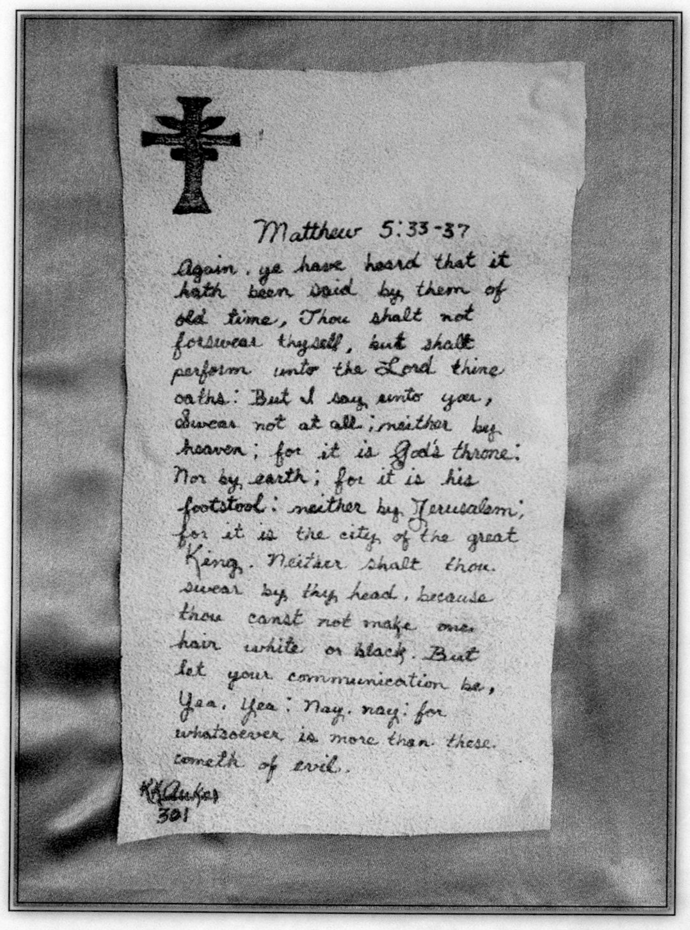

Matthew 5:33-37

Again, ye have heard that it hath been said by them of old time, Thou shalt not forswear thyself, but shalt perform unto the Lord thine oaths: But I say unto you, Swear not at all; neither by heaven; for it is God's throne: Nor by earth; for it is his footstool: neither by Jerusalem; for it is the city of the great King. Neither shalt thou swear by thy head, because thou canst not make one hair white or black. But let your communication be, Yea, Yea; Nay, nay: for whatsoever is more than these cometh of evil.

KKAuker 301

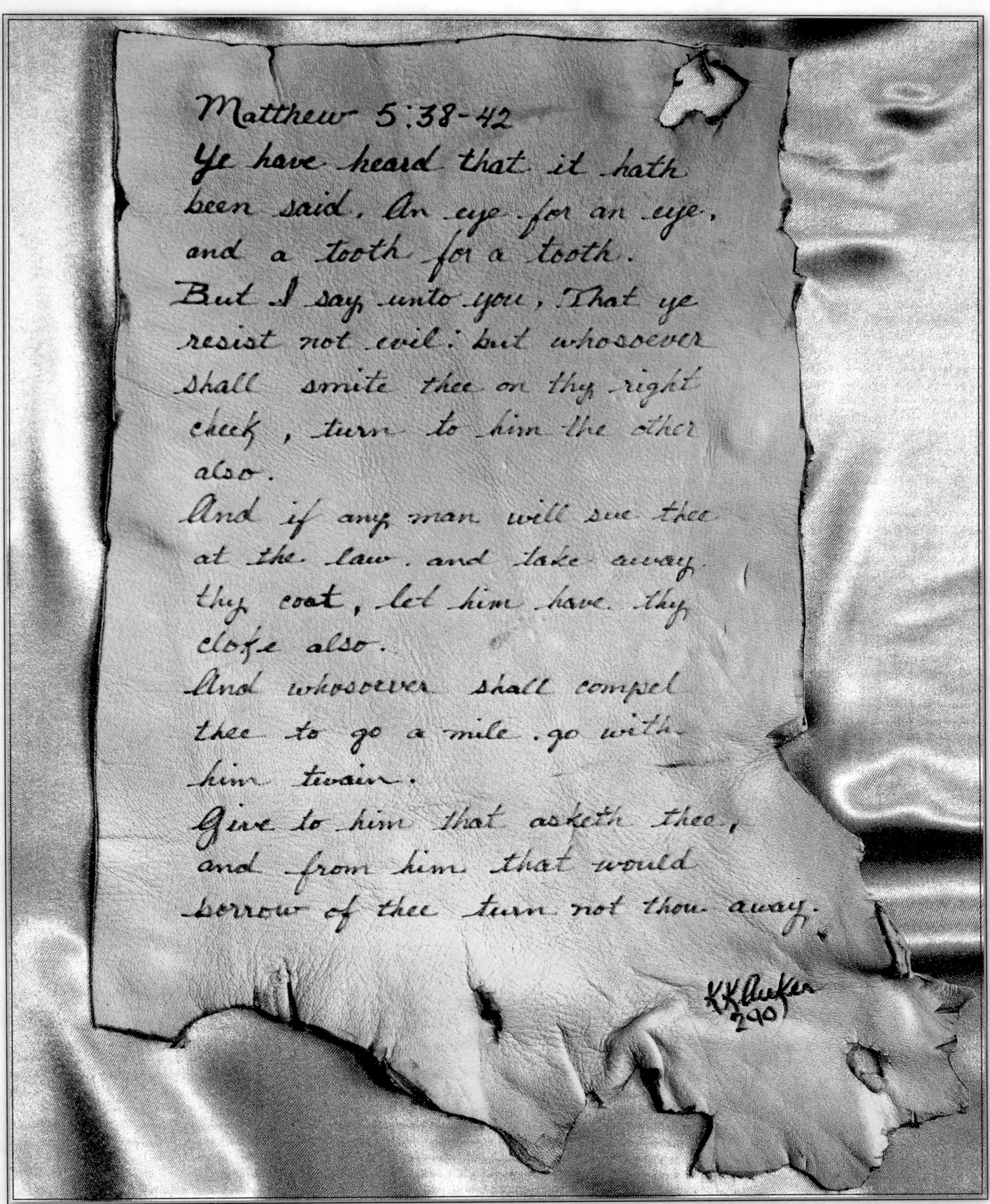
Matthew 5:38-42
Ye have heard that it hath been said, An eye for an eye, and a tooth for a tooth.
But I say unto you, That ye resist not evil: but whosoever shall smite thee on thy right cheek, turn to him the other also.
And if any man will sue thee at the law, and take away thy coat, let him have thy cloke also.
And whosoever shall compel thee to go a mile, go with him twain.
Give to him that asketh thee, and from him that would borrow of thee turn not thou away.

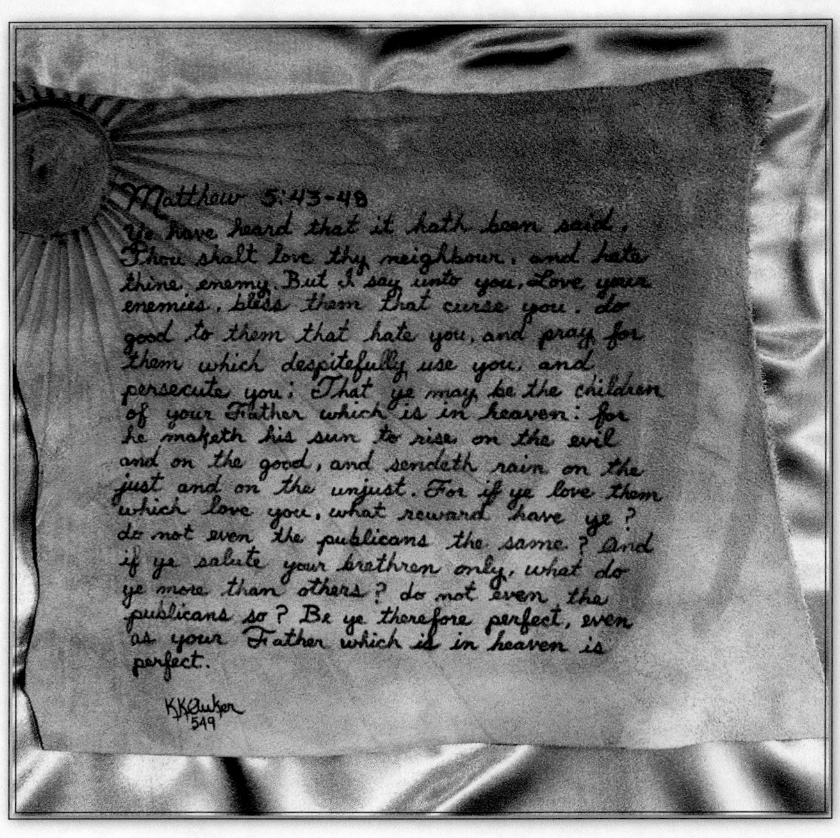
Matthew 5:43-48
Ye have heard that it hath been said,
Thou shalt love thy neighbour, and hate
thine enemy. But I say unto you, Love your
enemies, bless them that curse you, do
good to them that hate you, and pray for
them which despitefully use you, and
persecute you; That ye may be the children
of your Father which is in heaven: for
he maketh his sun to rise on the evil
and on the good, and sendeth rain on the
just and on the unjust. For if ye love them
which love you, what reward have ye?
do not even the publicans the same? And
if ye salute your brethren only, what do
ye more than others? do not even the
publicans so? Be ye therefore perfect, even
as your Father which is in heaven is
perfect.
KKAuker
549

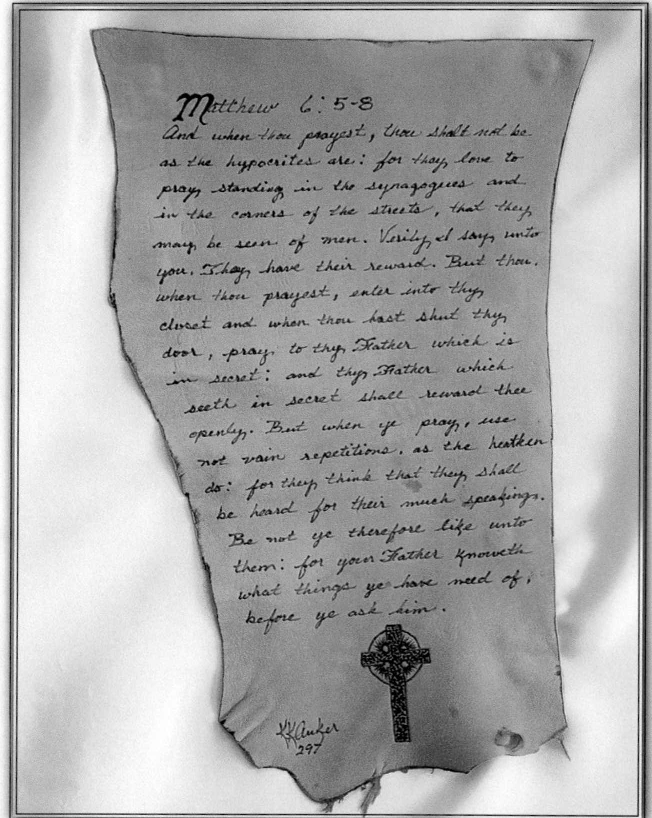
Matthew 6:5-8
And when thou prayest, thou shalt not be
as the hypocrites are: for they love to
pray standing in the synagogues and
in the corners of the streets, that they
may be seen of men. Verily I say unto
you, They have their reward. But thou,
when thou prayest, enter into thy
closet and when thou hast shut thy
door, pray to thy Father which is
in secret; and thy Father which
seeth in secret shall reward thee
openly. But when ye pray, use
not vain repetitions, as the heathen
do: for they think that they shall
be heard for their much speakings.
Be not ye therefore like unto
them: for your Father knoweth
what things ye have need of,
before ye ask him.
KKAuker
297

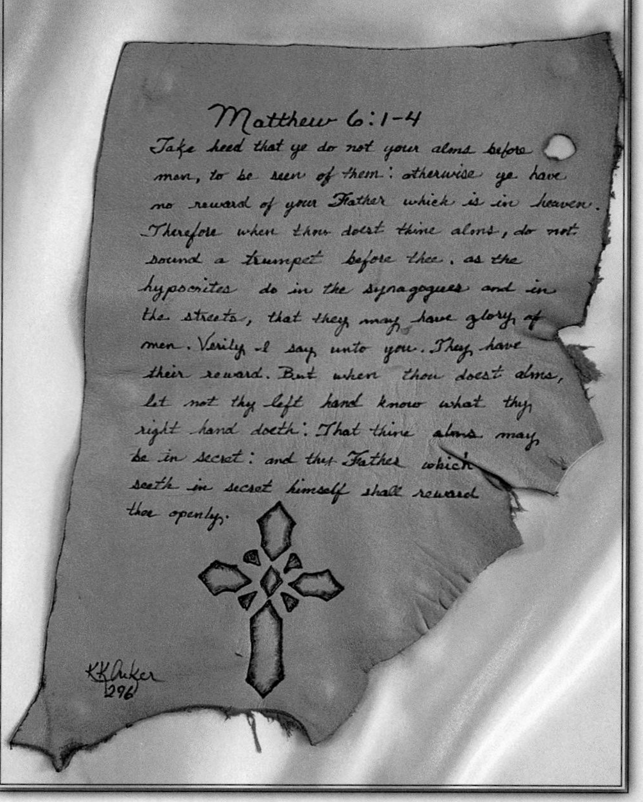
Matthew 6:1-4
Take heed that ye do not your alms before
men, to be seen of them: otherwise ye have
no reward of your Father which is in heaven.
Therefore when thou doest thine alms, do not
sound a trumpet before thee, as the
hypocrites do in the synagogues and in
the streets, that they may have glory of
men. Verily I say unto you, They have
their reward. But when thou doest alms,
let not thy left hand know what thy
right hand doeth: That thine alms may
be in secret: and thy Father which
seeth in secret himself shall reward
thee openly.
KKAuker
296

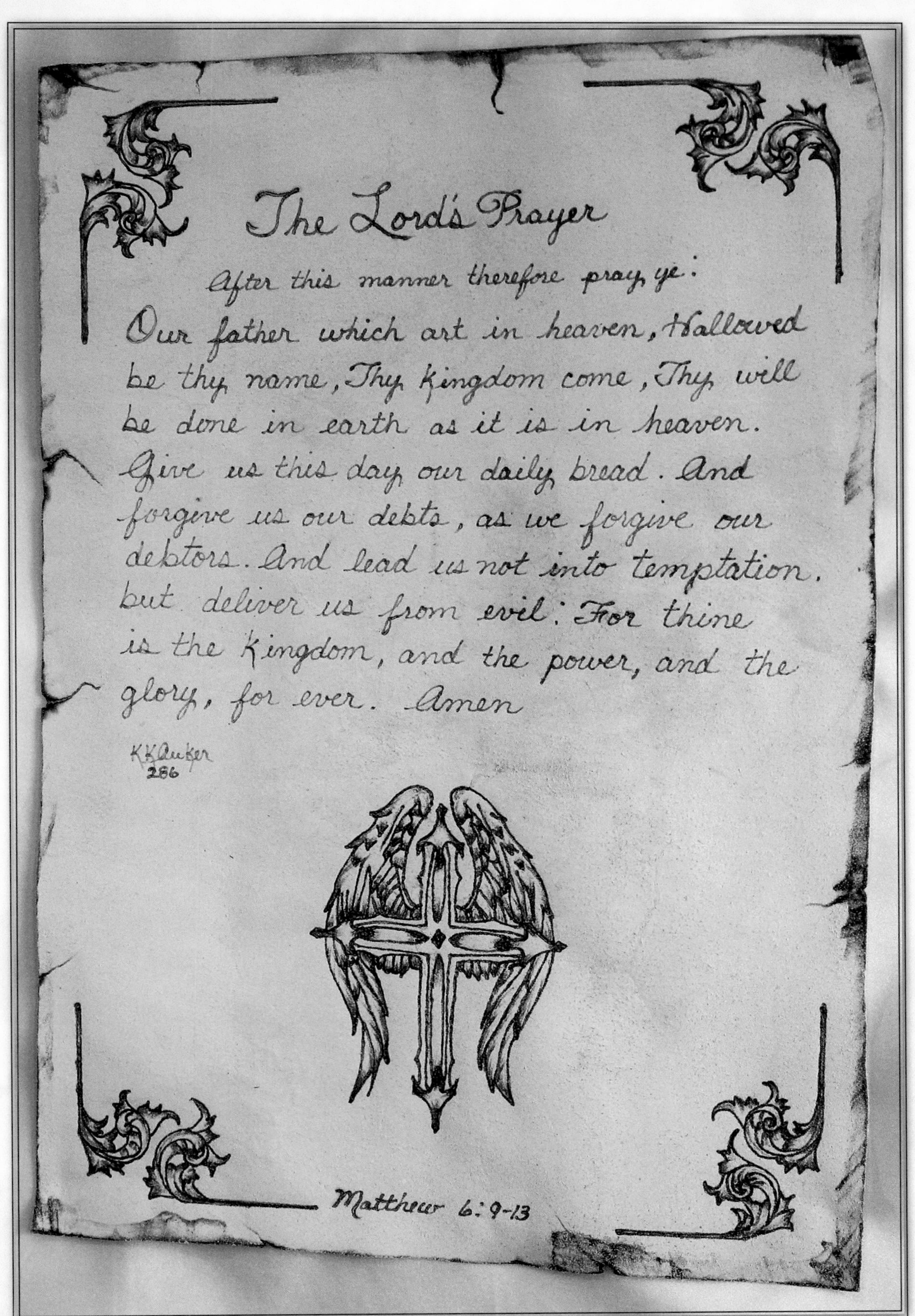
The Lord's Prayer
After this manner therefore pray ye:
Our father which art in heaven, Hallowed be thy name, Thy kingdom come, Thy will be done in earth as it is in heaven. Give us this day our daily bread. And forgive us our debts, as we forgive our debtors. And lead us not into temptation, but deliver us from evil: For thine is the kingdom, and the power, and the glory, for ever. Amen
KKlauker
286
Matthew 6:9-13

Matthew 6:14-18

For if ye forgive men their tresspasses, your heavenly Father will also forgive you: But if ye forgive not men their tresspasses, neither will your Father forgive your tresspasses. Moreover when ye fast, be not, as the hypocrites, of a sad countenance: for they disfigure their faces, that they may appear unto men to fast. Verily I say unto you, They have their reward. But thou, when thou fastest, anoint thine head and wash thy face. That thou appear not unto men to fast, but unto thy Father which is in secret: and thy Father, which seeth in secret, shall reward thee openly.

KKlunker
298

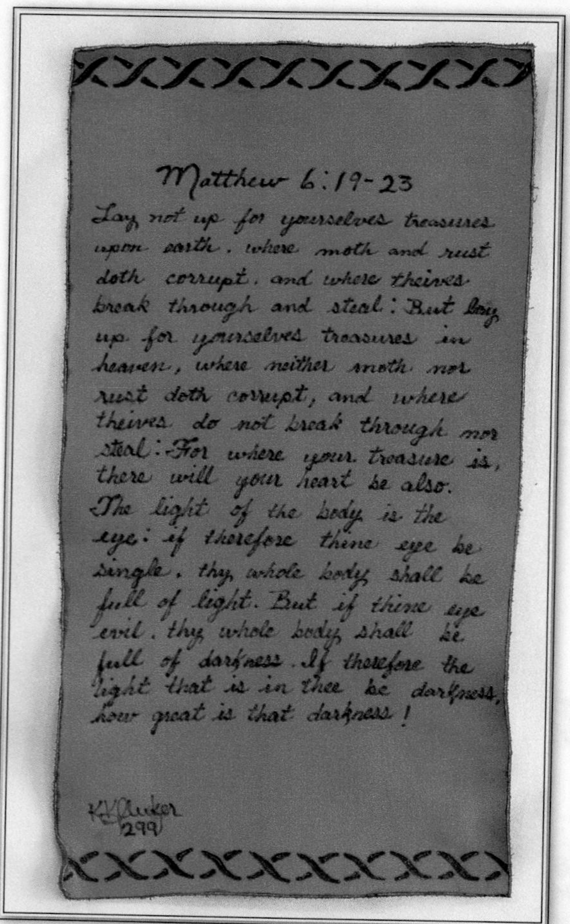

Matthew 6:19-23

Lay not up for yourselves treasures upon earth, where moth and rust doth corrupt, and where theives break through and steal: But lay up for yourselves treasures in heaven, where neither moth nor rust doth corrupt, and where theives do not break through nor steal: For where your treasure is, there will your heart be also. The light of the body is the eye: if therefore thine eye be single, thy whole body shall be full of light. But if thine eye evil, thy whole body shall be full of darkness. If therefore the light that is in thee be darkness, how great is that darkness!

KKlunker
299

Matthew 6:24-34

No man can serve two masters: for either he will hate the one, and love the other; or else he will hold to one, and despise the other. Ye cannot serve God and mammon. Therefore I say unto you, Take no thought for your life, what ye shall eat, or what ye shall drink; nor yet for your body, what ye shall put on. Is not the life more than meat, and the body than raiment? Behold the fowls of the air: for they sow not, neither do they reap, nor gather into barns; yet your heavenly Father feedeth them. Are ye not much better than they? Which of you by taking thought can add one cubit unto his stature? And why take ye thought for raiment? Consider the lilies of the field, how they grow; they toil not, neither do they spin: And yet I say unto you, That even Solomon in all his glory was not arrayed like one of these. Wherefore, if God so clothe the grass of the field, which to day is, and to morrow is cast into the oven, shall he not much more clothe you, O ye of little faith? Therefore take no thought, saying, What shall we eat? or, What shall we drink? or, Wherewithal shall we be clothed? (For after all these things do the Gentiles seek:) for your heavenly Father knoweth that ye have need of all of these things. But seek ye first the kingdom of God, and his righteousness; and all these things shall be added unto you. Take therefore no thought for the morrow: for the morrow shall take thought for the things of itself. Sufficient unto the day is the evil thereof.

KLAnker
300

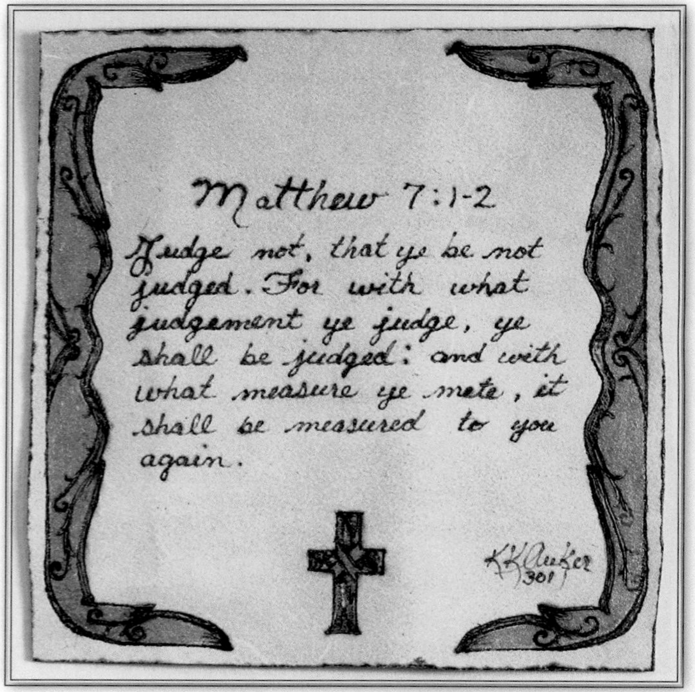

Matthew 7:3-5
And why beholdest thou the mote that
is in thy brothers eye, but considerest
not the beam that is in thy own eye?
Or how wilt thou say to thy brother,
Let me pull out the mote out of
thine eye; and behold, a beam
is in thy own eye? Thou hypo-
crite, first cast out the beam
out of thine own eye; and
then shalt thou see clearly
to cast out the mote out of
thy brothers eye.

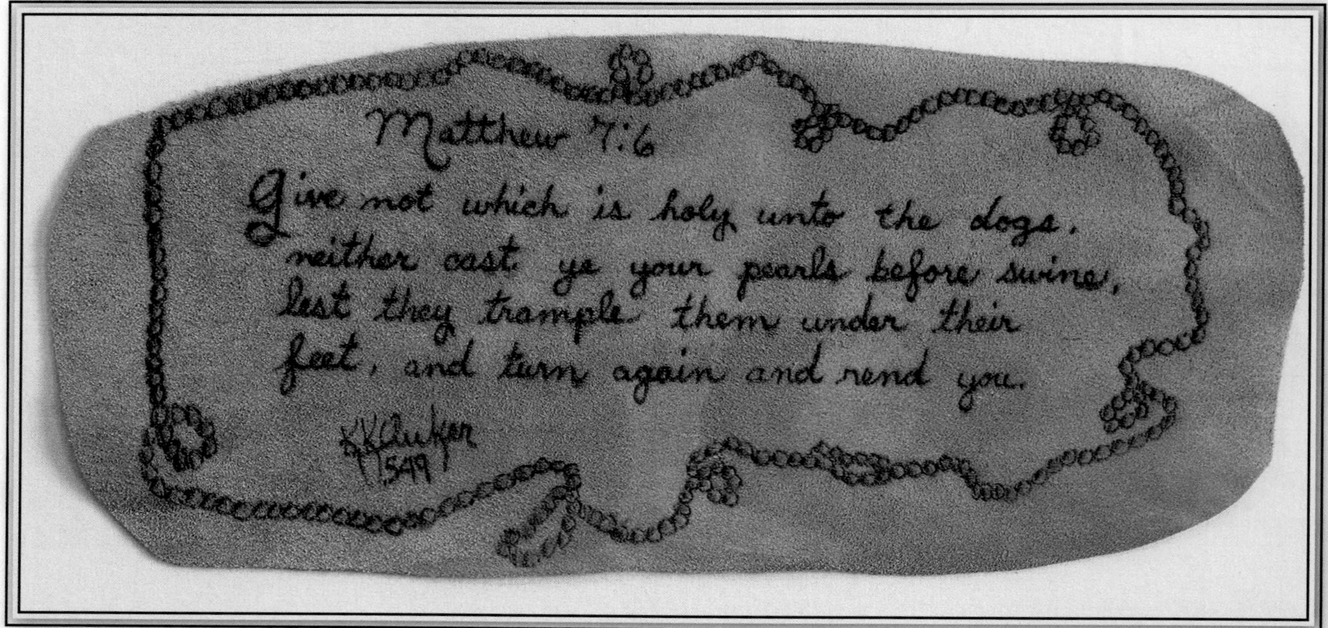

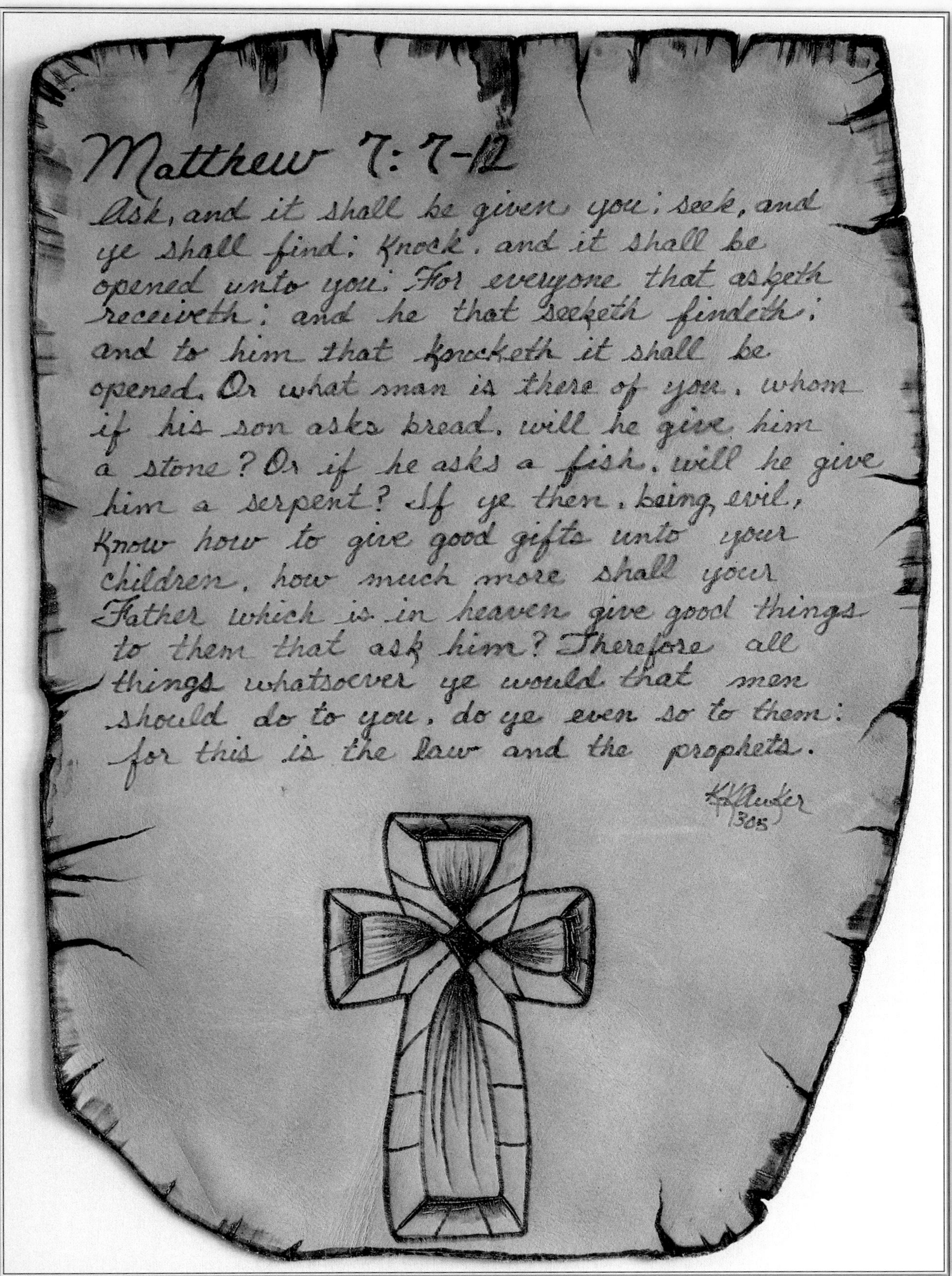
Matthew 7: 7-12
Ask, and it shall be given you; seek, and
ye shall find; knock, and it shall be
opened unto you: For everyone that asketh
receiveth; and he that seeketh findeth;
and to him that knocketh it shall be
opened. Or what man is there of you, whom
if his son asks bread, will he give him
a stone? Or if he asks a fish, will he give
him a serpent? If ye then, being evil,
know how to give good gifts unto your
children, how much more shall your
Father which is in heaven give good things
to them that ask him? Therefore all
things whatsoever ye would that men
should do to you, do ye even so to them:
for this is the law and the prophets.

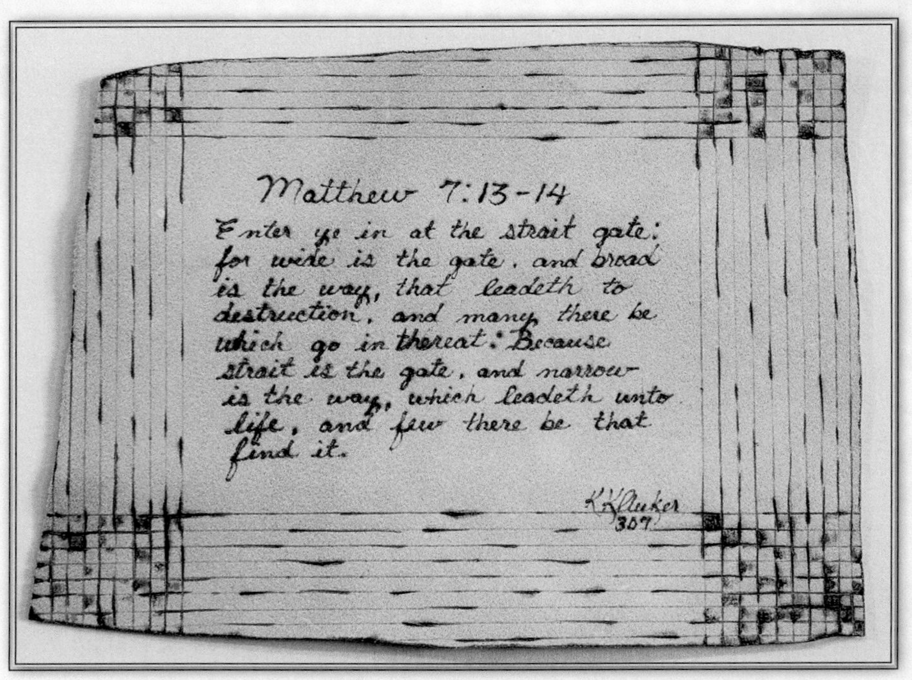
Matthew 7:13-14
Enter ye in at the strait gate:
for wide is the gate, and broad
is the way, that leadeth to
destruction, and many there be
which go in thereat: Because
strait is the gate, and narrow
is the way, which leadeth unto
life, and few there be that
find it.
KKlauker
307

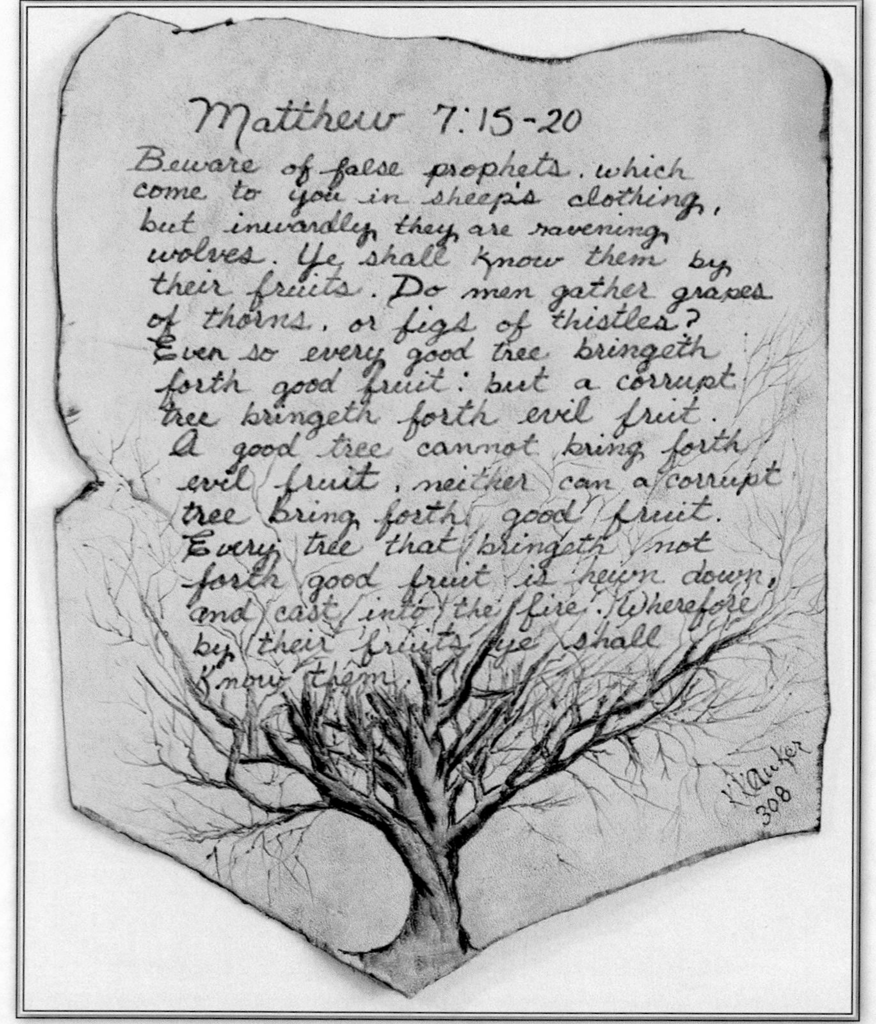
Matthew 7:15-20
Beware of false prophets, which
come to you in sheep's clothing,
but inwardly they are ravening
wolves. Ye shall know them by
their fruits. Do men gather grapes
of thorns, or figs of thistles?
Even so every good tree bringeth
forth good fruit; but a corrupt
tree bringeth forth evil fruit.
A good tree cannot bring forth
evil fruit, neither can a corrupt
tree bring forth good fruit.
Every tree that bringeth not
forth good fruit is hewn down,
and cast into the fire. Wherefore
by their fruits ye shall
know them.
KKlauker
308

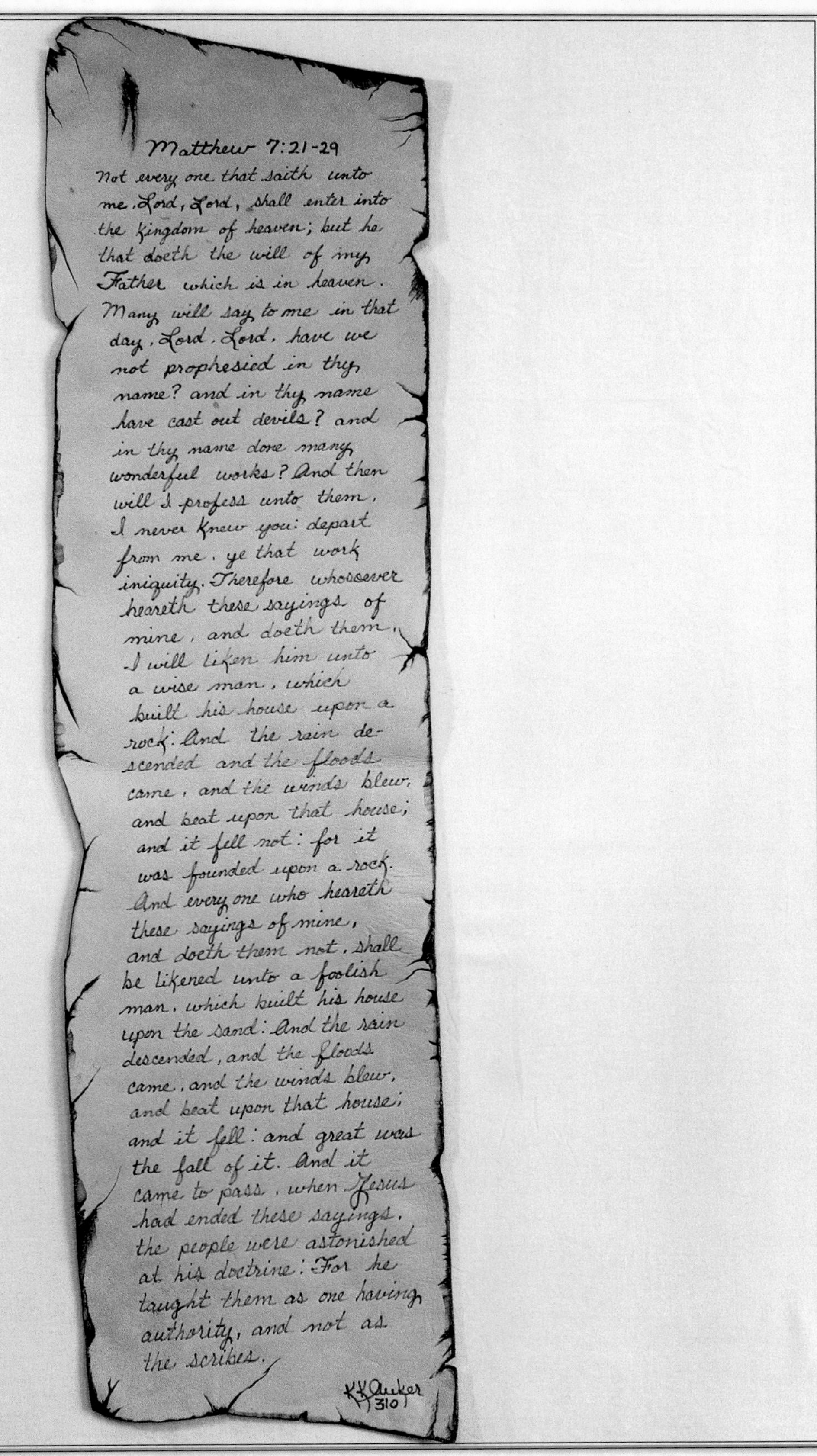
Matthew 7:21-29
Not every one that saith unto
me, Lord, Lord, shall enter into
the kingdom of heaven; but he
that doeth the will of my
Father which is in heaven.
Many will say to me in that
day, Lord, Lord, have we
not prophesied in thy
name? and in thy name
have cast out devils? and
in thy name done many
wonderful works? And then
will I profess unto them,
I never knew you: depart
from me, ye that work
iniquity. Therefore whosoever
heareth these sayings of
mine, and doeth them,
I will liken him unto
a wise man, which
built his house upon a
rock: And the rain de-
scended and the floods
came, and the winds blew,
and beat upon that house;
and it fell not: for it
was founded upon a rock.
And every one who heareth
these sayings of mine,
and doeth them not, shall
be likened unto a foolish
man, which built his house
upon the sand: And the rain
descended, and the floods
came, and the winds blew,
and beat upon that house;
and it fell: and great was
the fall of it. And it
came to pass, when Jesus
had ended these sayings,
the people were astonished
at his doctrine: For he
taught them as one having
authority, and not as
the scribes.

Matthew 8:1
When he was come down from the mountain,
great multitudes followed him.
KKAnker
311

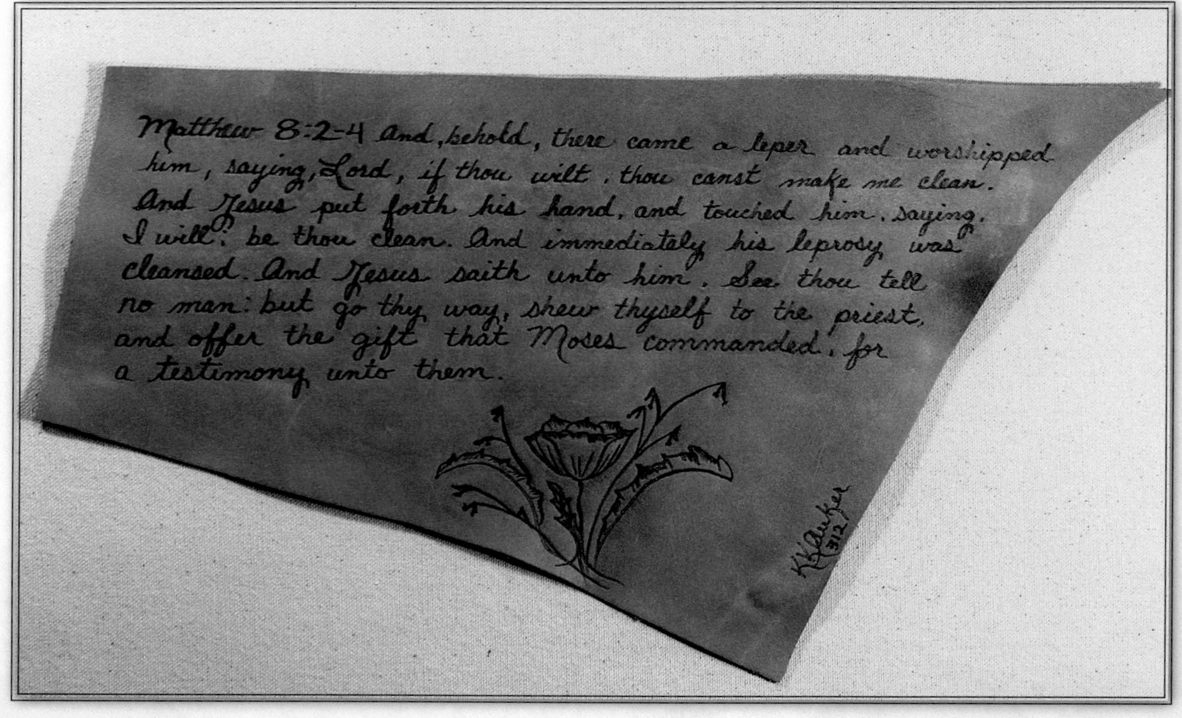

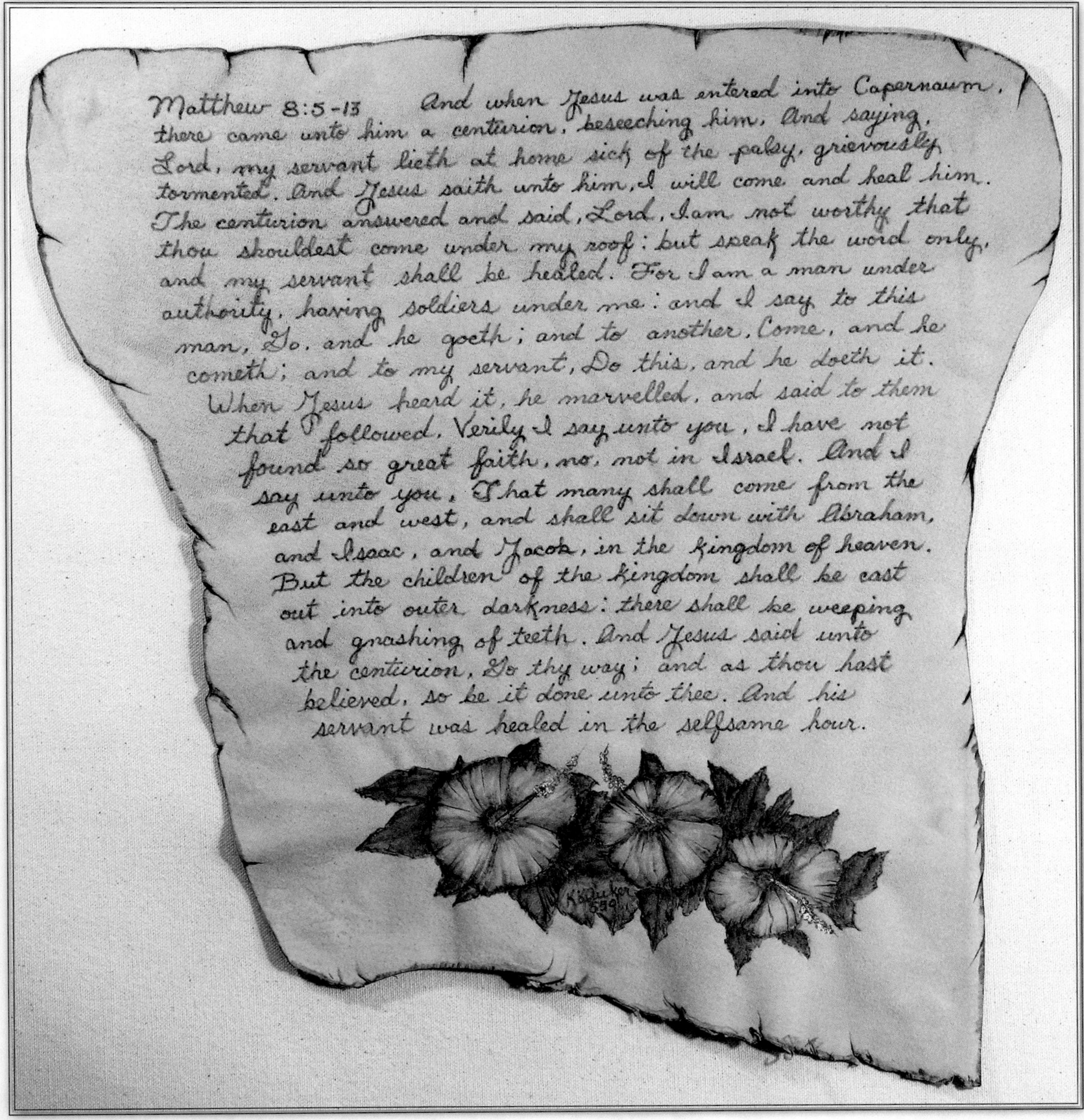
Matthew 8:5-13 And when Jesus was entered into Capernaum,
there came unto him a centurion, beseeching him, And saying,
Lord, my servant lieth at home sick of the palsy, grievously
tormented. And Jesus saith unto him, I will come and heal him.
The centurion answered and said, Lord, I am not worthy that
thou shouldest come under my roof: but speak the word only,
and my servant shall be healed. For I am a man under
authority, having soldiers under me: and I say to this
man, Go, and he goeth; and to another, Come, and he
cometh; and to my servant, Do this, and he doeth it.
When Jesus heard it, he marvelled, and said to them
that followed, Verily I say unto you, I have not
found so great faith, no, not in Israel. And I
say unto you, That many shall come from the
east and west, and shall sit down with Abraham,
and Isaac, and Jacob, in the kingdom of heaven.
But the children of the kingdom shall be cast
out into outer darkness: there shall be weeping
and gnashing of teeth. And Jesus said unto
the centurion, Go thy way; and as thou hast
believed, so be it done unto thee. And his
servant was healed in the selfsame hour.

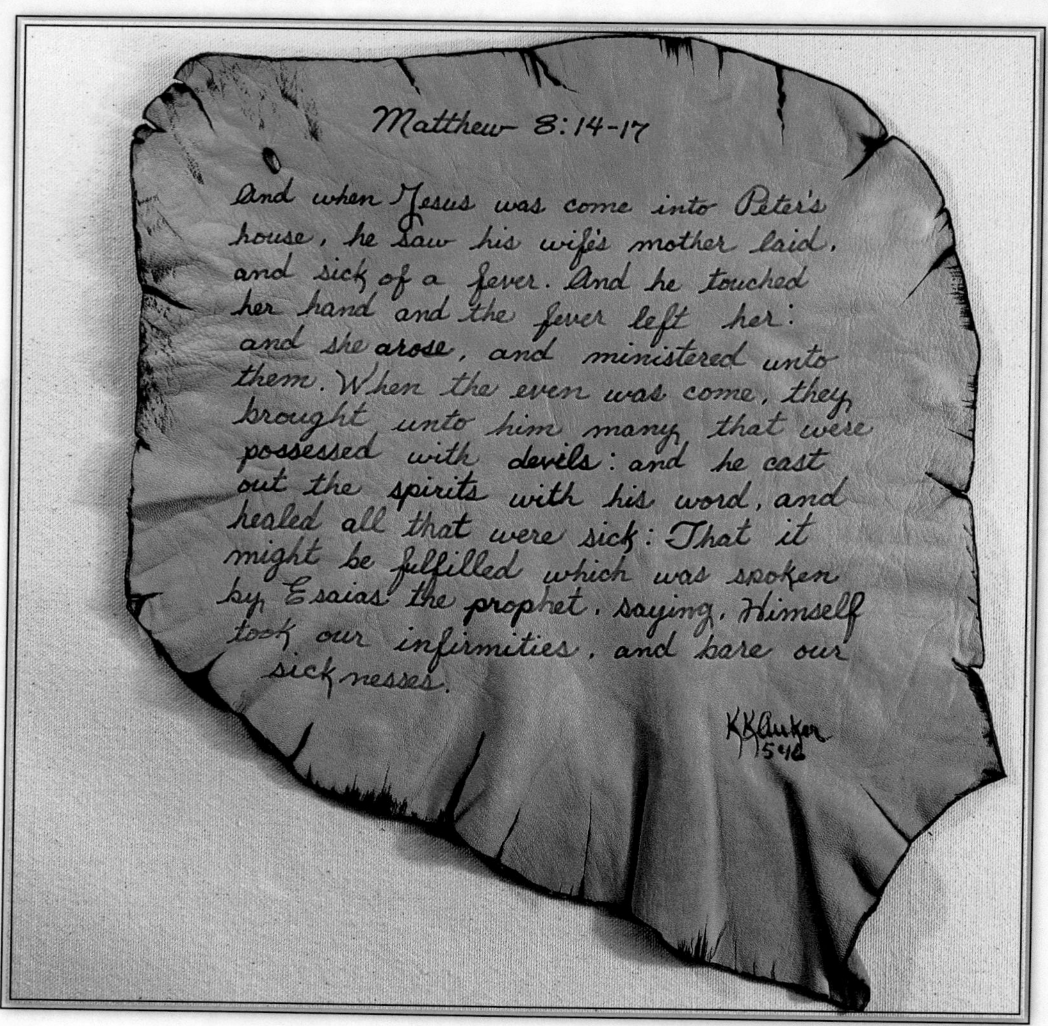
Matthew 8:14-17
And when Jesus was come into Peter's
house, he saw his wife's mother laid,
and sick of a fever. And he touched
her hand and the fever left her:
and she arose, and ministered unto
them. When the even was come, they
brought unto him many that were
possessed with devils: and he cast
out the spirits with his word, and
healed all that were sick: That it
might be fulfilled which was spoken
by Esaias the prophet, saying, Himself
took our infirmities, and bare our
sicknesses.
KKAuker
546

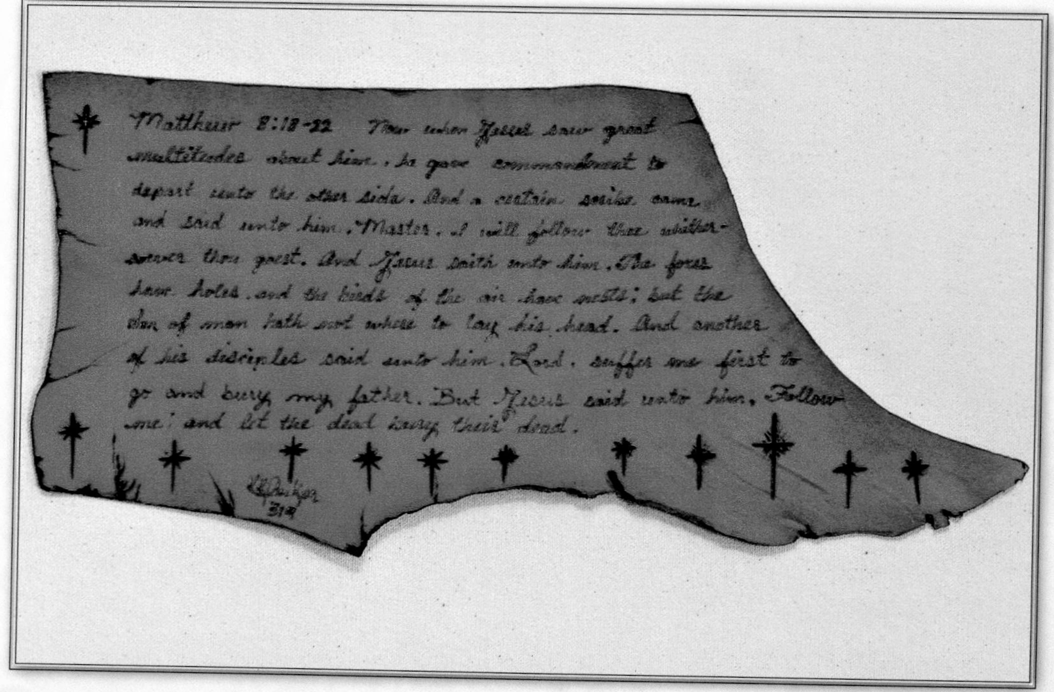
Matthew 8:18-22 Now when Jesus saw great
multitudes about him, he gave commandment to
depart unto the other side. And a certain scribe came,
and said unto him, Master, I will follow thee whither-
soever thou goest. And Jesus saith unto him, The foxes
have holes, and the birds of the air have nests; but the
Son of man hath not where to lay his head. And another
of his disciples said unto him, Lord, suffer me first to
go and bury my father. But Jesus said unto him, Follow
me; and let the dead bury their dead.

Matthew 8:23-27
And when he was entered into a ship,
his desciples followed him. And, behold,
there arose a great tempest in the sea,
insomuch that the ship was covered with
the waves: but he was asleep. And his
desciples came to him, and awoke him,
saying, Lord, save us: we perish.
And he saith unto them, Why are ye
fearful, O ye of little faith? Then he
arose, and rebuked the winds and the
sea; and there was a great calm. But
the men marvelled,
saying, What manner
of man is this,
that even the
winds and the
sea obey him!

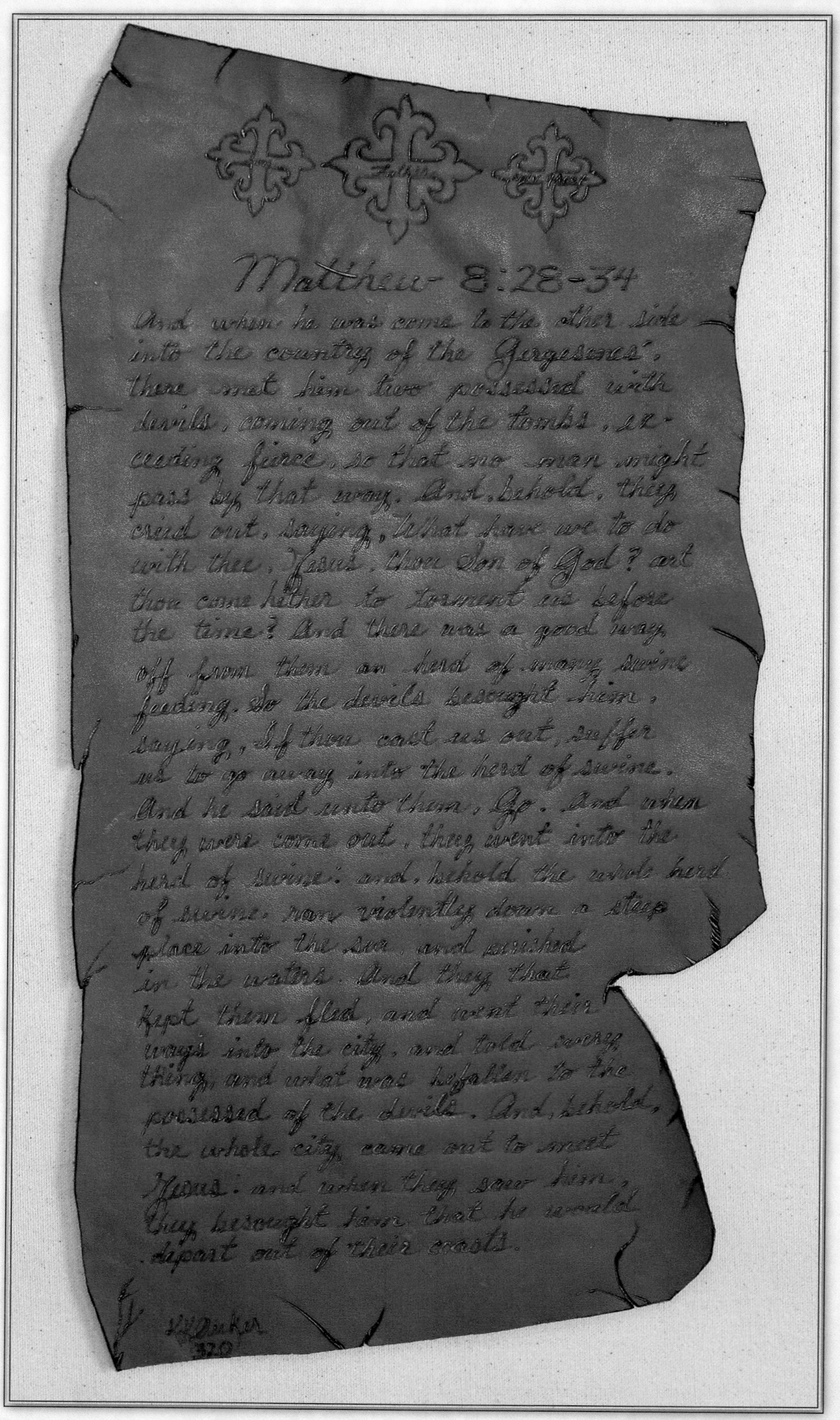
Matthew 8:28-34
And when he was come to the other side
into the country of the Gergesenes,
there met him two possessed with
devils, coming out of the tombs, exceeding fierce, so that no man might
pass by that way. And, behold, they
cried out, saying, What have we to do
with thee, Jesus, thou Son of God? art
thou come hither to torment us before
the time? And there was a good way
off from them an herd of many swine
feeding. So the devils besought him,
saying, If thou cast us out, suffer
us to go away into the herd of swine.
And he said unto them, Go. And when
they were come out, they went into the
herd of swine: and, behold the whole herd
of swine ran violently down a steep
place into the sea, and perished
in the waters. And they that
kept them fled, and went their
ways into the city, and told every
thing, and what was befallen to the
possessed of the devils. And, behold,
the whole city came out to meet
Jesus: and when they saw him,
they besought him that he would
depart out of their coasts.

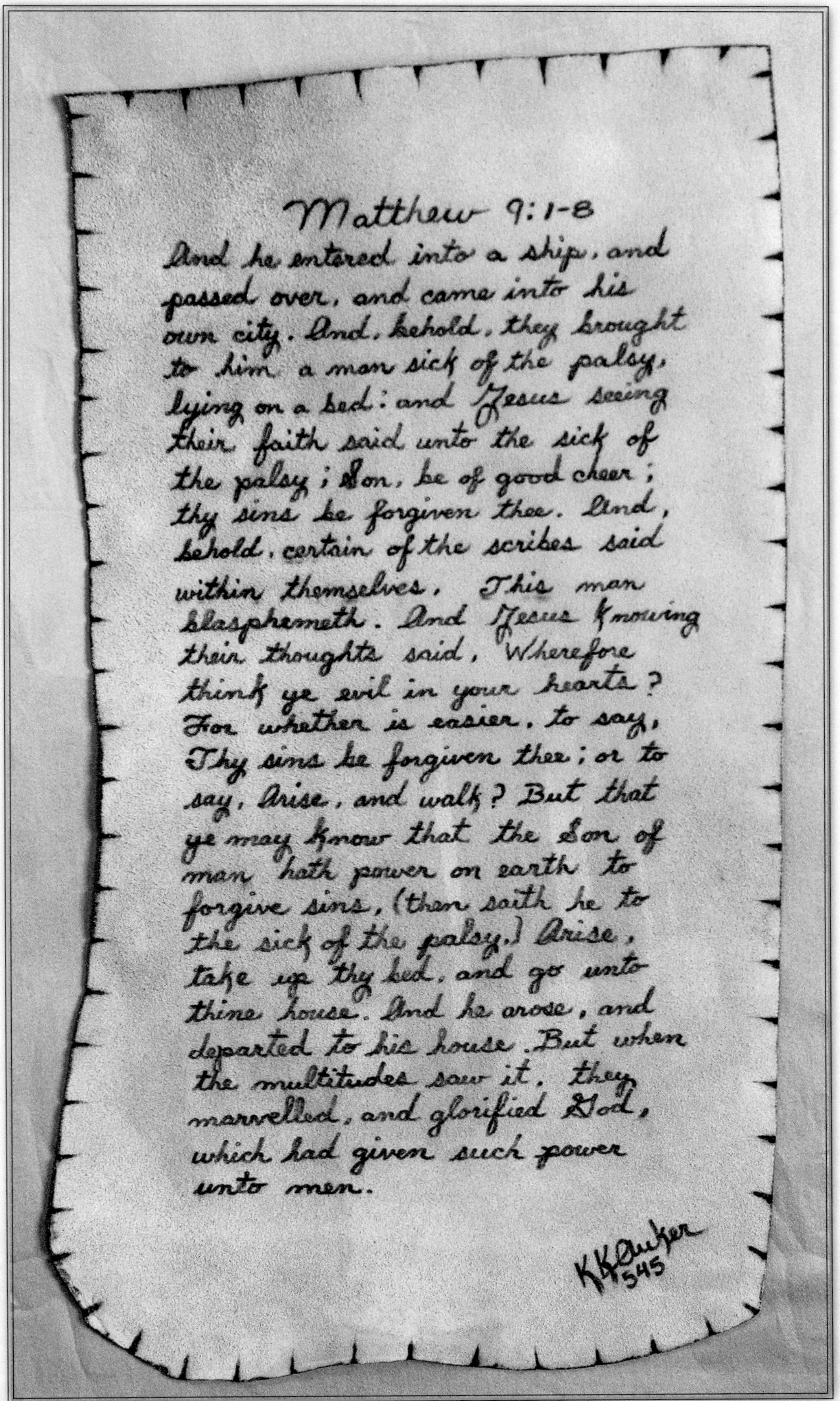

Matthew 9:1-8
And he entered into a ship, and
passed over, and came into his
own city. And, behold, they brought
to him a man sick of the palsy,
lying on a bed: and Jesus seeing
their faith said unto the sick of
the palsy; Son, be of good cheer;
thy sins be forgiven thee. And,
behold, certain of the scribes said
within themselves, This man
blasphemeth. And Jesus knowing
their thoughts said, Wherefore
think ye evil in your hearts?
For whether is easier, to say,
Thy sins be forgiven thee; or to
say, Arise, and walk? But that
ye may know that the Son of
man hath power on earth to
forgive sins, (then saith he to
the sick of the palsy,) Arise,
take up thy bed, and go unto
thine house. And he arose, and
departed to his house. But when
the multitudes saw it, they
marvelled, and glorified God,
which had given such power
unto men.
545

Matthew 9:9 And as Jesus passed forth from thence, he saw
a man, named Matthew, sitting at the receipt of custom: and he
saith unto him, Follow me. And he arose, and followed him.
KKDunker
552

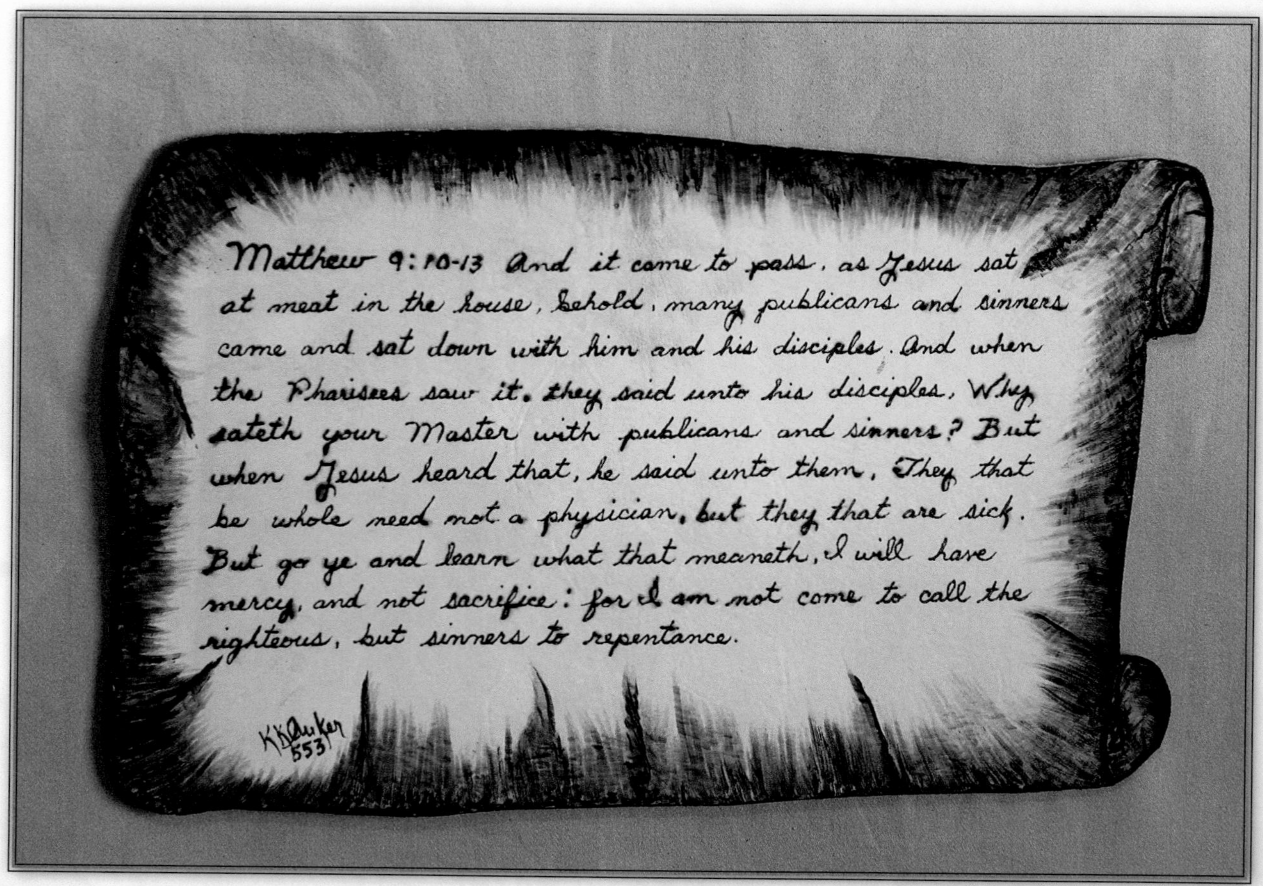
Matthew 9:10-13 And it came to pass, as Jesus sat
at meat in the house, behold, many publicans and sinners
came and sat down with him and his disciples. And when
the Pharisees saw it, they said unto his disciples, Why
eateth your Master with publicans and sinners? But
when Jesus heard that, he said unto them, They that
be whole need not a physician, but they that are sick.
But go ye and learn what that meaneth, I will have
mercy, and not sacrifice: for I am not come to call the
righteous, but sinners to repentance.
KKDunker
553

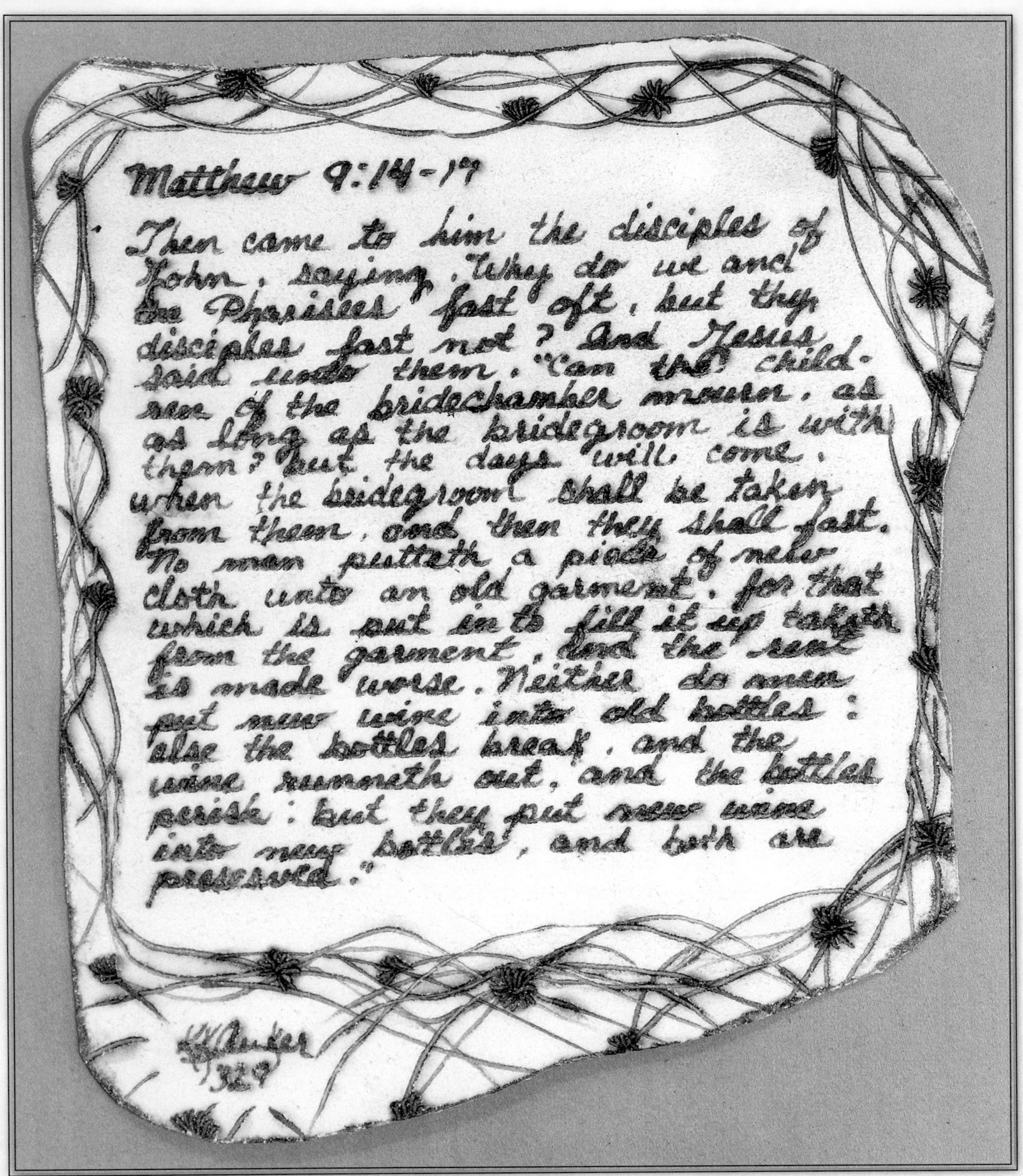
Matthew 9:14-17
Then came to him the disciples of
John, saying, Why do we and
the Pharisees fast oft, but thy
disciples fast not? And Jesus
said unto them, "Can the children of the bridechamber mourn, as
as long as the bridegroom is with
them? but the days will come,
when the bridegroom shall be taken
from them, and then they shall fast.
No man putteth a piece of new
cloth unto an old garment, for that
which is put in to fill it up taketh
from the garment, and the rent
is made worse. Neither do men
put new wine into old bottles:
else the bottles break, and the
wine runneth out, and the bottles
perish: but they put new wine
into new bottles, and both are
preserved."

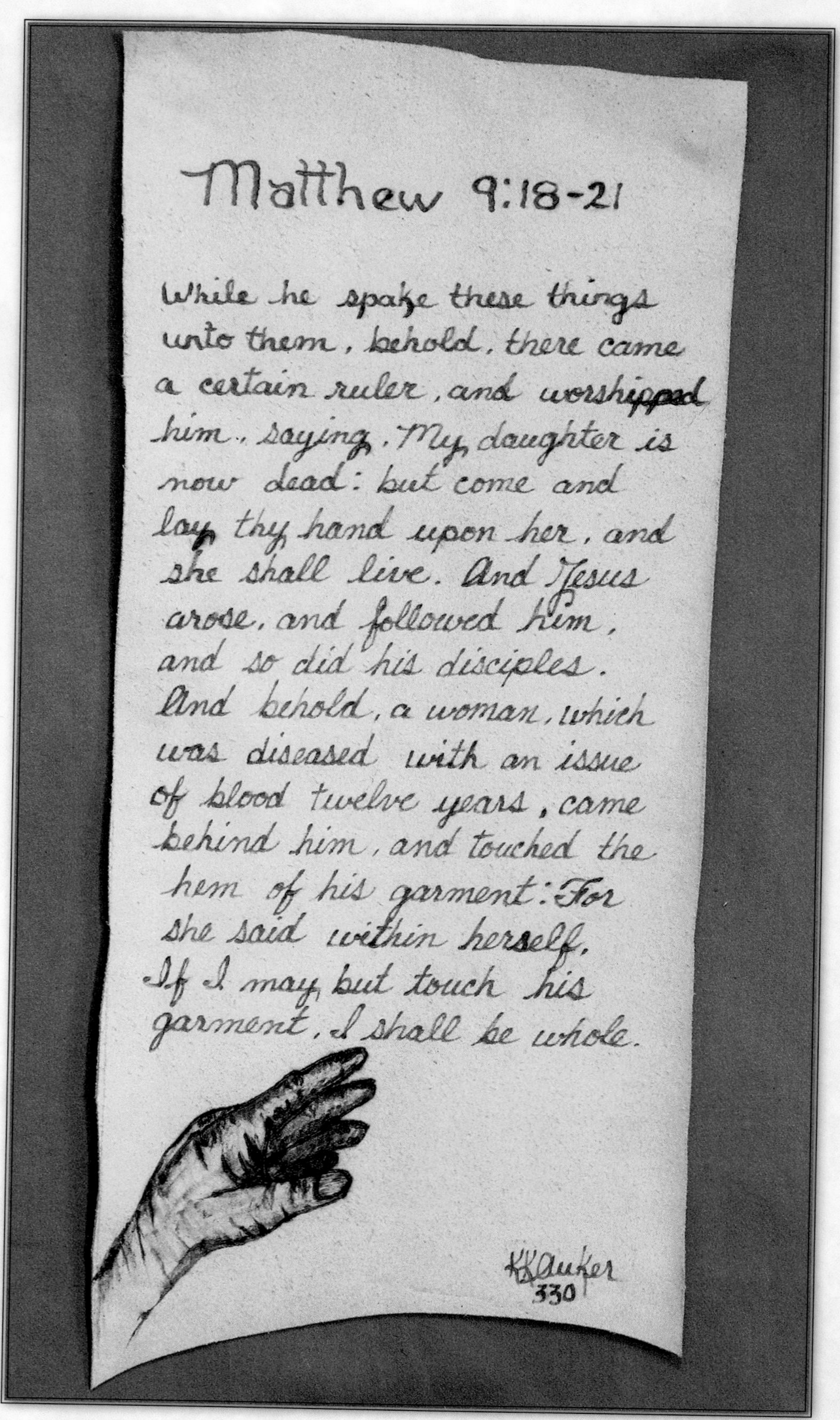
Matthew 9:18-21
While he spake these things
unto them, behold, there came
a certain ruler, and worshipped
him, saying, My daughter is
now dead: but come and
lay thy hand upon her, and
she shall live. And Jesus
arose, and followed him,
and so did his disciples.
And behold, a woman, which
was diseased with an issue
of blood twelve years, came
behind him, and touched the
hem of his garment: For
she said within herself,
If I may but touch his
garment, I shall be whole.
KKauker
330

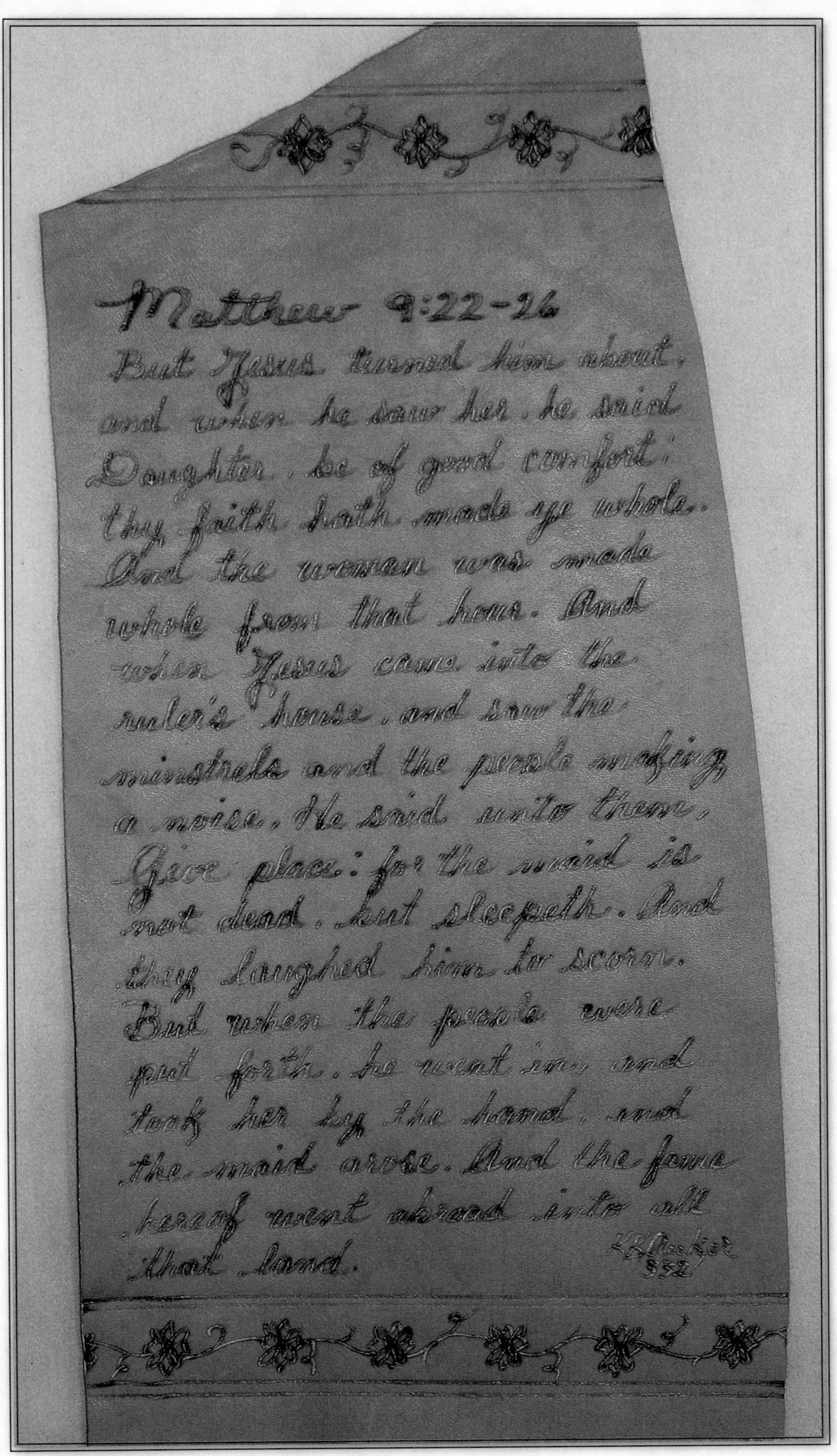
Matthew 9:22-26
But Jesus turned him about,
and when he saw her, he said
Daughter, be of good comfort;
thy faith hath made ye whole.
And the woman was made
whole from that hour. And
when Jesus came into the
ruler's house, and saw the
minstrels and the people making
a noise, He said unto them,
Give place: for the maid is
not dead, but sleepeth. And
they laughed him to scorn.
But when the people were
put forth, he went in, and
took her by the hand, and
the maid arose. And the fame
hereof went abroad into all
that land.

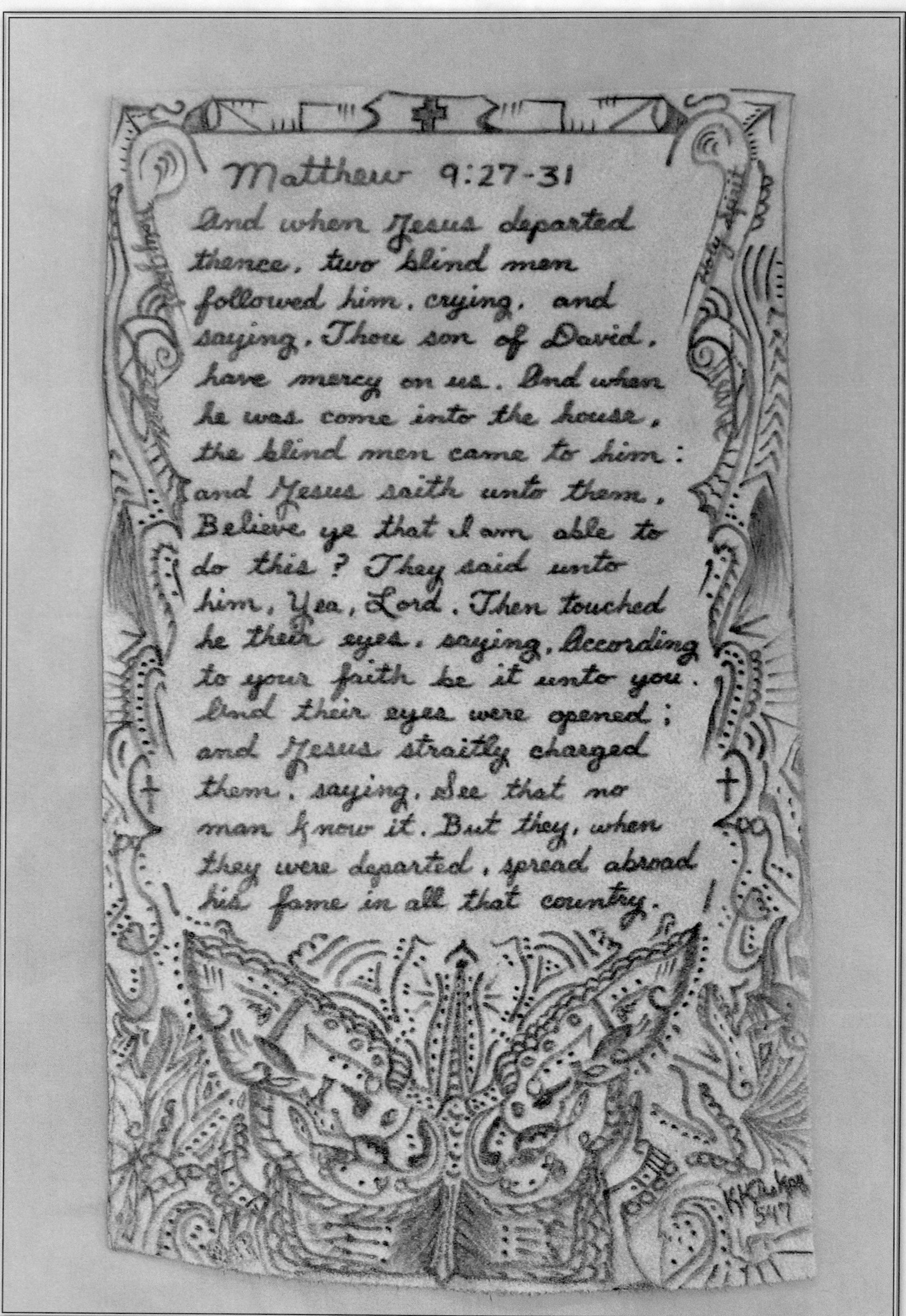

Matthew 9:27-31
And when Jesus departed
thence, two blind men
followed him, crying, and
saying, Thou son of David,
have mercy on us. And when
he was come into the house,
the blind men came to him:
and Jesus saith unto them,
Believe ye that I am able to
do this? They said unto
him, Yea, Lord. Then touched
he their eyes, saying, According
to your faith be it unto you.
And their eyes were opened;
and Jesus straitly charged
them, saying, See that no
man know it. But they, when
they were departed, spread abroad
his fame in all that country.

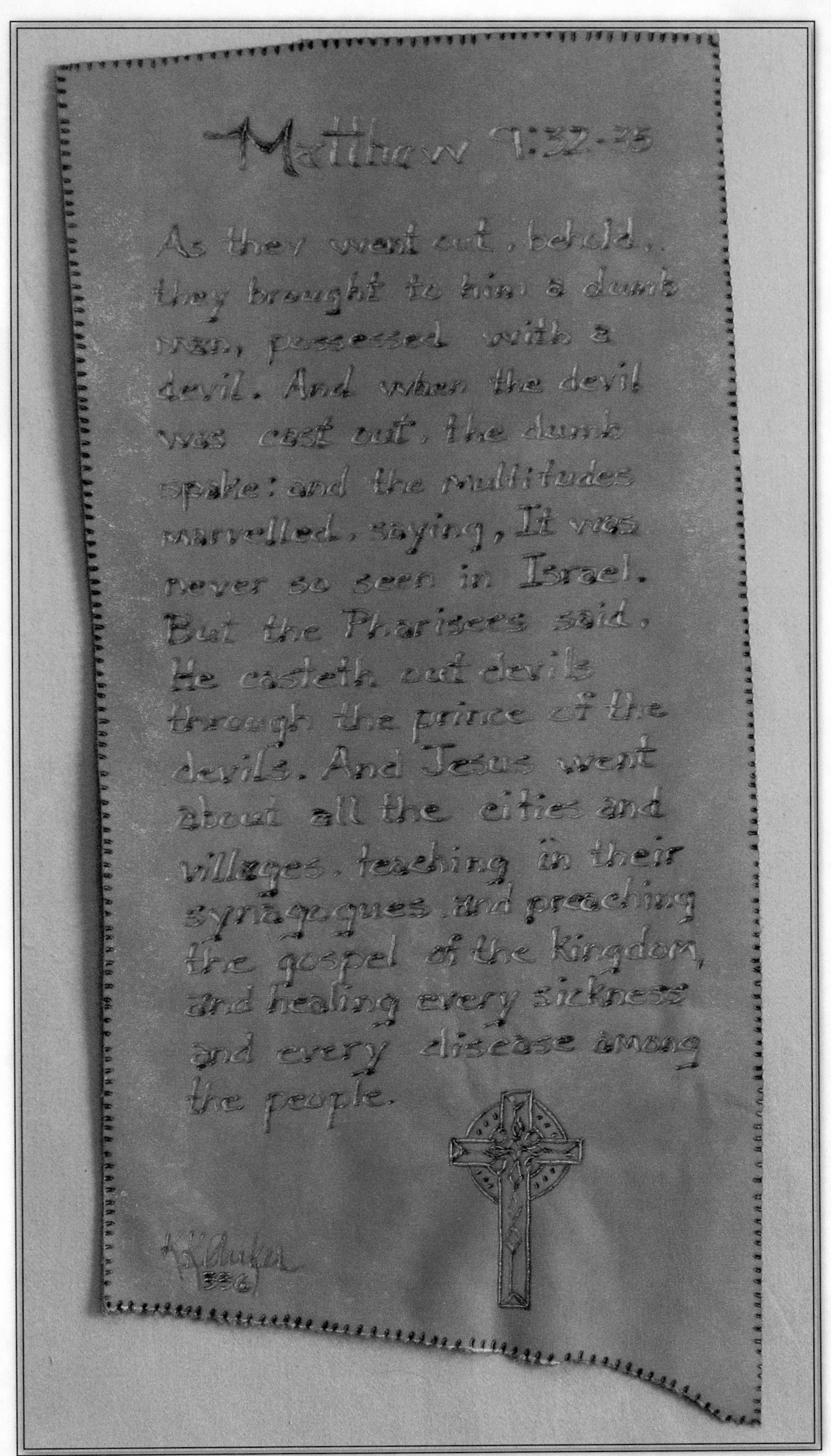
Matthew 9:32-35
As they went out, behold,
they brought to him a dumb
man, possessed with a
devil. And when the devil
was cast out, the dumb
spake: and the multitudes
marvelled, saying, It was
never so seen in Israel.
But the Pharisees said,
He casteth out devils
through the prince of the
devils. And Jesus went
about all the cities and
villages, teaching in their
synagogues, and preaching
the gospel of the kingdom,
and healing every sickness
and every disease among
the people.

Matthew 9:36-38
But when he saw the multitudes,
he was moved with compassion
on them, because they fainted,
and were scattered abroad, as
sheep having no shepard. Then
saith he unto his disciples, The
harvest truely is plenteous, but
the labourers are few; Pray ye
therefore the Lord of the harvest,
that he will send forth labourers
into his harvest.

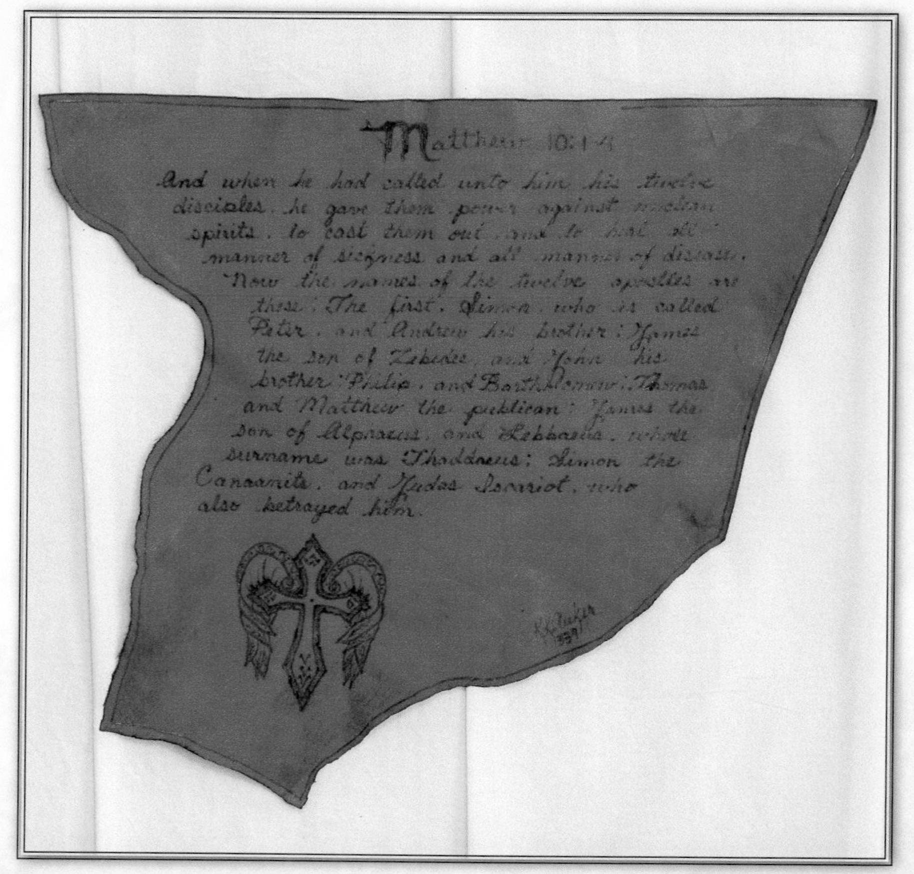
Matthew 10:1-4
And when he had called unto him his twelve
disciples, he gave them power against unclean
spirits, to cast them out, and to heal all
manner of sickness and all manner of disease.
Now the names of the twelve apostles are
these; The first, Simon, who is called
Peter, and Andrew his brother; James
the son of Zebedee, and John his
brother; Philip, and Bartholomew; Thomas
and Matthew the publican; James the
son of Alphaeus, and Lebbaeus, whose
surname was Thaddaeus; Simon the
Canaanite, and Judas Iscariot, who
also betrayed him.

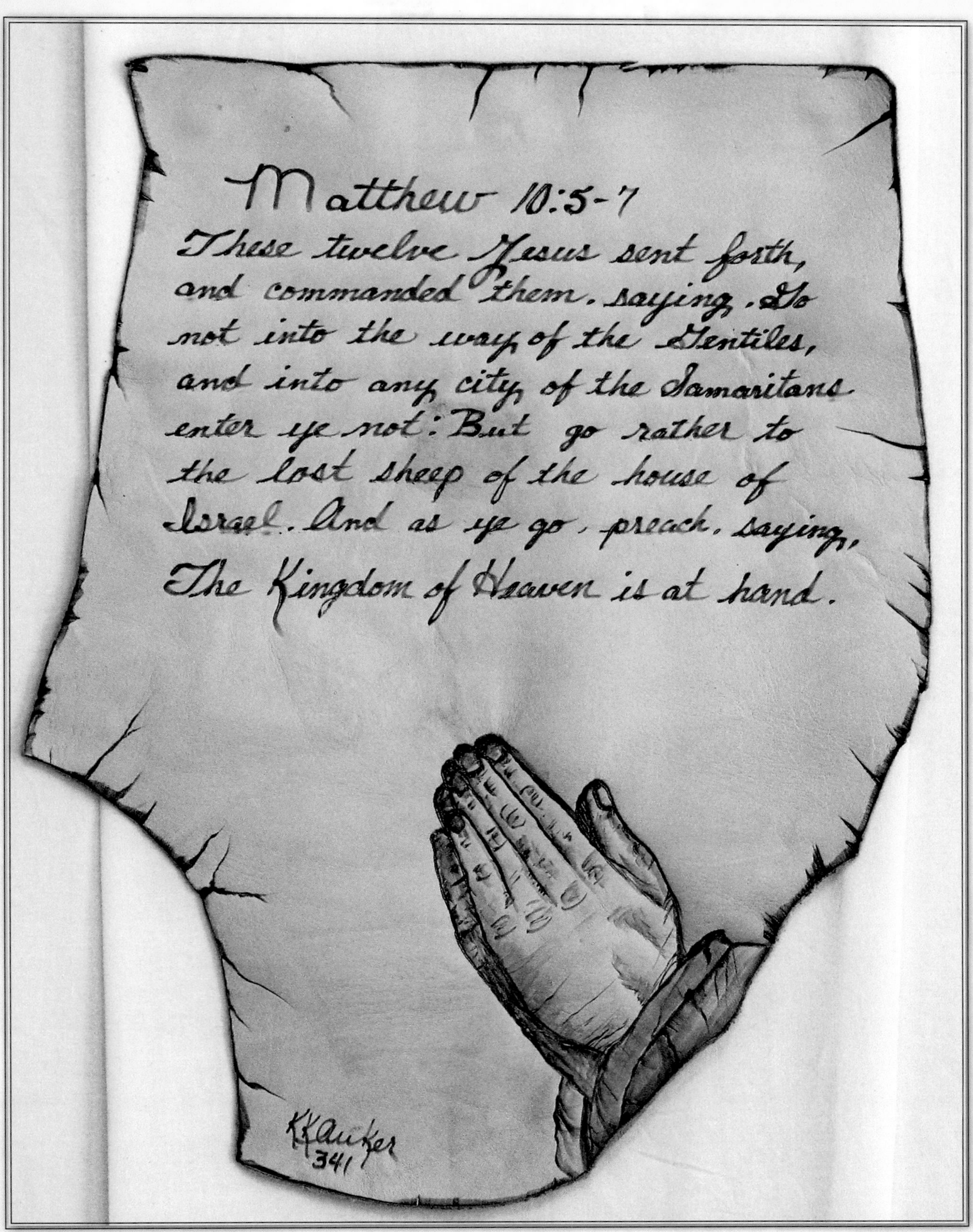
Matthew 10:5-7
These twelve Jesus sent forth,
and commanded them, saying, Go
not into the way of the Gentiles,
and into any city of the Samaritans
enter ye not: But go rather to
the lost sheep of the house of
Israel. And as ye go, preach, saying,
The Kingdom of Heaven is at hand.
KKancker
341

Matthew 10:8-10
Heal the sick, cleanse the lepers,
raise the dead, cast out devils: freely ye
have received, freely give. Provide neither
gold, nor silver, nor brass in your
purses, Nor script for your journey,
neither two coats, neither shoes, nor
yet staves: for the workman is worthy
of his meat.

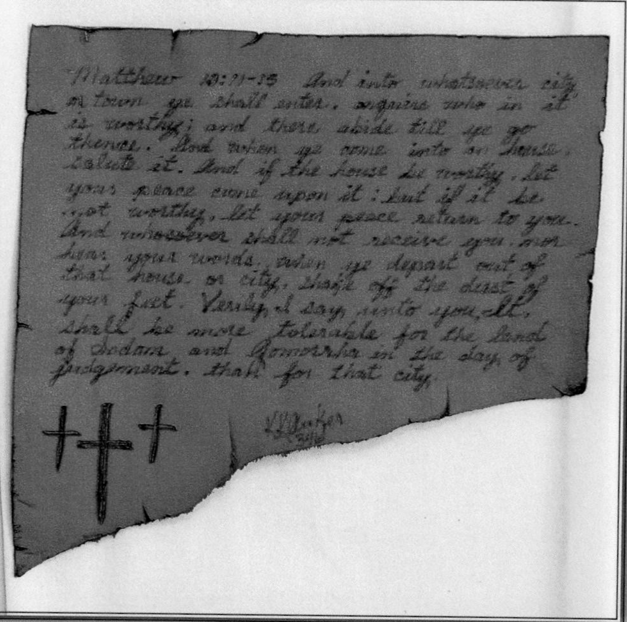
Matthew 10:11-15 And into whatsoever city
or town ye shall enter, enquire who in it
is worthy; and there abide till ye go
thence. And when ye come into an house,
salute it. And if the house be worthy, let
your peace come upon it: but if it be
not worthy, let your peace return to you.
And whosoever shall not receive you, nor
hear your words, when ye depart out of
that house or city, shake off the dust of
your feet. Verily, I say unto you, It
shall be more tolerable for the land
of Sodom and Gomorrha in the day of
judgement, than for that city.
KKDuker

Matthew 10:16-18
Behold, I send you forth as sheep
in the midst of wolves: be ye therefore wise as serpents, and harmless
as doves. But beware of men: for
they will deliver you up to the coun-
cils, and they will scourge you in
their synagogues: And ye shall
be brought before governors and
kings for my sake, for a testimony
against them and the Gentiles.
KKDuker
350

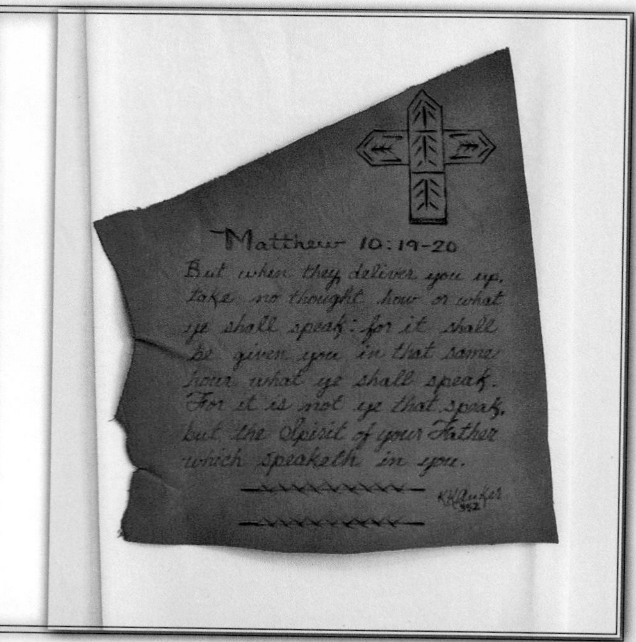
Matthew 10:19-20
But when they deliver you up,
take no thought how or what
ye shall speak: for it shall
be given you in that same
hour what ye shall speak.
For it is not ye that speak,
but the Spirit of your Father
which speaketh in you.
KKDuker
352

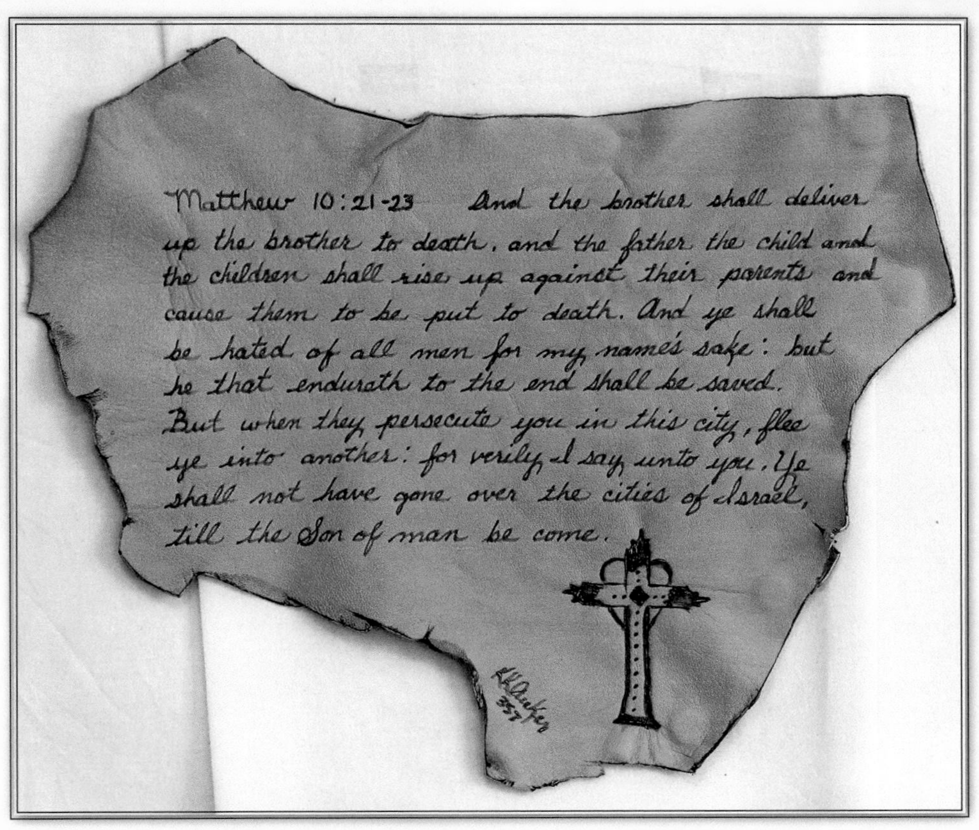

Matthew 10:21-23 And the brother shall deliver
up the brother to death, and the father the child and
the children shall rise up against their parents and
cause them to be put to death. And ye shall
be hated of all men for my name's sake: but
he that endurath to the end shall be saved.
But when they persecute you in this city, flee
ye into another: for verily I say unto you, Ye
shall not have gone over the cities of Israel,
till the Son of man be come.

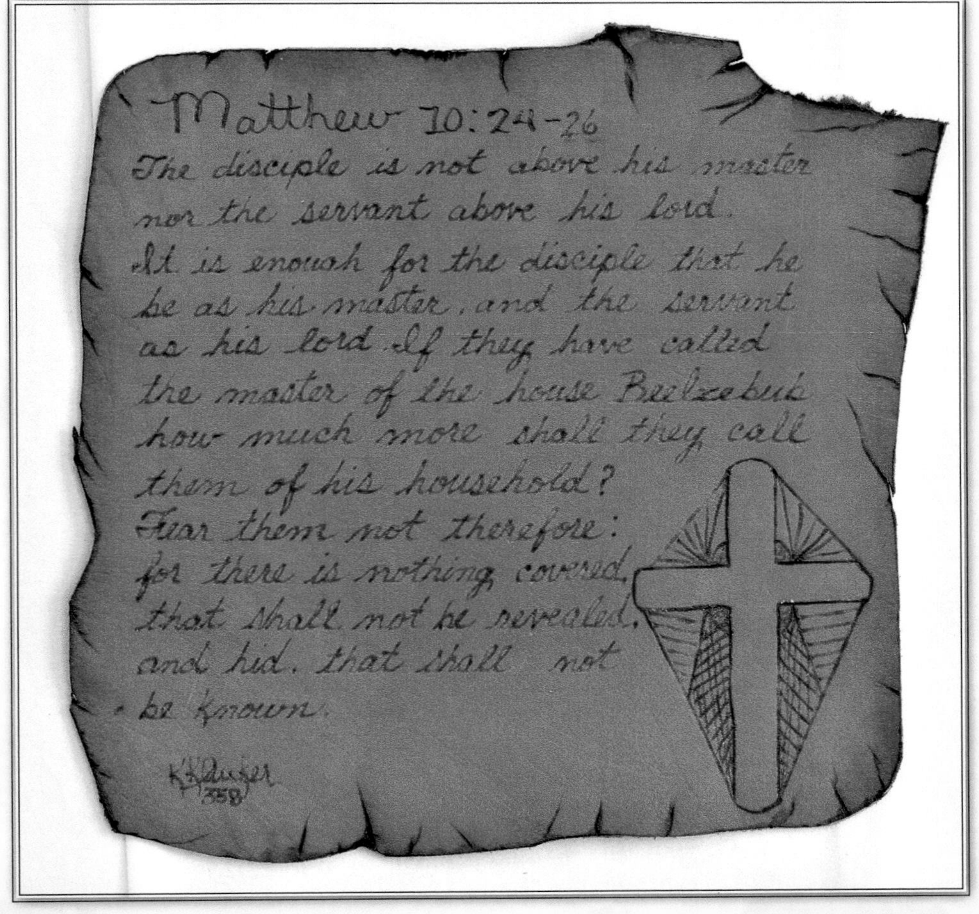

Matthew 10:24-26
The disciple is not above his master
nor the servant above his lord.
It is enouah for the disciple that he
be as his master, and the servant
as his lord. If they have called
the master of the house Beelzebub
how much more shall they call
them of his household?
Fear them not therefore:
for there is nothing covered,
that shall not be revealed,
and hid, that shall not
be known.

Matthew 10:27-28
What I tell you in darkness, that speak ye in light: and what ye hear in the ear, that preach ye upon the housetops. And fear not them which kill the body, but are not able to kill the soul: but rather fear him which is able to destroy both soul and body in hell.

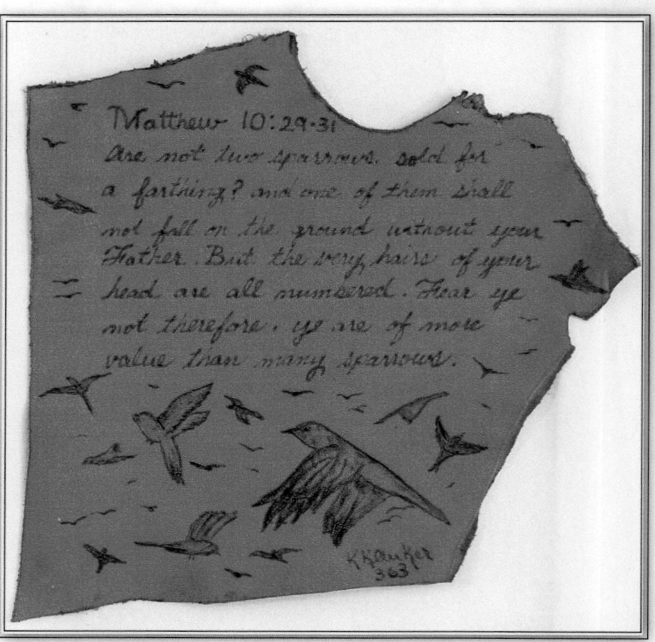

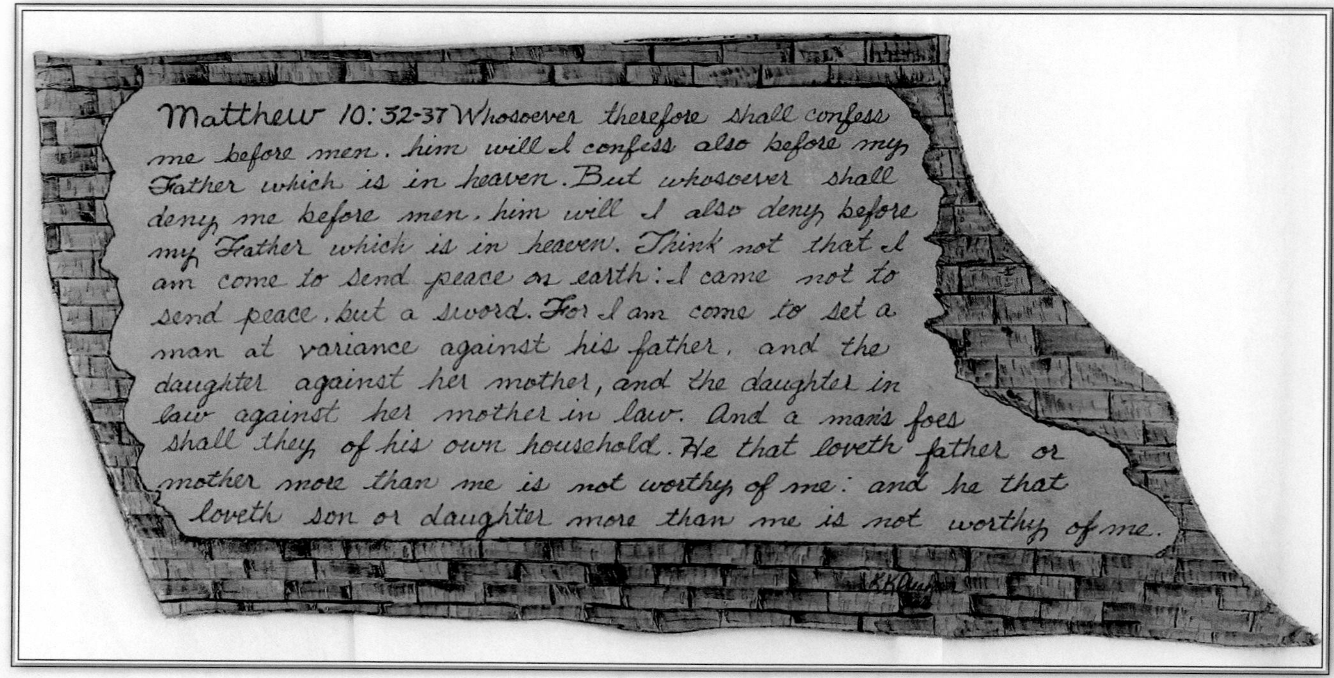

Matthew 10:38-42.

And he that taketh not his cross, and followeth after me, is not worthy of me. He that findeth his life shall lose it: and he that loseth his life for my sake shall find it. He that receiveth you receiveth me, and he that receiveth me recieveth him that sent me. He that receiveth a prophet in the name of a prophet shall receive a prophets reward: and he that receiveth a righteous man in the name of a righteous man shall receive a righteous man's reward. And whosoever shall give to drink unto one of these little ones a cup of cold water only in the name of a disciple, verily, I say unto you, he shall in no wise lose his reward.

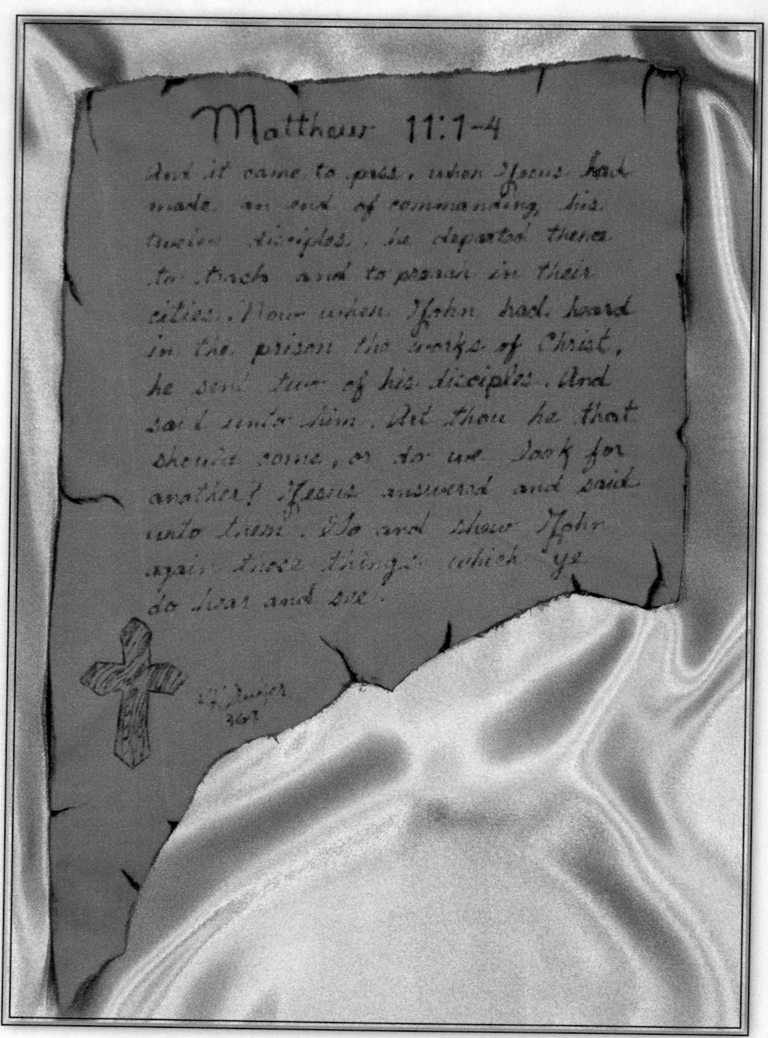
Matthew 11:1-4
And it came to pass, when Jesus had
made an end of commanding his
twelve disciples, he departed thence
to teach and to preach in their
cities. Now when John had heard
in the prison the works of Christ,
he sent two of his disciples. And
said unto him, Art thou he that
should come, or do we look for
another? Jesus answered and said
unto them, Go and shew John
again those things which ye
do hear and see.

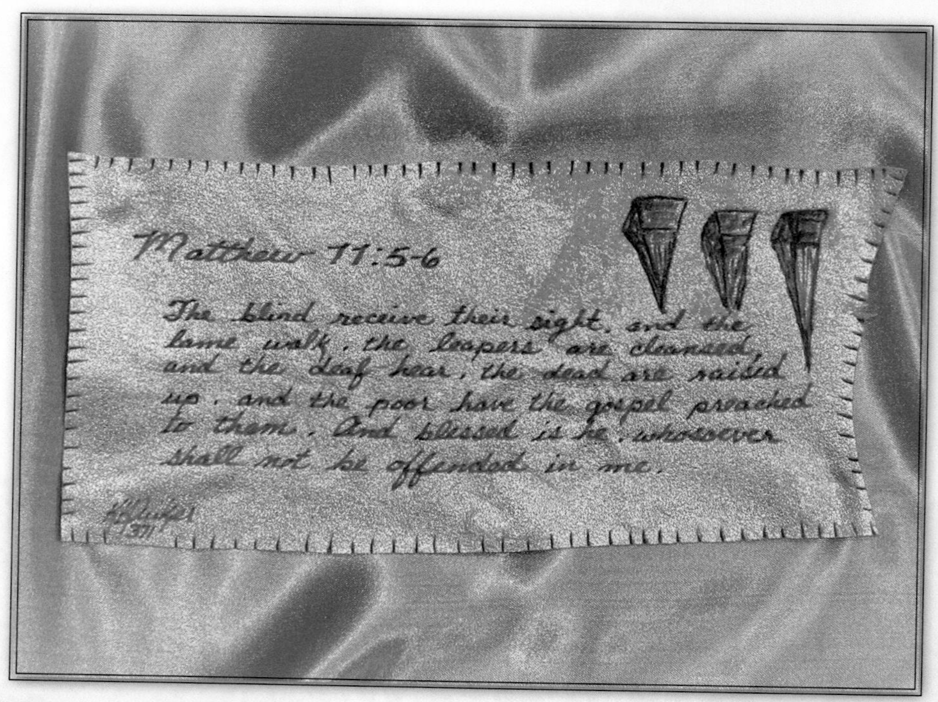
Matthew 11:5-6
The blind receive their sight, and the
lame walk, the leapers are cleansed,
and the deaf hear, the dead are raised
up, and the poor have the gospel preached
to them. And blessed is he, whosoever
shall not be offended in me.
1371

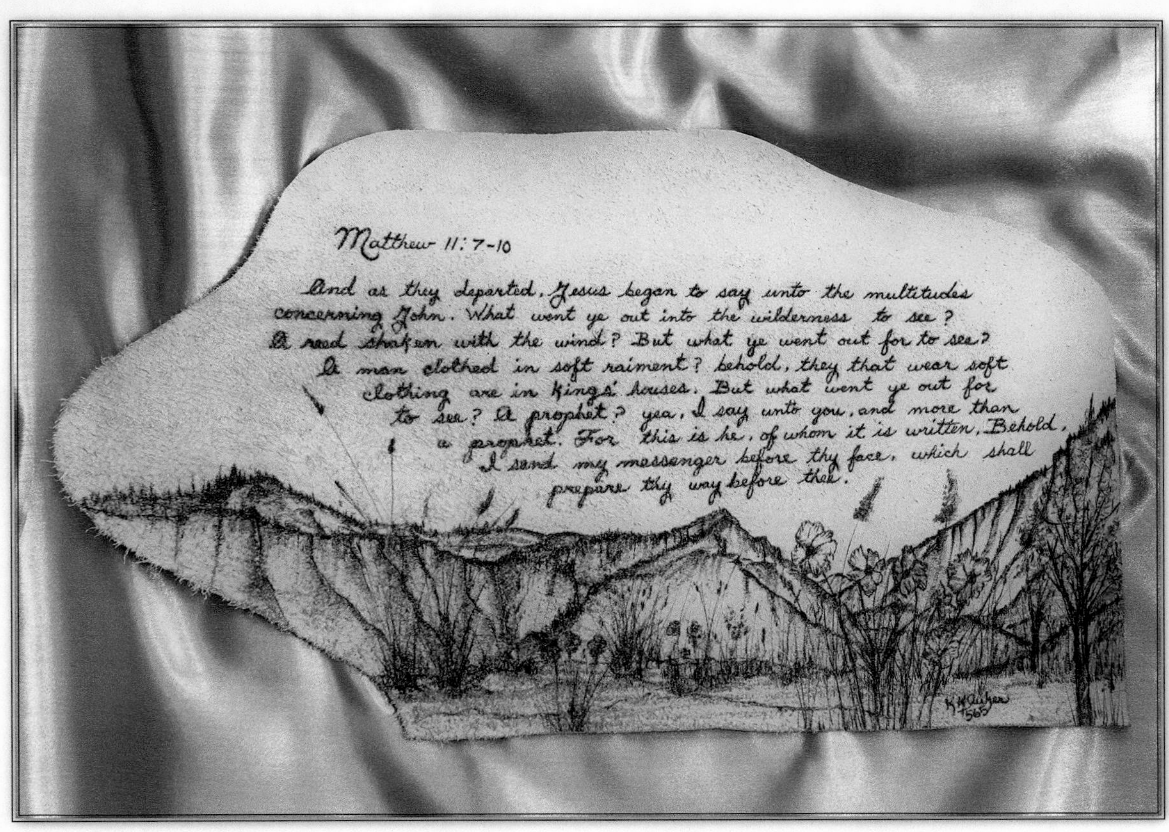
Matthew 11:7-10
And as they departed, Jesus began to say unto the multitudes
concerning John. What went ye out into the wilderness to see?
A reed shaken with the wind? But what ye went out for to see?
A man clothed in soft raiment? behold, they that wear soft
clothing are in kings' houses. But what went ye out for
to see? A prophet? yea, I say unto you, and more than
a prophet. For this is he, of whom it is written, Behold,
I send my messenger before thy face, which shall
prepare thy way before thee.

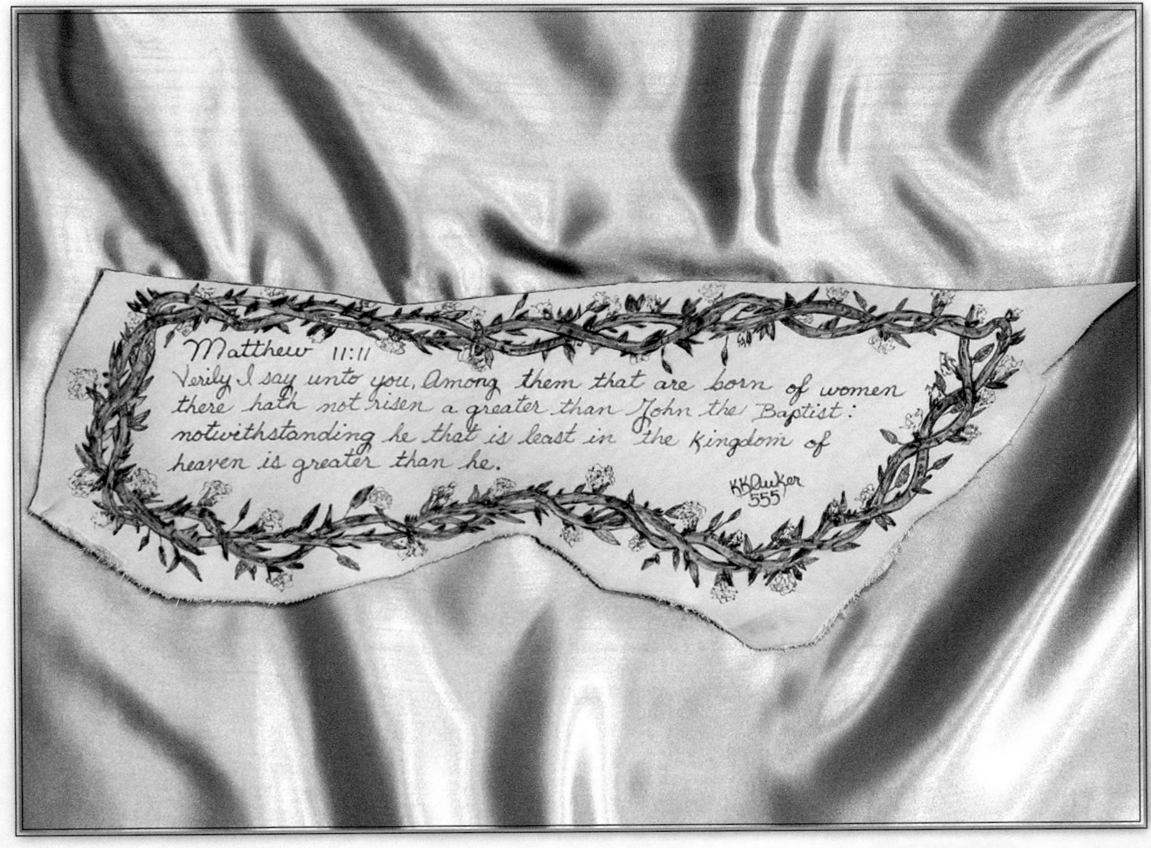
Matthew 11:11
Verily I say unto you, Among them that are born of women
there hath not risen a greater than John the Baptist:
notwithstanding he that is least in the kingdom of
heaven is greater than he.

Matthew 11:12-19

And from the days of John the Baptist until now the kingdom of heaven suffereth violence, and the violent take it by force. For all the prophets and the law prophesied until John. And if ye will receive it, thie is Elias, which was for to come. He that hath ears to hear, let him hear. But whereunto shall I liken this generation? It is like unto children sitting in the markets and calling unto their fellows. And saying, We have piped unto you, and ye have not danced; we have mourned unto you, and ye have not lamented. For John came neither eating nor drinking, and they say, He hath a devil. The Son of man came eating and drinking, and they say, Behold a man gluttonous, and a winebibber, a friend of publicans and sinners. But wisdom is justified of her children.

K.K.Duker
576

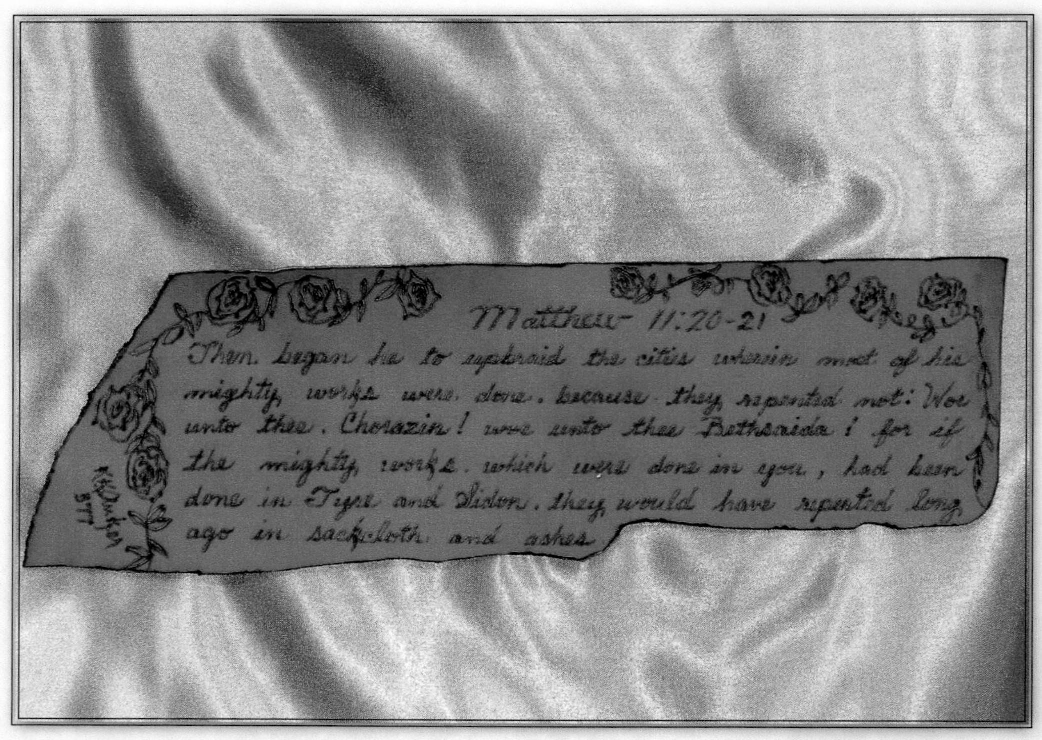

Matthew 11:20-21

Then began he to upbraid the cities wherein most of his mighty works were done, because they repented not: Woe unto thee, Chorazin! woe unto thee Bethsaida! for if the mighty works, which were done in you, had been done in Tyre and Sidon, they would have repented long ago in sackcloth and ashes

K.K.Duker
577

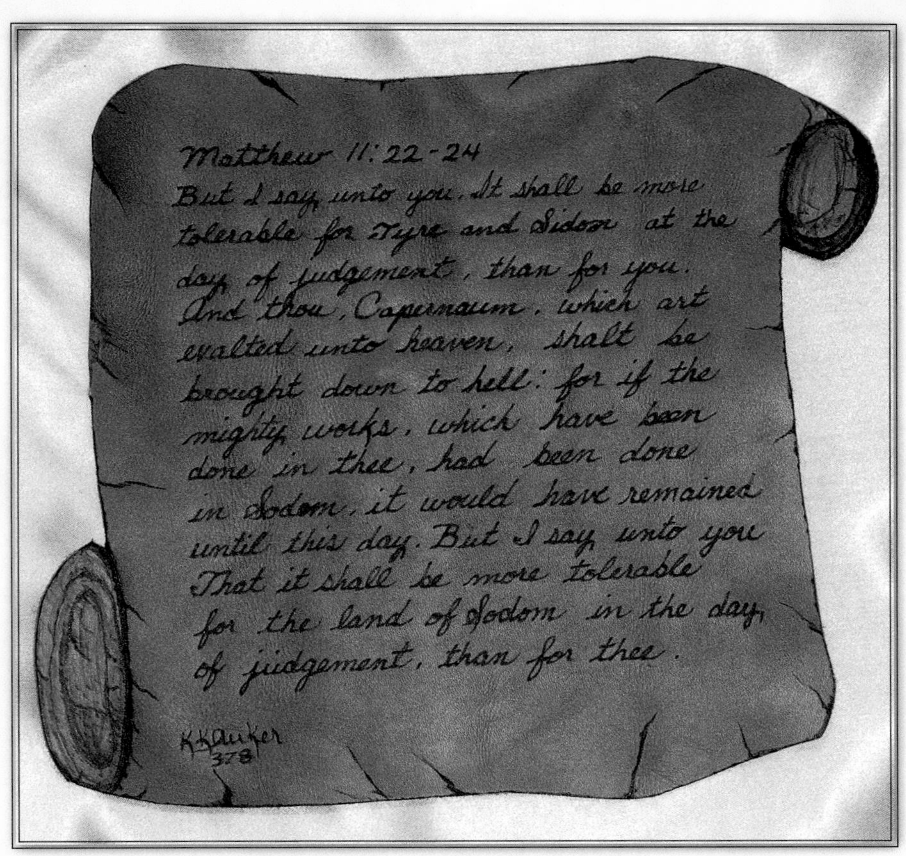
Matthew 11:22-24
But I say unto you, It shall be more
tolerable for Tyre and Sidon at the
day of judgement, than for you.
And thou, Capernaum, which art
exalted unto heaven, shalt be
brought down to hell: for if the
mighty works, which have been
done in thee, had been done
in Sodom, it would have remained
until this day. But I say unto you
That it shall be more tolerable
for the land of Sodom in the day
of judgement, than for thee.
KKlinker
378

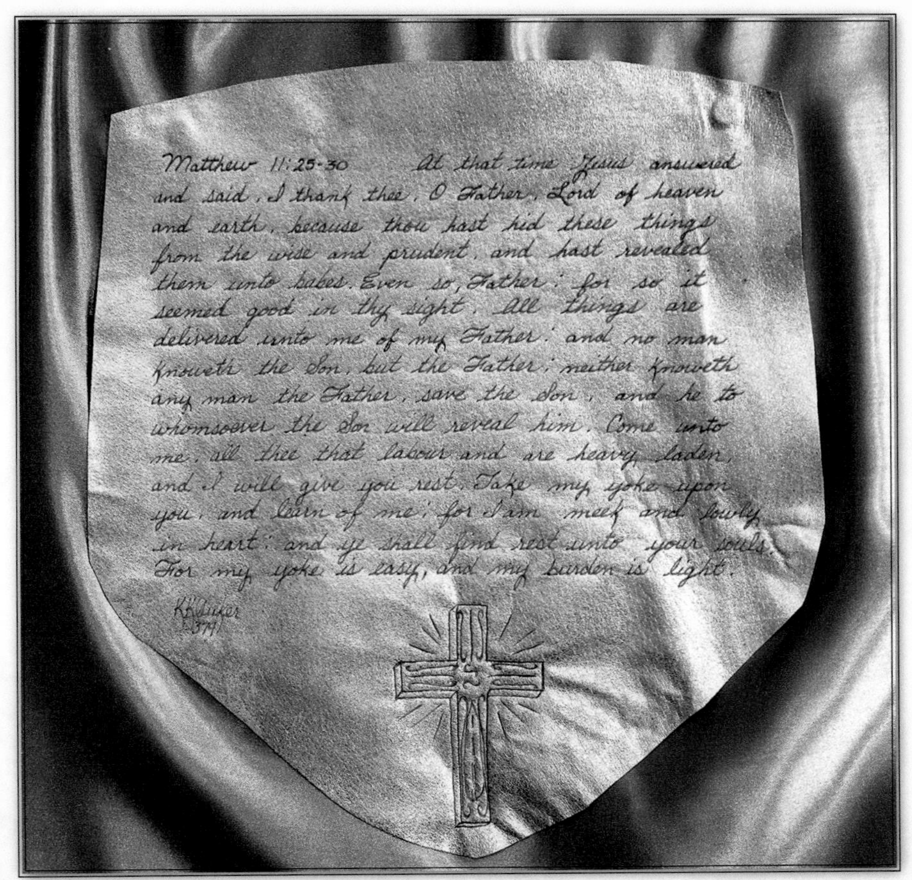
Matthew 11:25-30 At that time Jesus answered
and said, I thank thee, O Father, Lord of heaven
and earth, because thou hast hid these things
from the wise and prudent, and hast revealed
them unto babes. Even so, Father: for so it
seemed good in thy sight. All things are
delivered unto me of my Father: and no man
knoweth the Son, but the Father; neither knoweth
any man the Father, save the Son, and he to
whomsoever the Son will reveal him. Come unto
me, all thee that labour and are heavy laden,
and I will give you rest. Take my yoke upon
you, and learn of me; for I am meek and lowly
in heart: and ye shall find rest unto your souls.
For my yoke is easy, and my burden is light.

Matthew 12:1-2 At that time Jesus went on
the sabbath day through the corn; and his disciples
were an hungred, and began to pluck the ears
of corn, and to eat. But when the Pharisees saw
it, they said unto him, Behold, thy disciples do
that which is not lawful to do upon the
sabbath day.
K Kiluker
1536

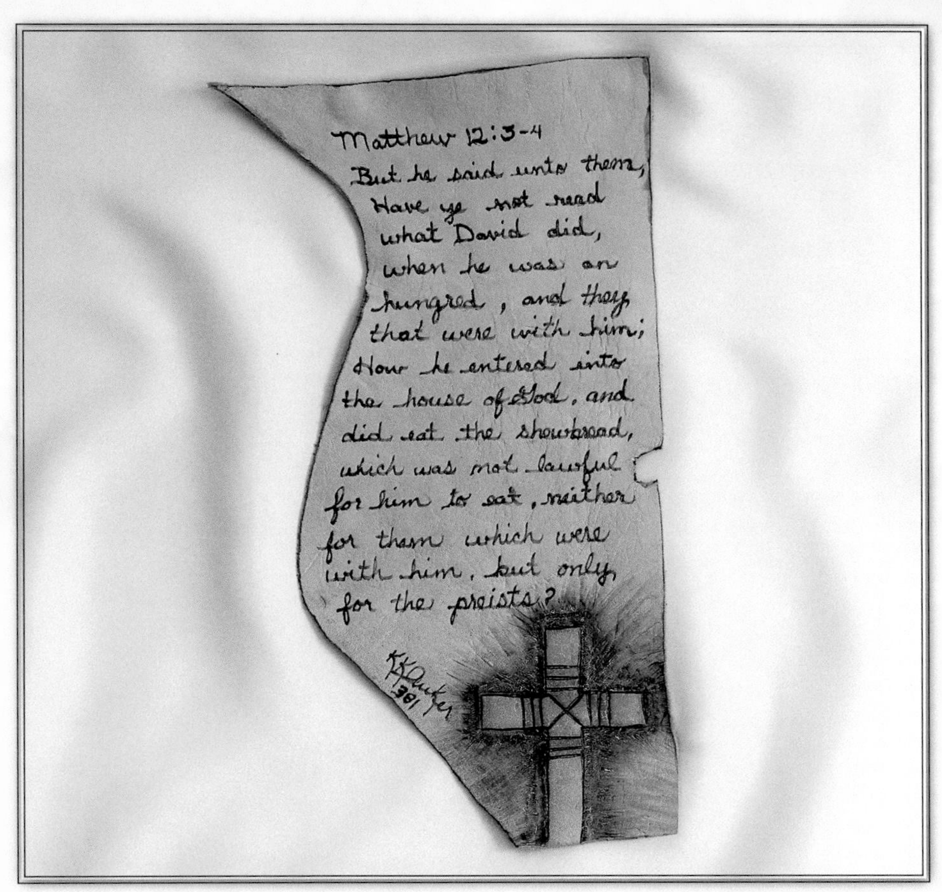

Matthew 12:5-7
Or have ye not read in
the law, how that on the
sabbath days the preists
in the temple profane
the sabbath, and are
blameless? But I say
unto you, That in this
place is one greater than
the temple, But if ye
had known what this
meaneth, I will have
mercy and not sacri-
fice, ye would not
have condemned
the guiltless.

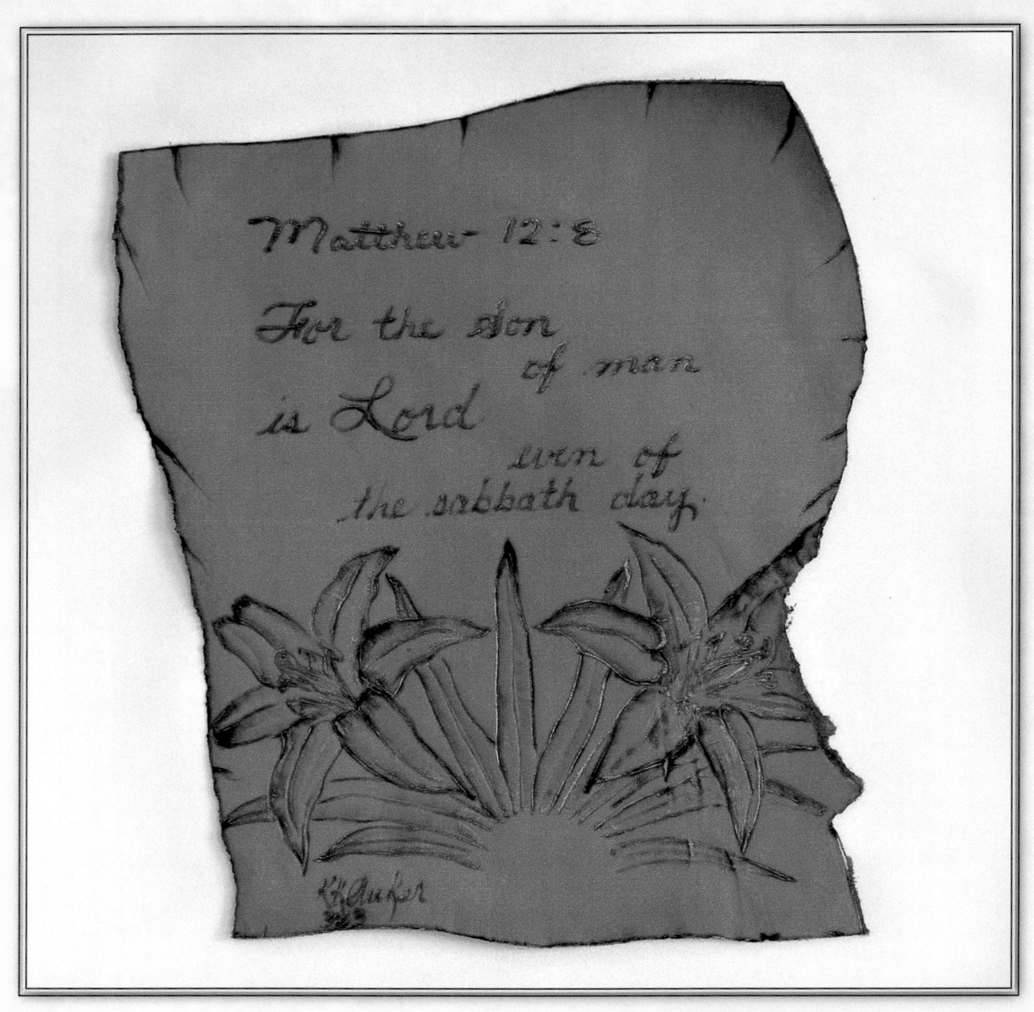
Matthew 12:8
For the Son
of man
is Lord
even of
the sabbath day.

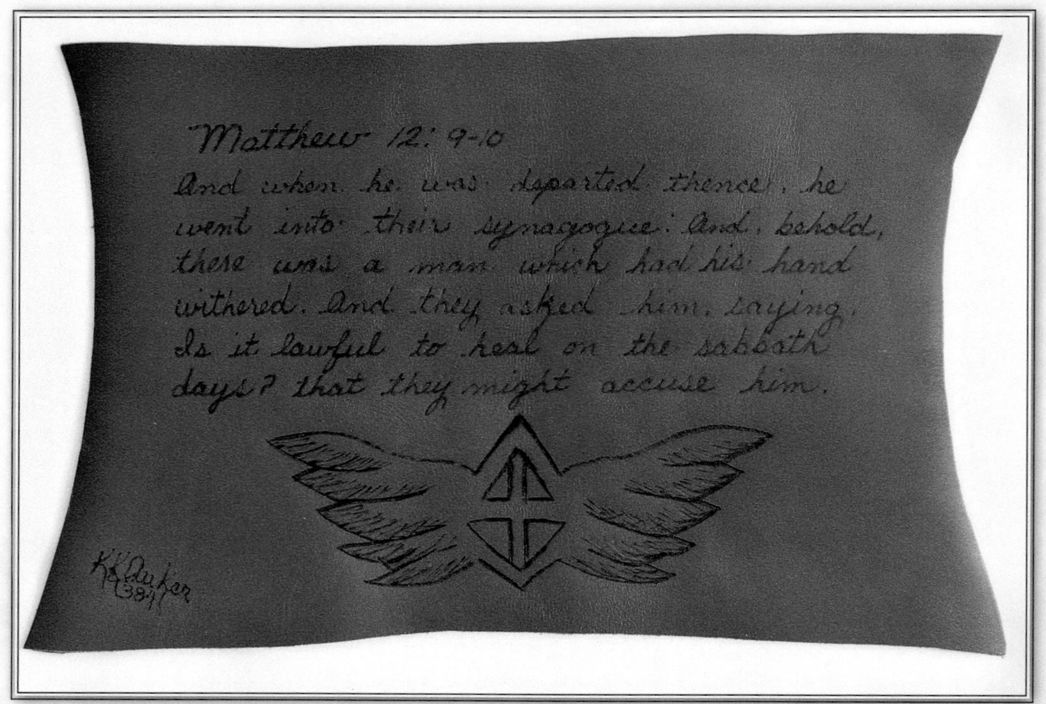
Matthew 12: 9-10
And when he was departed thence, he
went into their synagogue: And, behold,
there was a man which had his hand
withered. And they asked him, saying,
Is it lawful to heal on the sabbath
days? that they might accuse him.

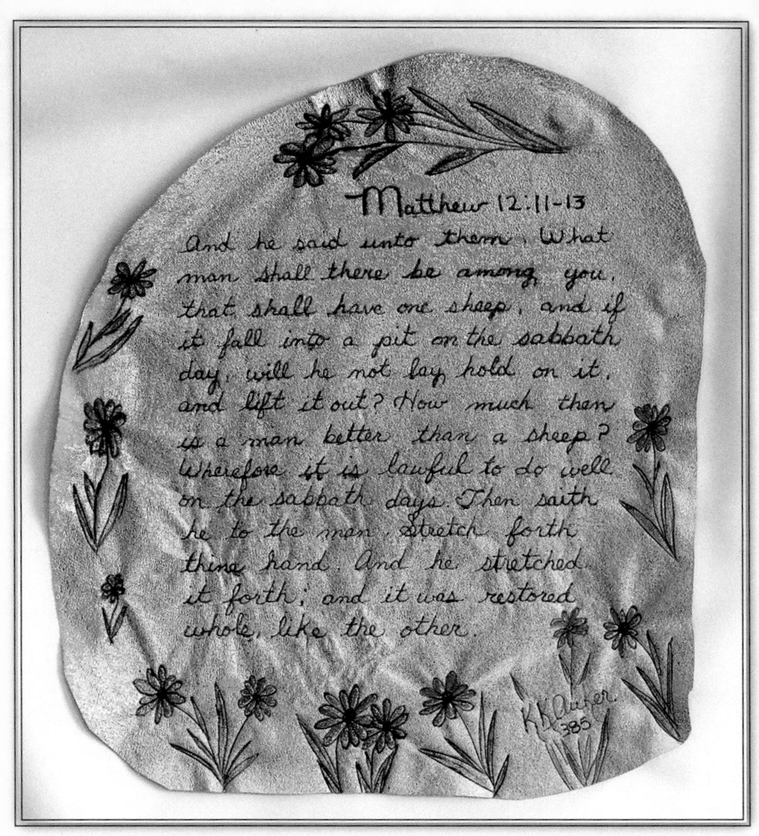
Matthew 12:11-13
And he said unto them, What
man shall there be among you,
that shall have one sheep, and if
it fall into a pit on the sabbath
day, will he not lay hold on it,
and lift it out? How much then
is a man better than a sheep?
Wherefore it is lawful to do well
on the sabbath days. Then saith
he to the man, Stretch forth
thine hand. And he stretched
it forth; and it was restored
whole, like the other.
K.K.Luzer
385

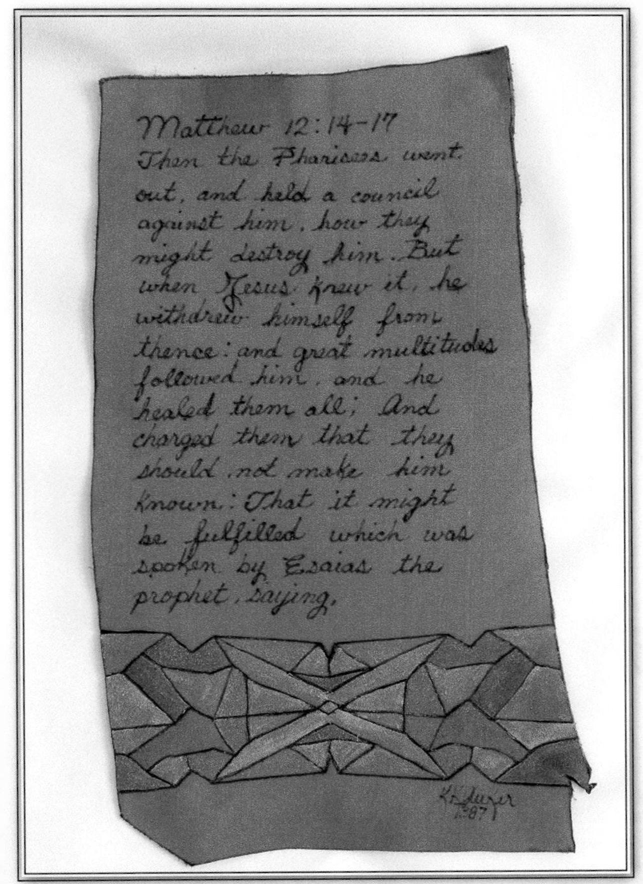
Matthew 12:14-17
Then the Pharisees went
out, and held a council
against him, how they
might destroy him. But
when Jesus knew it, he
withdrew himself from
thence: and great multitudes
followed him, and he
healed them all; And
charged them that they
should not make him
known: That it might
be fulfilled which was
spoken by Esaias the
prophet, saying,
K.K.Luzer
387

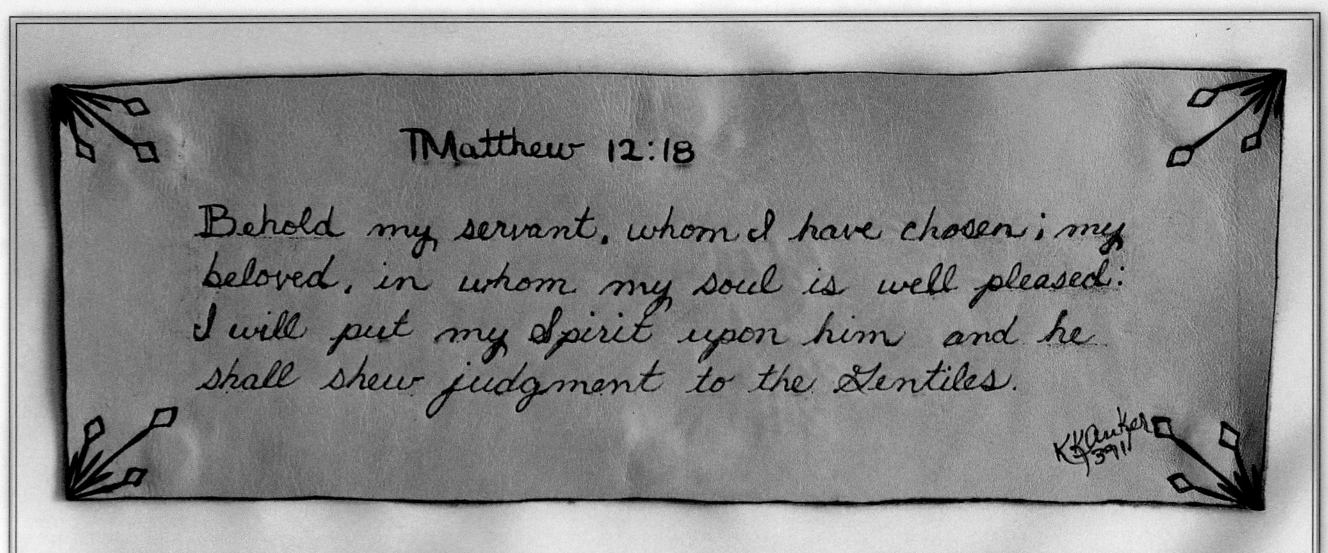
Matthew 12:18
Behold my servant, whom I have chosen; my
beloved, in whom my soul is well pleased:
I will put my Spirit upon him and he
shall shew judgment to the Gentiles.
KKlunker 3911

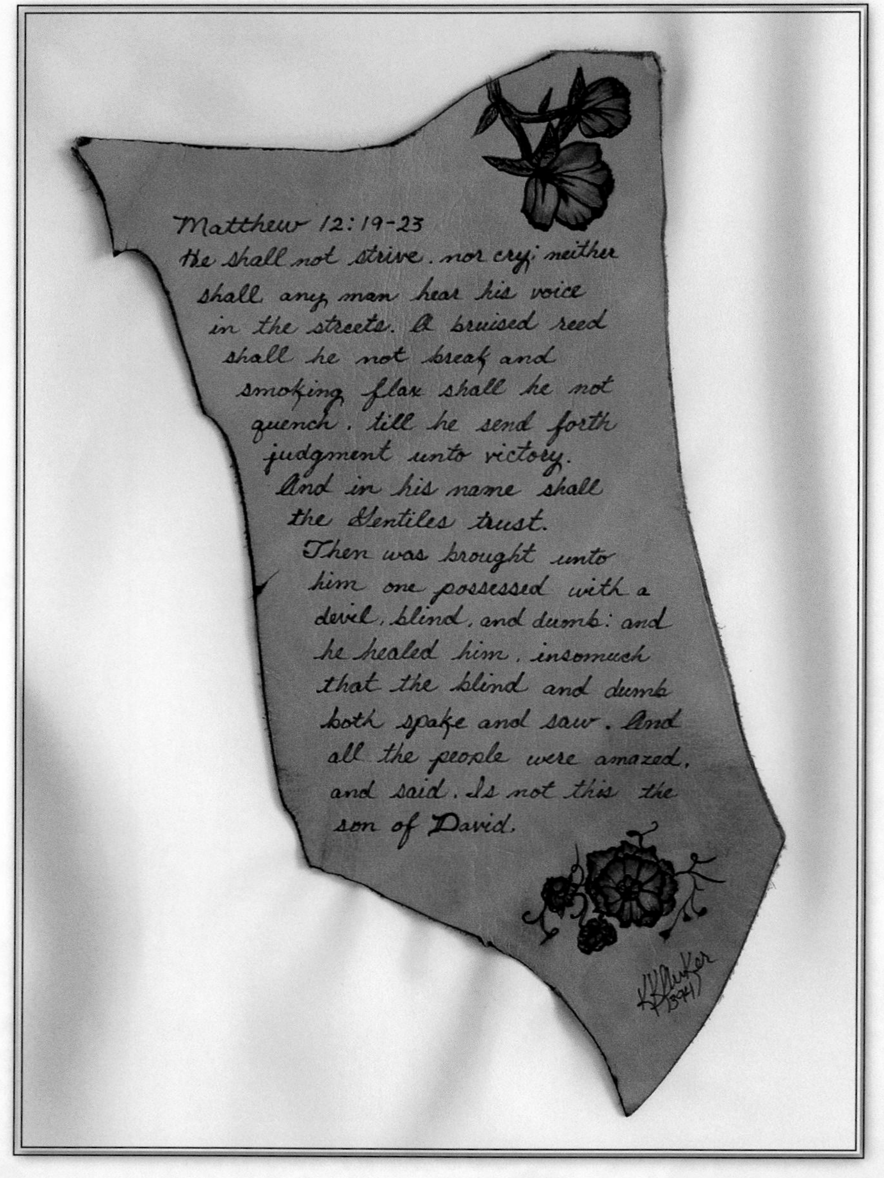
Matthew 12:19-23
He shall not strive, nor cry; neither
shall any man hear his voice
in the streets. A bruised reed
shall he not break and
smoking flax shall he not
quench, till he send forth
judgment unto victory.
And in his name shall
the Gentiles trust.
Then was brought unto
him one possessed with a
devil, blind, and dumb: and
he healed him, insomuch
that the blind and dumb
both spake and saw. And
all the people were amazed,
and said, Is not this the
son of David.

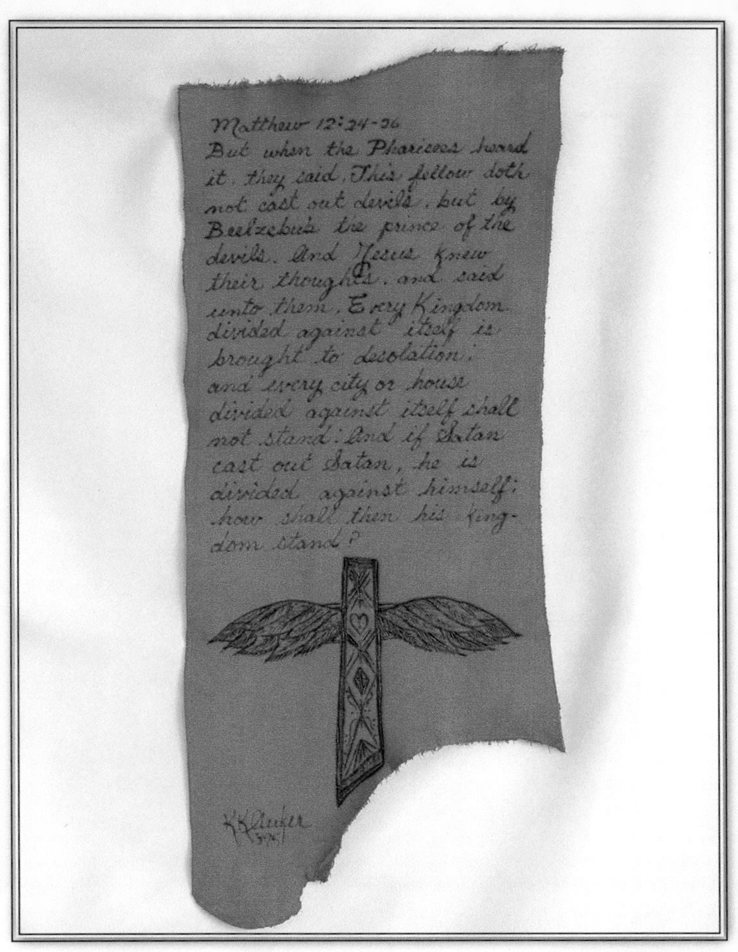
Matthew 12:24-26
But when the Pharisees heard it, they said, This fellow doth not cast out devils, but by Beelzebub the prince of the devils. And Jesus knew their thoughts, and said unto them, Every Kingdom divided against itself is brought to desolation; and every city or house divided against itself shall not stand: And if Satan cast out Satan, he is divided against himself; how shall then his kingdom stand?

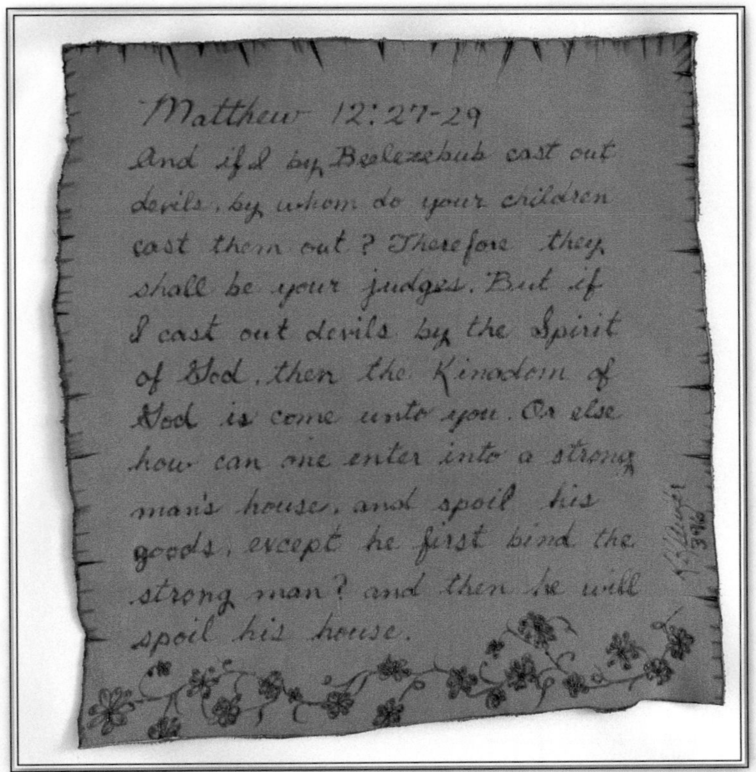
Matthew 12:27-29
And if I by Beelezebub cast out devils, by whom do your children cast them out? Therefore they shall be your judges. But if I cast out devils by the Spirit of God, then the Kingdom of God is come unto you. Or else how can one enter into a strong man's house, and spoil his goods, except he first bind the strong man? and then he will spoil his house.

Matthew 12:30-32
He that is not with me is against
me; and he that gathereth not with
me scattereth abroad. Wherefore I
say unto you, All matter of sin
and blasphemy shall be forgiven
unto men: but the blasphemy
against the Holy Ghost shall
not be forgiven unto men. And
whosoever speaketh a word against
the Son of man, it shall be
forgiven him: but whosoever speaketh against the Holy Ghost, it
shall not be forgiven him neither
in this world, neither in the
world to come.

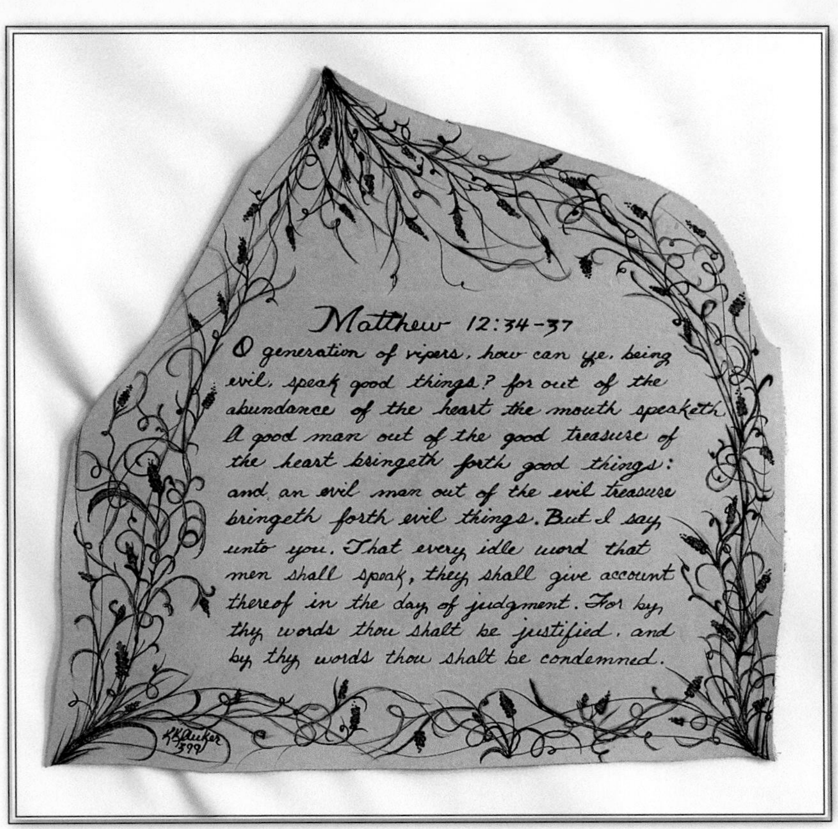
Matthew 12:34-37
O generation of vipers, how can ye, being evil, speak good things? for out of the abundance of the heart the mouth speaketh. A good man out of the good treasure of the heart bringeth forth good things: and an evil man out of the evil treasure bringeth forth evil things. But I say unto you, That every idle word that men shall speak, they shall give account thereof in the day of judgment. For by thy words thou shalt be justified, and by thy words thou shalt be condemned.
KKRuker 3/99

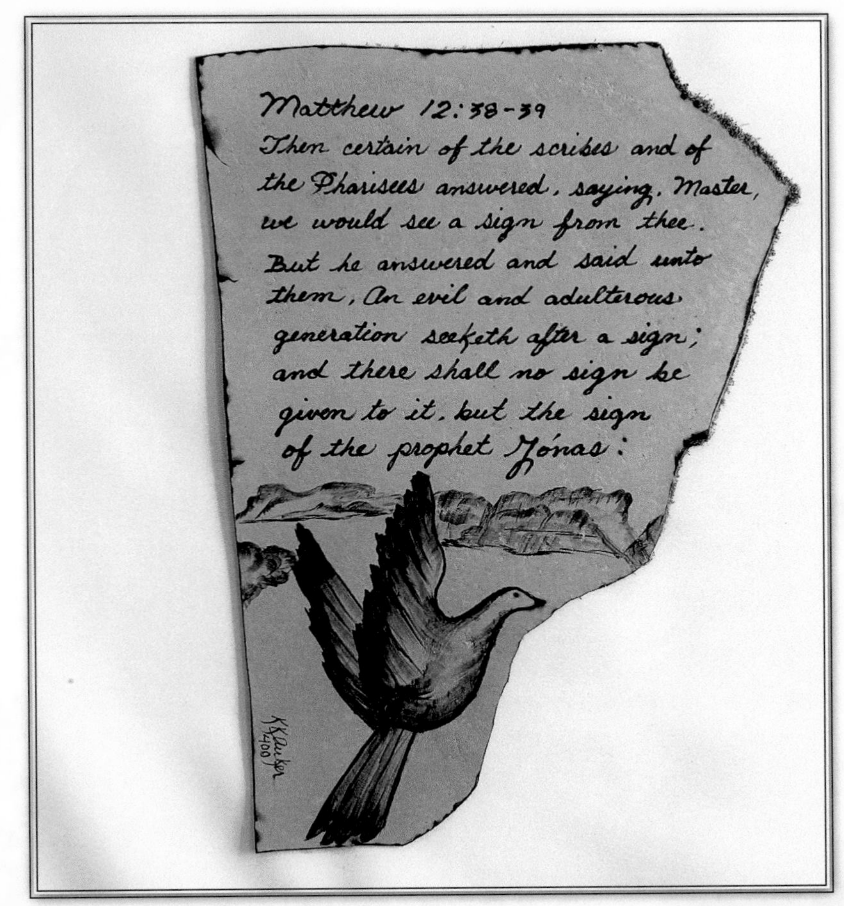
Matthew 12:38-39
Then certain of the scribes and of the Pharisees answered, saying, Master, we would see a sign from thee. But he answered and said unto them, An evil and adulterous generation seeketh after a sign; and there shall no sign be given to it, but the sign of the prophet Jonas:
KKRuker 4/00

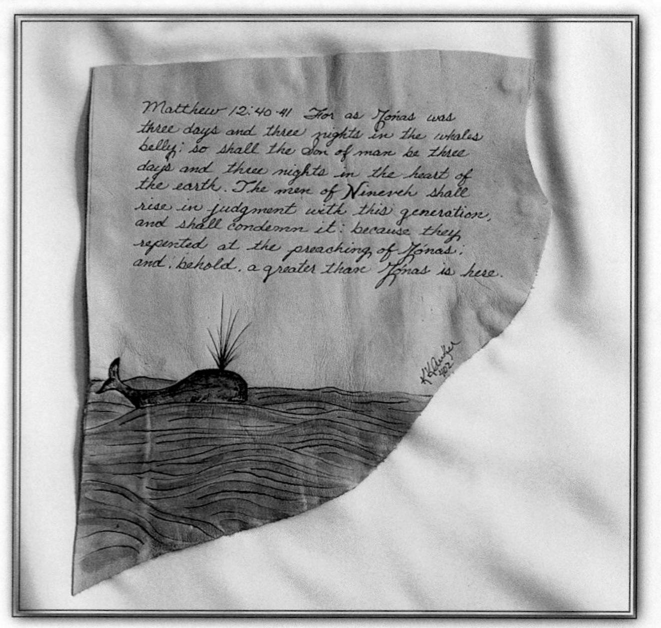
Matthew 12:40-41 For as Jonas was
three days and three nights in the whales
belly; so shall the Son of man be three
days and three nights in the heart of
the earth. The men of Nineveh shall
rise in judgment with this generation,
and shall condemn it: because they
repented at the preaching of Jonas;
and, behold, a greater than Jonas is here.

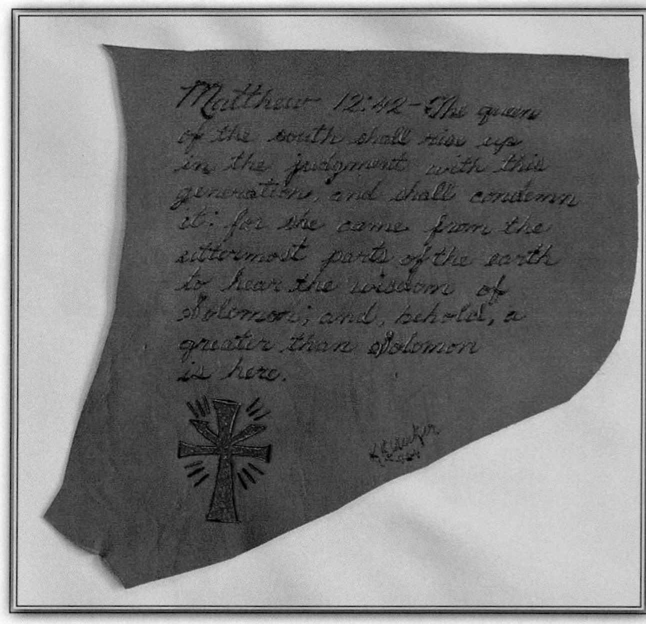
Matthew 12:42-The queen
of the south shall rise up
in the judgment with this
generation, and shall condemn
it: for she came from the
uttermost parts of the earth
to hear the wisdom of
Solomon; and, behold, a
greater than Solomon
is here.

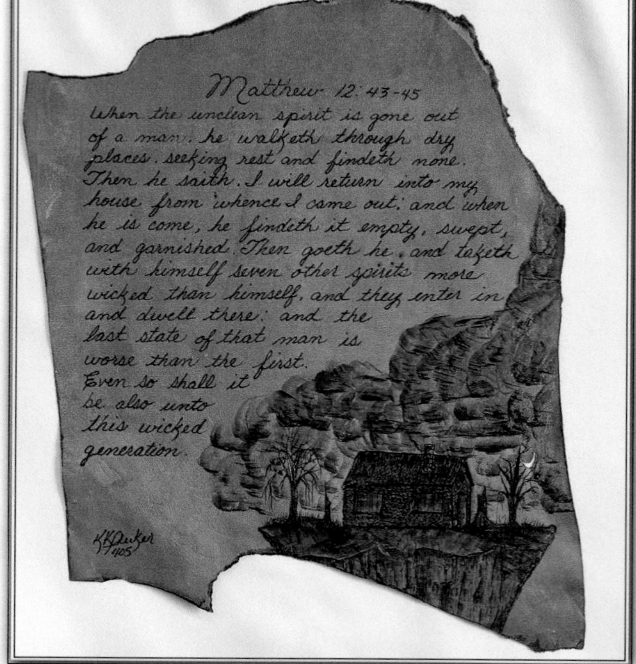
Matthew 12:43-45
When the unclean spirit is gone out
of a man, he walketh through dry
places, seeking rest and findeth none.
Then he saith, I will return into my
house from whence I came out; and when
he is come, he findeth it empty, swept,
and garnished. Then goeth he, and taketh
with himself seven other spirits more
wicked than himself, and they enter in
and dwell there: and the
last state of that man is
worse than the first.
Even so shall it
be also unto
this wicked
generation.
KKDuker
405

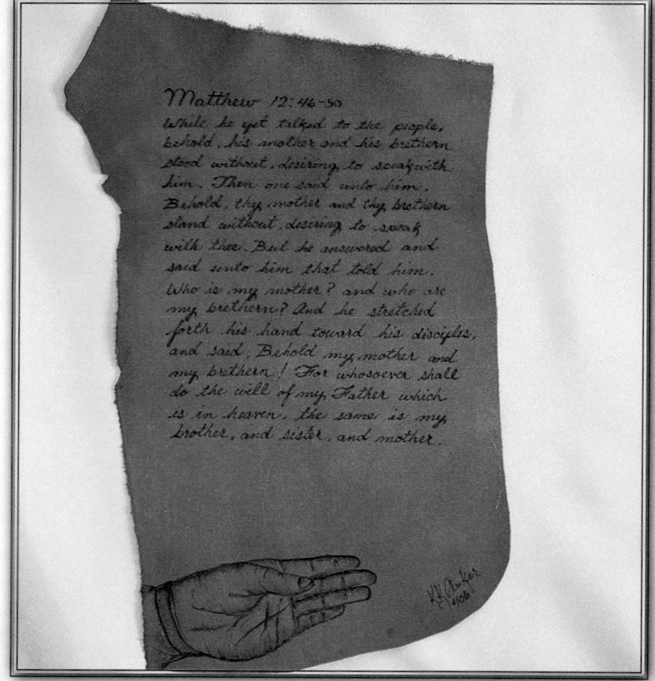
Matthew 12:46-50
While he yet talked to the people,
behold, his mother and his brethern
stood without, desiring to speak with
him. Then one said unto him,
Behold, thy mother and thy brethern
stand without, desiring to speak
with thee. But he answered and
said unto him that told him,
Who is my mother? and who are
my brethern? And he stretched
forth his hand toward his disciples,
and said, Behold my mother and
my brethern! For whosoever shall
do the will of my Father which
is in heaven, the same is my
brother, and sister, and mother.

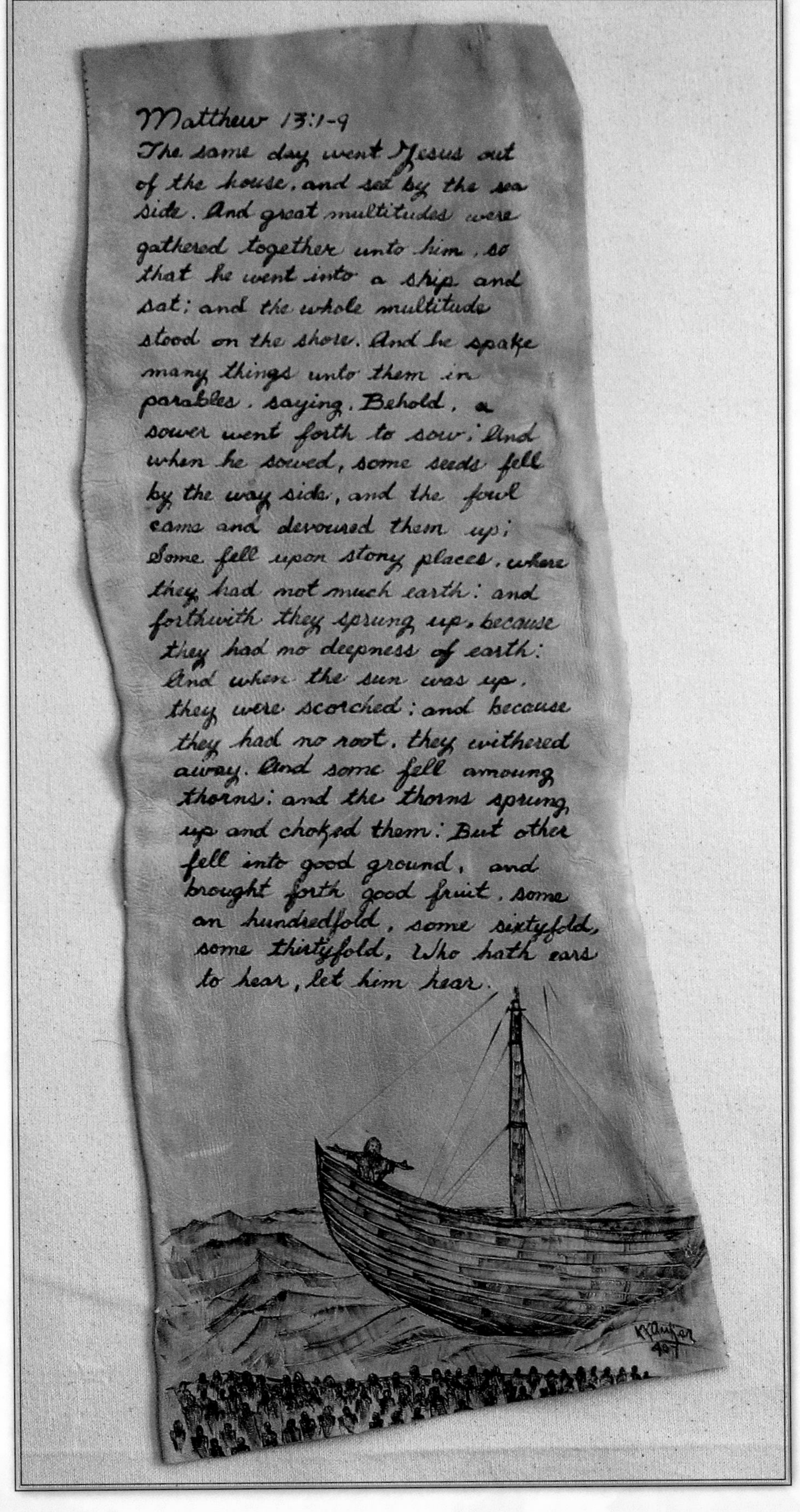
Matthew 13:1-9
The same day went Jesus out
of the house, and sat by the sea
side. And great multitudes were
gathered together unto him, so
that he went into a ship and
sat; and the whole multitude
stood on the shore. And he spake
many things unto them in
parables, saying, Behold, a
sower went forth to sow; And
when he sowed, some seeds fell
by the way side, and the fowl
came and devoured them up;
Some fell upon stony places, where
they had not much earth: and
forthwith they sprung up, because
they had no deepness of earth:
And when the sun was up,
they were scorched; and because
they had no root, they withered
away. And some fell amoung
thorns; and the thorns sprung
up and choked them: But other
fell into good ground, and
brought forth good fruit, some
an hundredfold, some sixtyfold,
some thirtyfold. Who hath ears
to hear, let him hear.

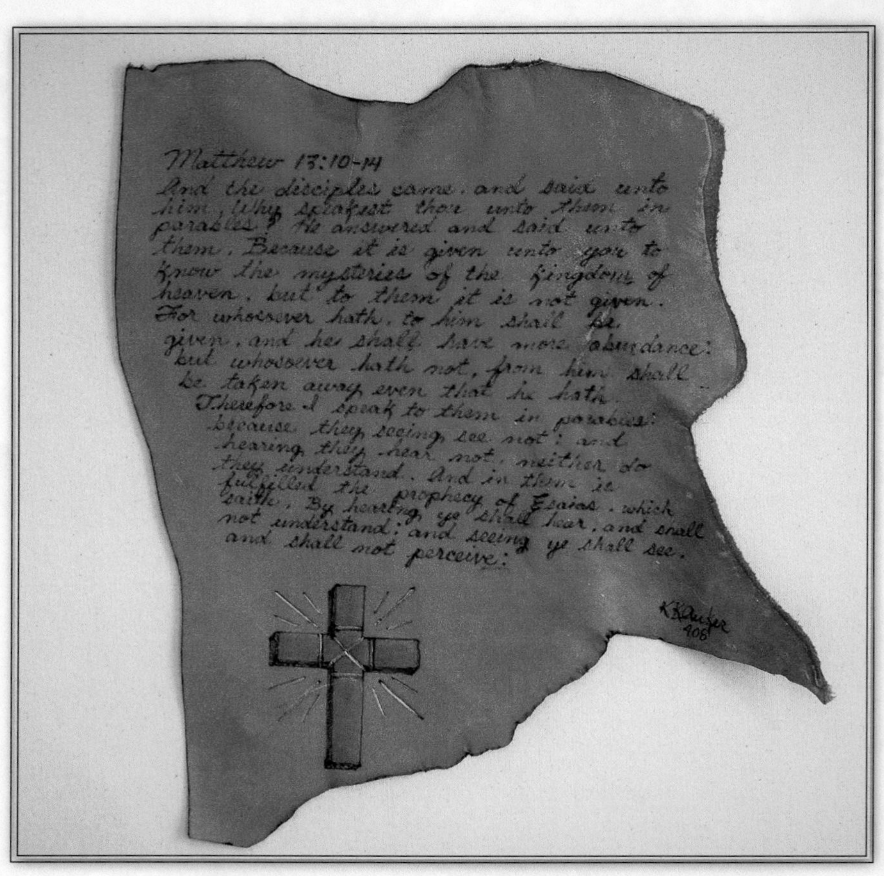
Matthew 13:10-14
And the disciples came, and said unto
him, Why speakest thou unto them in
parables? He answered and said unto
them, Because it is given unto you to
know the mysteries of the kingdom of
heaven, but to them it is not given.
For whosoever hath, to him shall be
given, and he shall have more abundance:
but whosoever hath not, from him shall
be taken away even that he hath.
Therefore I speak to them in parables:
because they seeing see not; and
hearing they hear not, neither do
they understand. And in them is
fulfilled the prophecy of Esaias, which
saith, By hearing ye shall hear, and shall
not understand; and seeing ye shall see,
and shall not perceive:

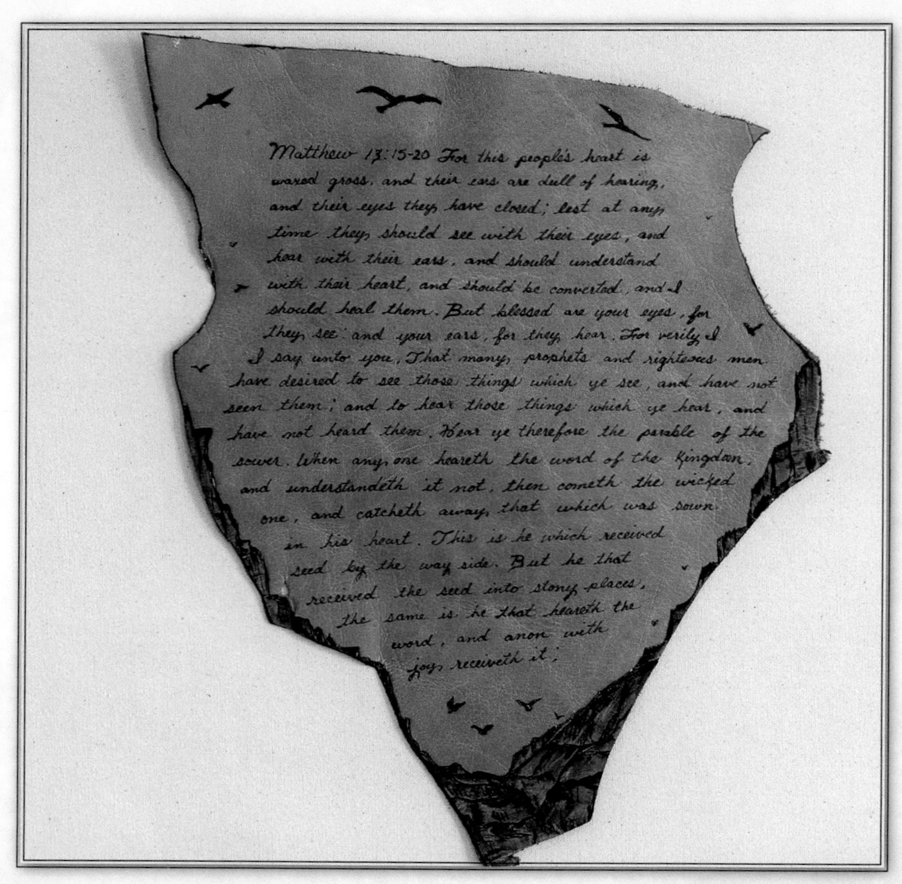
Matthew 13:15-20 For this people's heart is
waxed gross, and their ears are dull of hearing,
and their eyes they have closed; lest at any
time they should see with their eyes, and
hear with their ears, and should understand
with their heart, and should be converted, and I
should heal them. But blessed are your eyes, for
they see: and your ears, for they hear. For verily I
I say unto you, That many prophets and righteous men
have desired to see those things which ye see, and have not
seen them; and to hear those things which ye hear, and
have not heard them. Hear ye therefore the parable of the
sower. When any one heareth the word of the kingdom,
and understandeth it not, then cometh the wicked
one, and catcheth away that which was sown
in his heart. This is he which received
seed by the way side. But he that
received the seed into stony places,
the same is he that heareth the
word, and anon with
joy receiveth it;

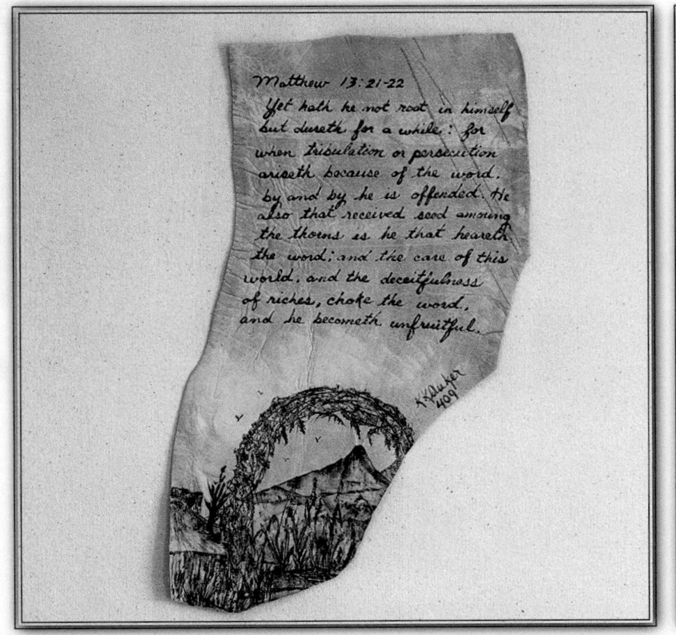
Matthew 13:21-22
Yet hath he not root in himself
but dureth for a while: for
when tribulation or persecution
ariseth because of the word,
by and by he is offended. He
also that received seed among
the thorns is he that heareth
the word; and the care of this
world, and the deceitfulness
of riches, choke the word,
and he becometh unfruitful.

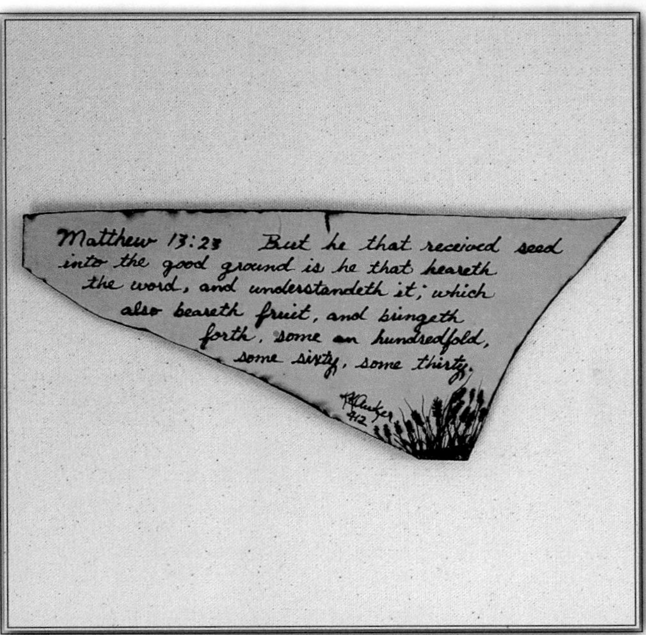
Matthew 13:23 But he that received seed
into the good ground is he that heareth
the word, and understandeth it; which
also beareth fruit, and bringeth
forth, some an hundredfold,
some sixty, some thirty.

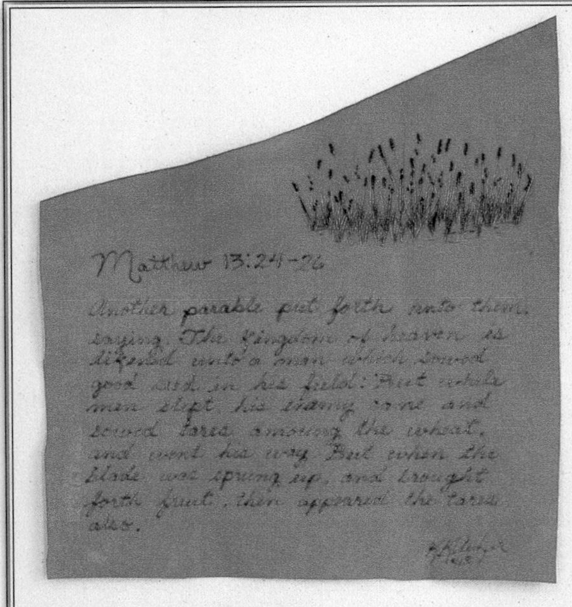
Matthew 13:24-26
Another parable put forth unto them,
saying, The kingdom of heaven is
likened unto a man which sowed
good seed in his field: But while
men slept, his enemy came and
sowed tares among the wheat,
and went his way. But when the
blade was sprung up, and brought
forth fruit, then appeared the tares
also.

Matthew 13:27-30 So the servants of the householder came
and said unto him, Sir, didst not thou sow good seed in thy field
from whence then hath it tares? He said unto them, An enemy
hath done this. The servants said unto him, Wilt thou then
that we gather them up? But he said, Nay; lest while ye
gather up the tares, ye root up also the wheat with them.
Let both grow together until the harvest: and in the
time of harvest I will say to the reapers, Gather ye
together first the tares, and bind them in bundles
to burn them: but gather the wheat into my barn.

Matthew 13:31-32
Another parable put he forth unto them,
saying, The kingdom of heaven is like to
a grain of mustard seed, which a man took,
and sowed in his field: Which indeed is the
least of all seeds: but when it is grown,
it is the greatest among herbs, and becometh
a tree, so that the birds of air come and
lodge in the branches thereof.

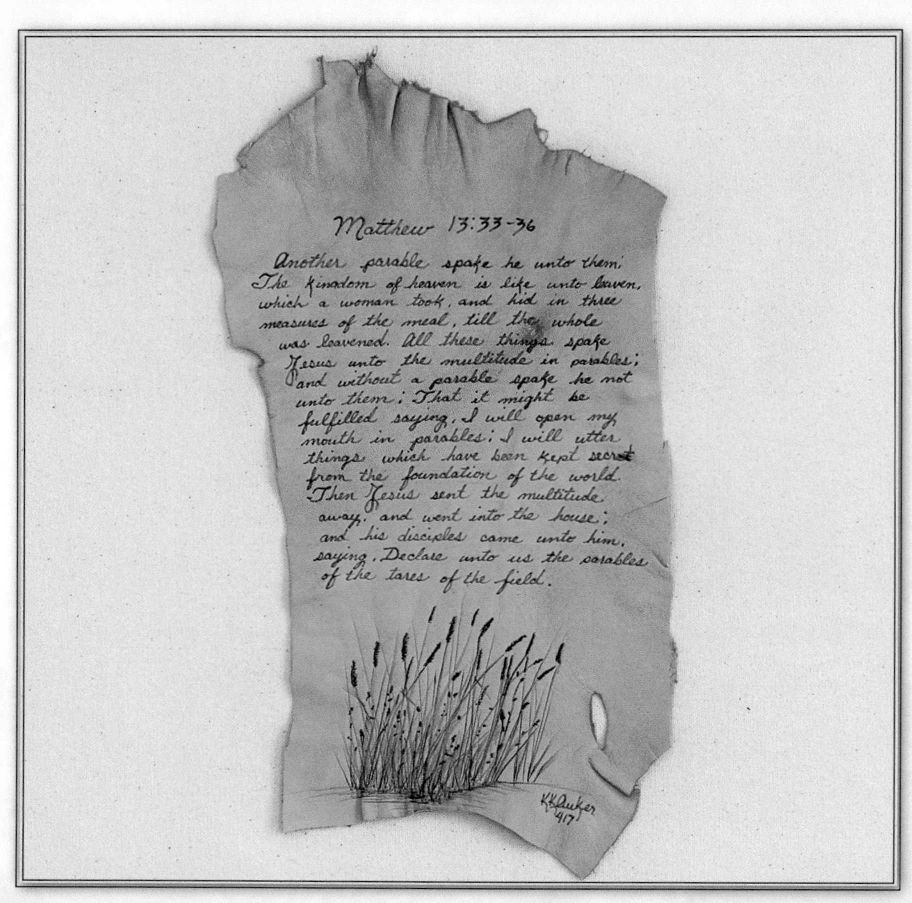
Matthew 13:33-36
Another parable spake he unto them;
The kingdom of heaven is like unto leaven,
which a woman took, and hid in three
measures of the meal, till the whole
was leavened. All these things spake
Jesus unto the multitude in parables;
and without a parable spake he not
unto them: That it might be
fulfilled saying, I will open my
mouth in parables; I will utter
things which have been kept secret
from the foundation of the world.
Then Jesus sent the multitude
away, and went into the house:
and his disciples came unto him,
saying, Declare unto us the parables
of the tares of the field.

Matthew 13:37-43

He answered and said unto them, He that soweth the good seed is the Son of man; The field is the world; the good seed are the children of the kingdom; but the tares are the children of the wicked one; The enemy that sowed them is the devil; the harvest is the end of the world; and the reapers are the angels. As therefore the tares are gathered and burned in the fire; so shall it be in the end of this world. The Son of man shall send forth his angels, and they shall gather out of his Kingdom all things that offend, and them which do iniquity; And shall cast them into a furnace of fire: there shall be wailing and gnashing of teeth. Then shall the righteous shine forth as the sun in the Kingdom of their Father.

Who hath ears to hear, let him hear.

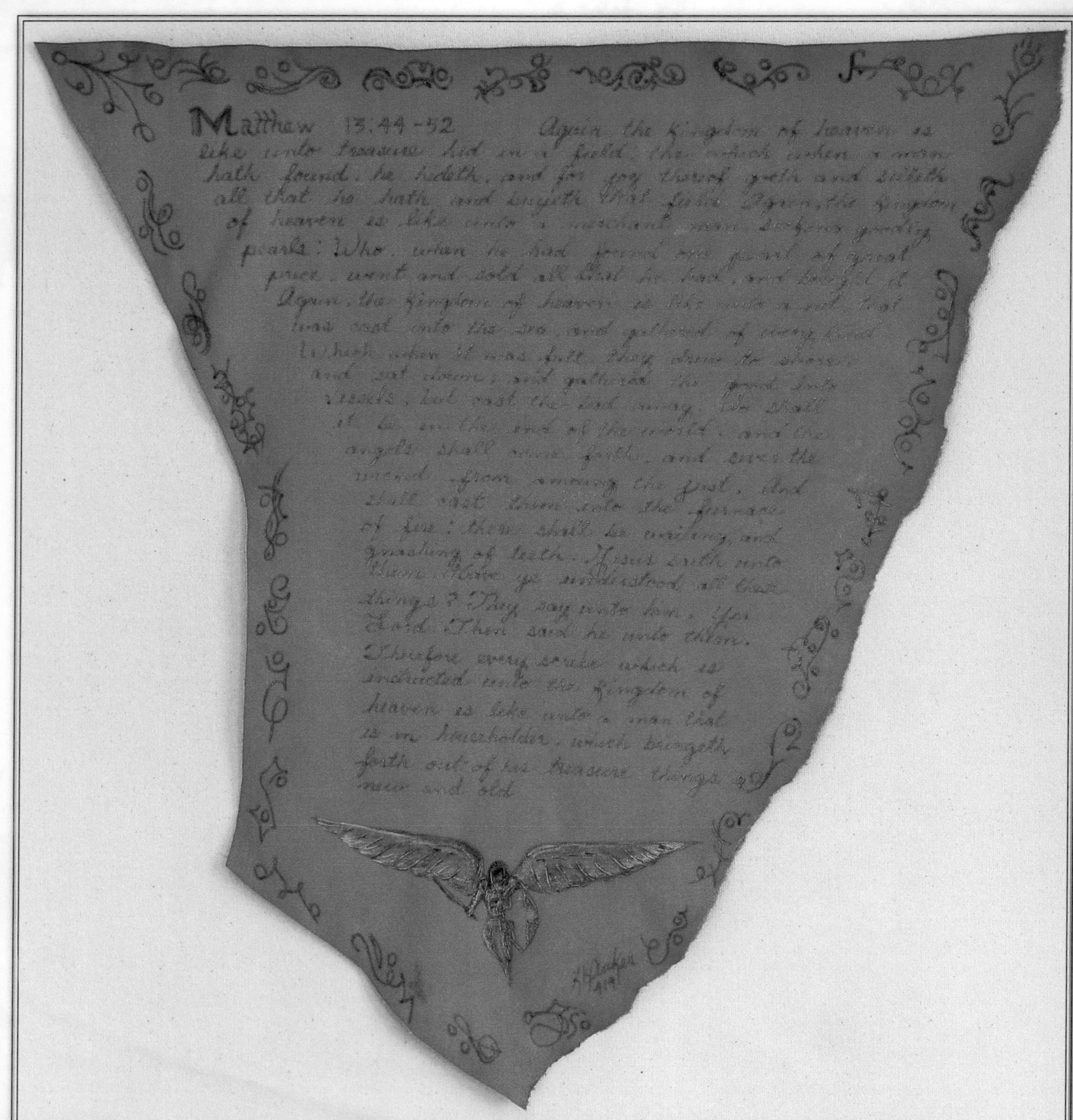
Matthew 13:44-52 Again, the kingdom of heaven is
like unto treasure hid in a field; the which when a man
hath found, he hideth, and for joy thereof goeth and selleth
all that he hath and buyeth that field. Again, the kingdom
of heaven is like unto a merchant man, seeking goodly
pearls: Who, when he had found one pearl of great
price, went and sold all that he had, and bought it.
Again, the kingdom of heaven is like unto a net, that
was cast into the sea, and gathered of every kind:
Which, when it was full, they drew to shore,
and sat down, and gathered the good into
vessels, but cast the bad away. So shall
it be in the end of the world: and the
angels shall come forth, and sever the
wicked from among the just, And
shall cast them into the furnace
of fire: there shall be wailing and
gnashing of teeth. Jesus saith unto
them, Have ye understood all these
things? They say unto him, Yea,
Lord. Then said he unto them,
Therefore every scribe which is
instructed unto the kingdom of
heaven is like unto a man that
is an householder, which bringeth
forth out of his treasure things
new and old.

Matthew 13:53-58
And it came to pass, that when Jesus had
finished these parables, he departed thence.
And when he was come into his own country,
he taught them in their synagogues, insomuch that they were astonished, and said,
Whence hath this man this wisdom, and
these mighty works? Is not this the
carpenter's son? is not his mother called
Mary? and his bretheren, James, and
Joses, and Simon and Judas? And his
sisters, are they not all with us? Whence
then hath this man all these things?
And they were offended in him. But
Jesus said unto them, A prophet is not
without honour, save in his own country
and in his own house. And he did not
many mighty works there because of
their unbelief.

KKlanker
420

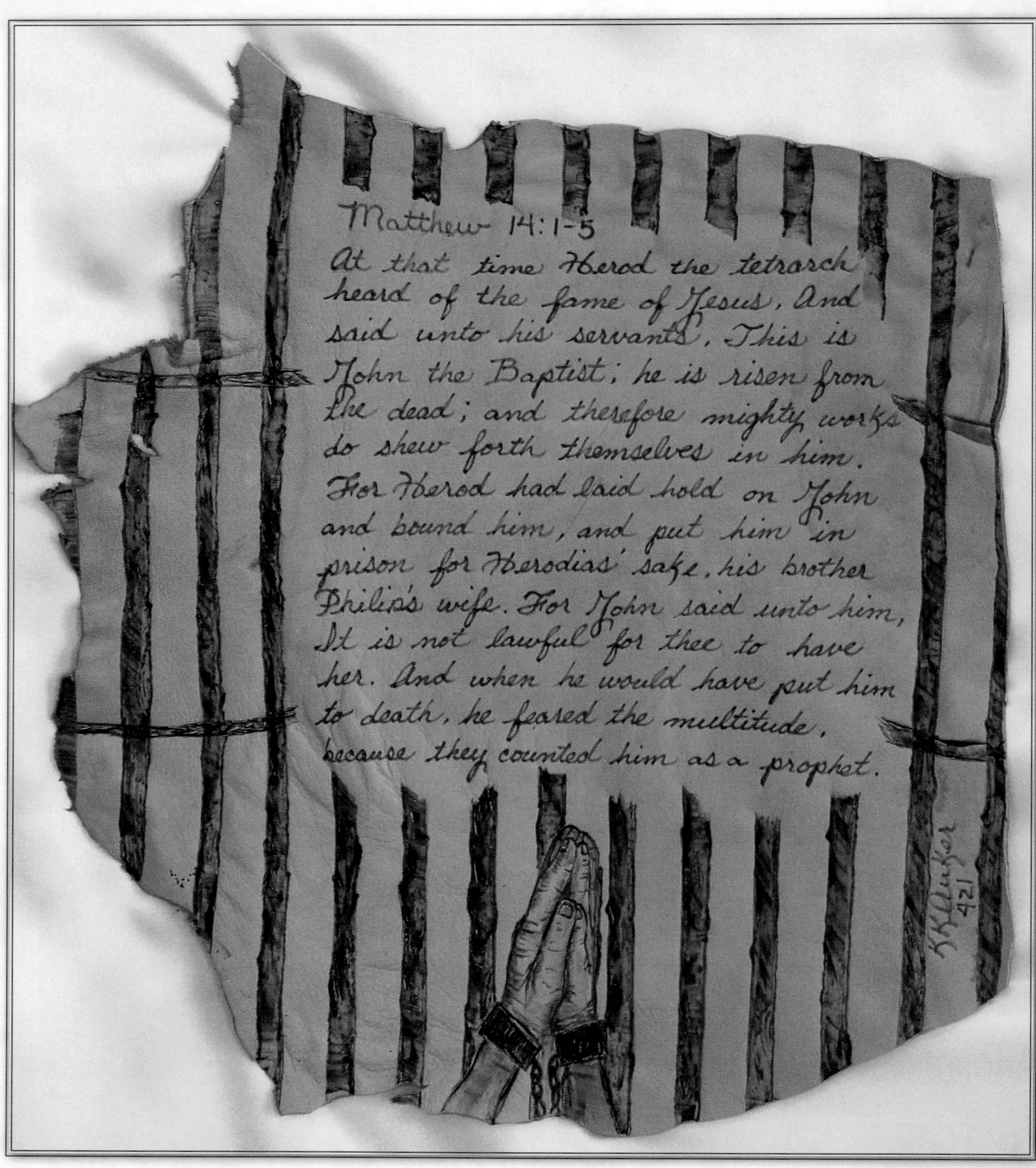
Matthew 14:1-5
At that time Herod the tetrarch heard of the fame of Jesus, And said unto his servants, This is John the Baptist; he is risen from the dead; and therefore mighty works do shew forth themselves in him. For Herod had laid hold on John and bound him, and put him in prison for Herodias' sake, his brother Philip's wife. For John said unto him, It is not lawful for thee to have her. And when he would have put him to death, he feared the multitude, because they counted him as a prophet.
KKlucker
421

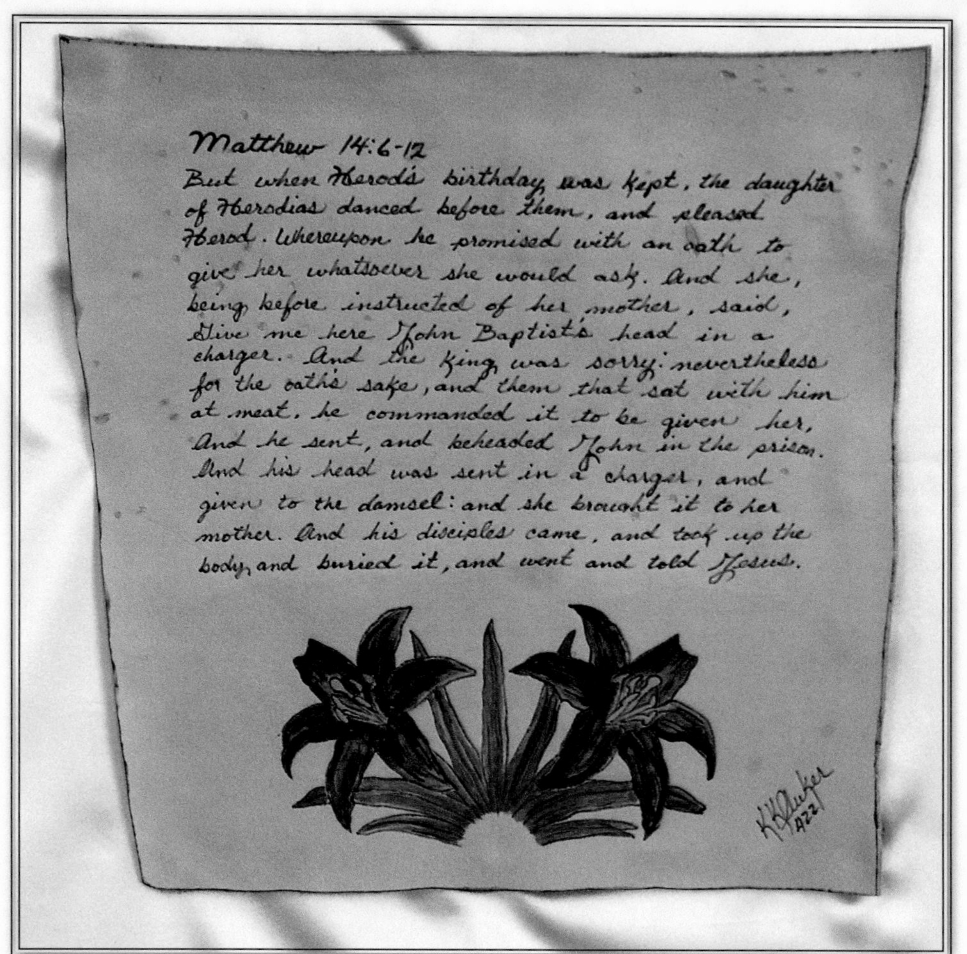
Matthew 14:6-12
But when Herod's birthday was kept, the daughter of Herodias danced before them, and pleased Herod. Whereupon he promised with an oath to give her whatsoever she would ask. And she, being before instructed of her mother, said, Give me here John Baptist's head in a charger. And the king was sorry: nevertheless for the oath's sake, and them that sat with him at meat, he commanded it to be given her. And he sent, and beheaded John in the prison. And his head was sent in a charger, and given to the damsel: and she brought it to her mother. And his disciples came, and took up the body, and buried it, and went and told Jesus.
KLShuker
A22

Matthew 14:13-14
When Jesus heard of it, he departed thence by ship into a desert place apart: and when the people had heard thereof, they followed him on foot out of the cities. And Jesus went forth, and saw a great multitude, and was moved with compassion toward them, and he healed their sick.
KLShuker
A23

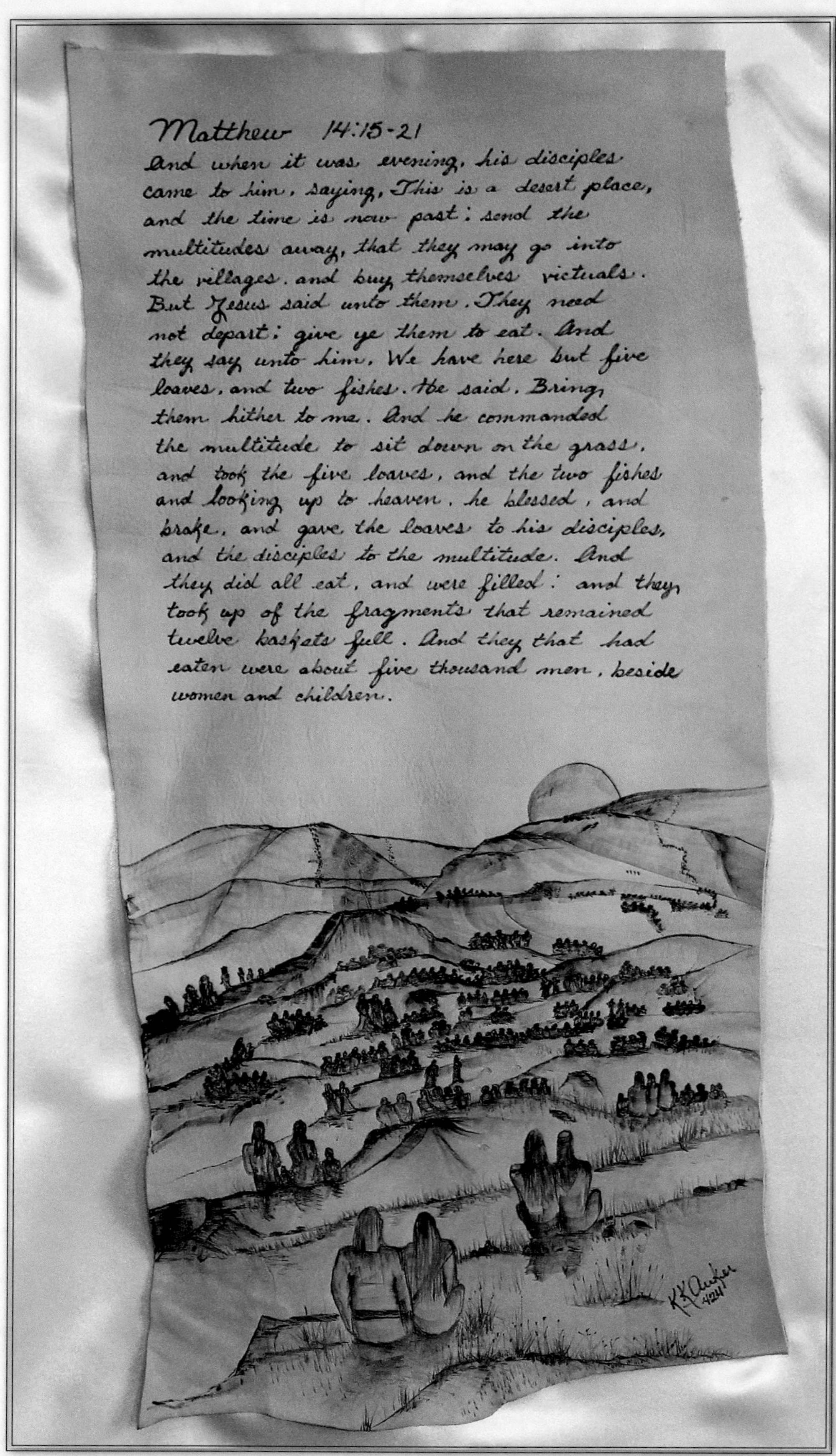
Matthew 14:15-21
And when it was evening, his disciples
came to him, saying, This is a desert place,
and the time is now past: send the
multitudes away, that they may go into
the villages. and buy themselves victuals.
But Jesus said unto them. They need
not depart; give ye them to eat. And
they say unto him. We have here but five
loaves. and two fishes. He said. Bring,
them hither to me. And he commanded
the multitude to sit down on the grass.
and took the five loaves. and the two fishes
and looking up to heaven. he blessed. and
brake. and gave the loaves to his disciples.
and the disciples to the multitude. And
they did all eat. and were filled: and they
took up of the fragments that remained
twelve baskets full. And they that had
eaten were about five thousand men. beside
women and children.

Matthew 14:22-23
And straightway Jesus constrained
his disciples to get into a ship, and
to go before him unto the other side, while
he sent the multitudes away. And when
he had sent the multitudes away, he
went up into a mountain apart to
pray: and when the evening was
come, he was there alone.
KKAnker

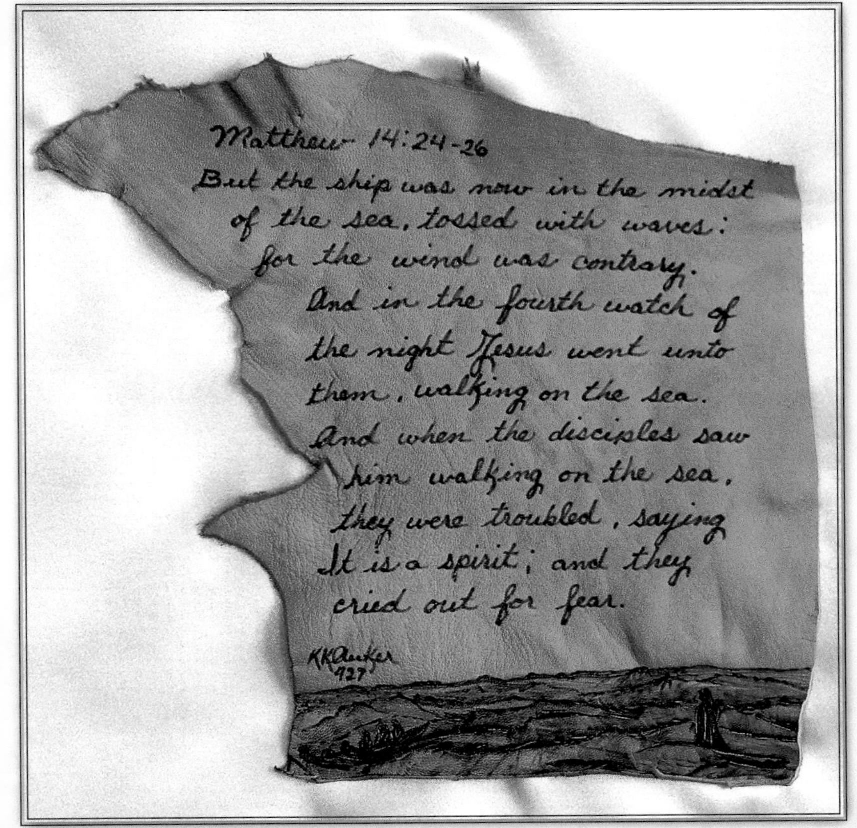
Matthew 14:24-26
But the ship was now in the midst
of the sea, tossed with waves:
for the wind was contrary.
And in the fourth watch of
the night Jesus went unto
them, walking on the sea.
And when the disciples saw
him walking on the sea,
they were troubled, saying
It is a spirit; and they
cried out for fear.
KKAnker

Matthew 14:27-31
But straightway Jesus spake
unto them, saying, Be of
good cheer; It is I; be not
afraid. And Peter answered
him and said, Lord, if it
be thou, bid me come unto
thee on the water. And he
said, Come. And when Peter
was come down out of the
ship, he walked on the
water, to go to Jesus. But
when he saw the wind
boisterous, he was afraid;
and beginning to sink,
he cried, saying, Lord,
save me. And immediately
Jesus stretched forth his
his hand, and caught him,
and said unto him, O thou
of little faith, wherefore
didst thou doubt?

Matthew 14:33-36

Then they that were in the ship came and worshipped him, saying, Of a truth thou art the Son of God. And they were gone over, they came into the land of Gennesaret. And when the men of that place had knowledge of him, they sent out into all that country round about, and brought unto him all that were diseased; And besought him that they might only touch the hem of his garment: and as many as touched were made perfectly whole.

KKlinger
430

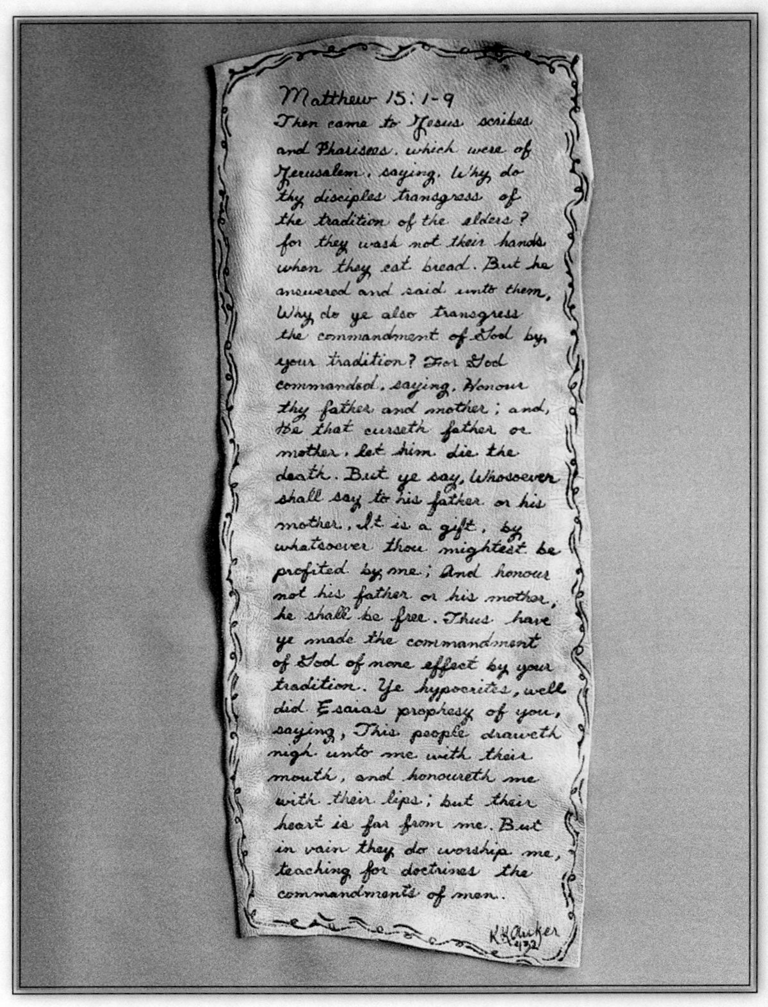
Matthew 15:1-9
Then came to Jesus scribes
and Pharisees, which were of
Jerusalem, saying, Why do
thy disciples transgress of
the tradition of the elders?
for they wash not their hands
when they eat bread. But he
answered and said unto them,
Why do ye also transgress
the commandment of God by
your tradition? For God
commanded, saying, Honour
thy father and mother; and,
He that curseth father or
mother, let him die the
death. But ye say, Whosoever
shall say to his father or his
mother, It is a gift, by
whatsoever thou mightest be
profited by me; And honour
not his father or his mother,
he shall be free. Thus have
ye made the commandment
of God of none effect by your
tradition. Ye hypocrites, well
did Esaias prophesy of you,
saying, This people draweth
nigh unto me with their
mouth, and honoureth me
with their lips; but their
heart is far from me. But
in vain they do worship me,
teaching for doctrines the
commandments of men.

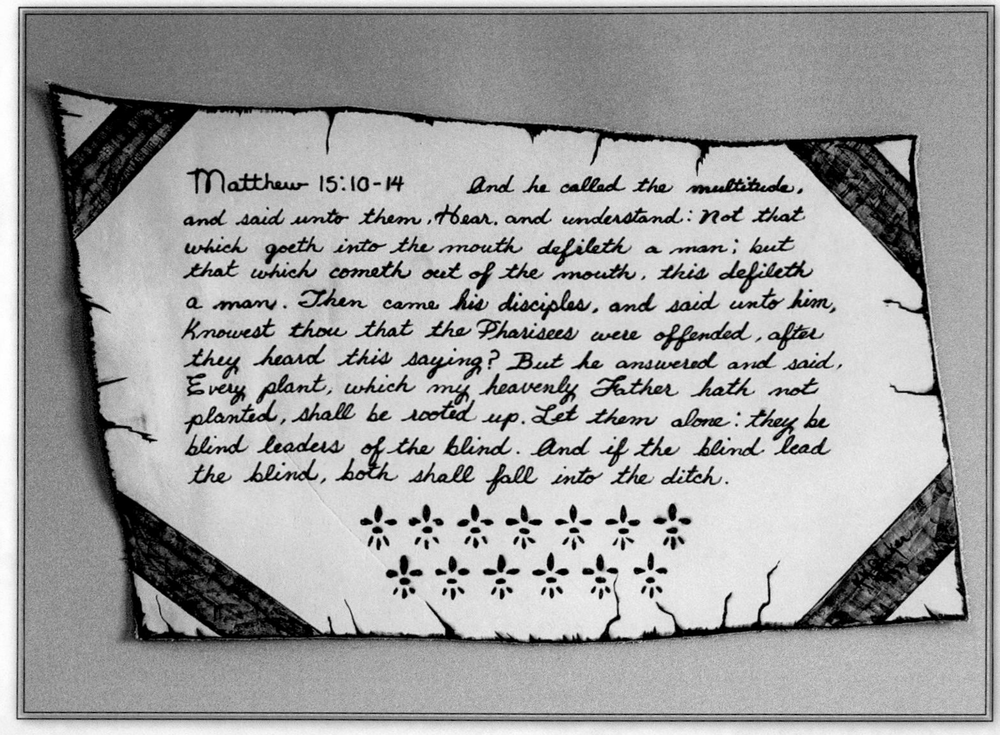
Matthew 15:10-14 And he called the multitude,
and said unto them, Hear, and understand: Not that
which goeth into the mouth defileth a man; but
that which cometh out of the mouth, this defileth
a man. Then came his disciples, and said unto him,
Knowest thou that the Pharisees were offended, after
they heard this saying? But he answered and said,
Every plant, which my heavenly Father hath not
planted, shall be rooted up. Let them alone: they be
blind leaders of the blind. And if the blind lead
the blind, both shall fall into the ditch.

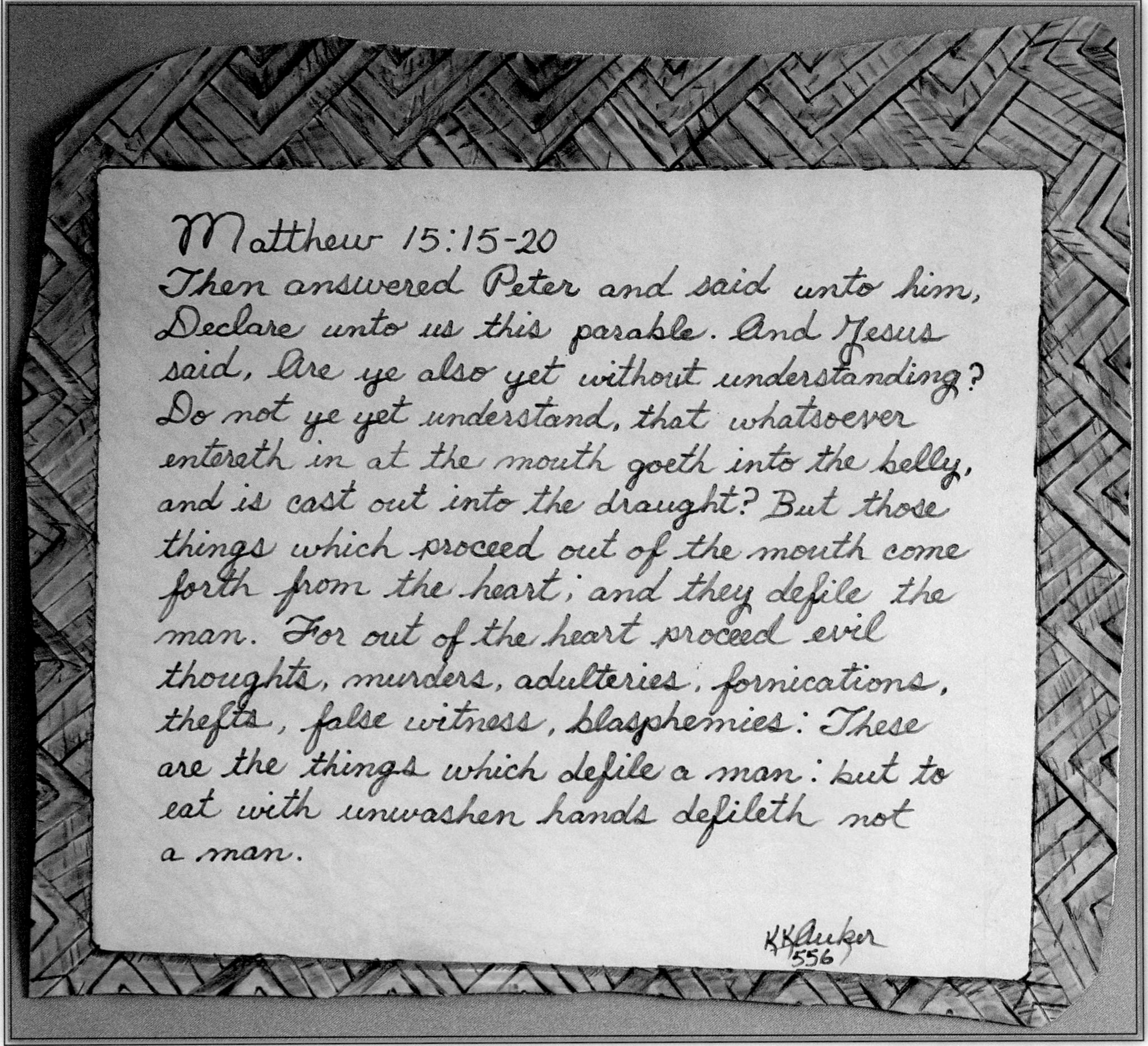
Matthew 15:15-20
Then answered Peter and said unto him,
Declare unto us this parable. And Jesus
said, Are ye also yet without understanding?
Do not ye yet understand, that whatsoever
entereth in at the mouth goeth into the belly,
and is cast out into the draught? But those
things which proceed out of the mouth come
forth from the heart; and they defile the
man. For out of the heart proceed evil
thoughts, murders, adulteries, fornications,
thefts, false witness, blasphemies: These
are the things which defile a man: but to
eat with unwashen hands defileth not
a man.
KKAuker
556

Matthew 15: 21-28

Then Jesus went thence, and departed
into the coasts of Tyre and Sidon.
And behold, a woman of Canaan came
out of the same coasts, and cried unto
him, saying, Have mercy on me,
O Lord, thou son of David; my
daughter is grievously vexed with a
devil. But he answered her not a word.
And his disciples came and besought him,
saying, Send her away; for she crieth after us.
But he answered and said, I am not sent but unto
the lost sheep of the house of Israel. Then came she and worshipped
him, saying, Lord, help me. But he answered and said, It is not
meet to take the children's bread, and to cast it to the dogs. And
she said, Truth, Lord: yet the dogs eat of the crumbs which fall from
their masters' table. Then Jesus answered and said unto her, O woman,
great is thy faith: be it unto thee even as thou wilt. And her daughter was
made whole from that very hour.

KKAuker
4/98

Matthew 15:29-31

And Jesus departed from thence, and
came nigh unto the sea of Galilee;
and went up into a mountain, and
sat down there. And great multitudes
came unto him, having with them
those that were lame, blind, dumb,
maimed, and many others, and cast
them down at Jesus' feet; and
he healed them: Insomuch that
the multitude wondered, when
they saw the dumb to speak, the
maimed to be whole, the lame to
walk, and the blind to see: and
they glorified the God of Israel.

KKAuker
2/96

Matthew 15:32-39

Then Jesus called his disciples
unto him and said, I have
compassion on the multitude,
because they continue with me
now three days, and have
nothing to eat: and I will
not send them away fasting,
lest they faint in the way.
And his disciples say unto
him, Whence should we have
so much bread in the wilderness,
as to fill so great a multitude?
And Jesus saith unto them,
How many loaves have ye?
And they said, Seven, and a
few little fishes. And he
commanded the multitude to
sit down on the ground. And
he took the seven loaves and
the fishes, and gave thanks,
and brake them, and gave to his
disciples, and the disciples to the
multitude. And they did all eat,
and were filled: and they took up
of the broken meat that was left
seven baskets full. And they that
did eat were four thousand men,
beside women and children. And
he sent away the multitude, and
took ship, and came into
the coasts of Magdala.

Matthew 16:1-4 The Pharisees also with the Sadducees came, and tempting desired him that he would shew them a sign from heaven. He answered and said unto them, When it is evening, ye say, It will be fair weather: for the sky is red. And in the morning, It will be foul weather to day: for the sky is red and lowring. O ye hypocrites, ye can discern the face of the sky; but can ye not discern the signs of the times? A wicked and adulterous generation seeketh after a sign; and there shall no sign be given unto it, but the sign of the prophet Jonas. And he left them, and departed.

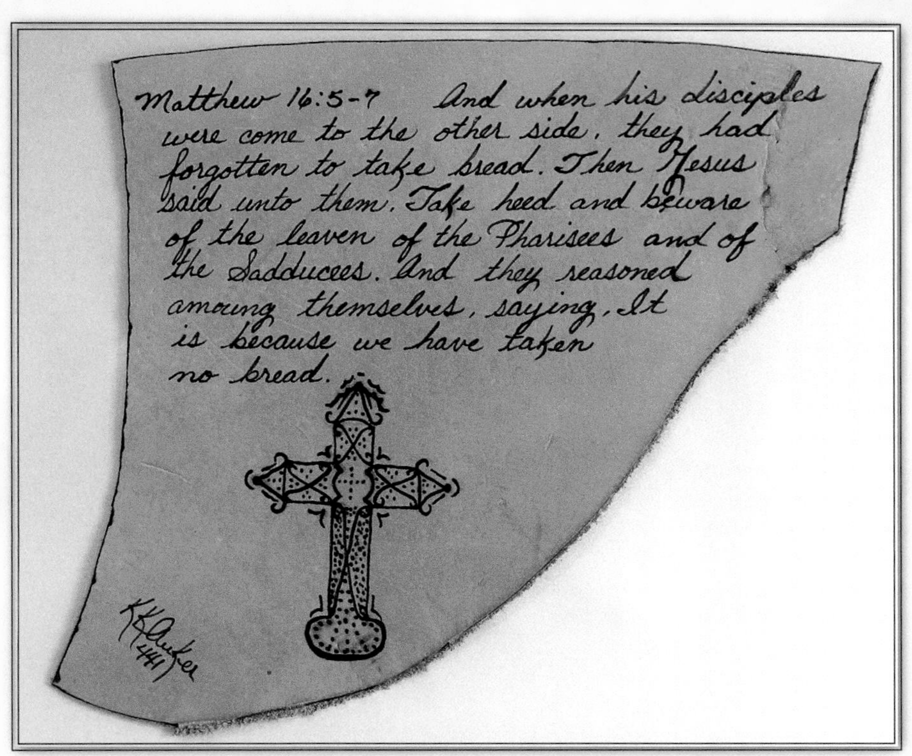
Matthew 16:5-7 And when his disciples
were come to the other side, they had
forgotten to take bread. Then Jesus
said unto them, Take heed and beware
of the leaven of the Pharisees and of
the Sadducees. And they reasoned
among themselves, saying, It
is because we have taken
no bread.
KKAuker
441

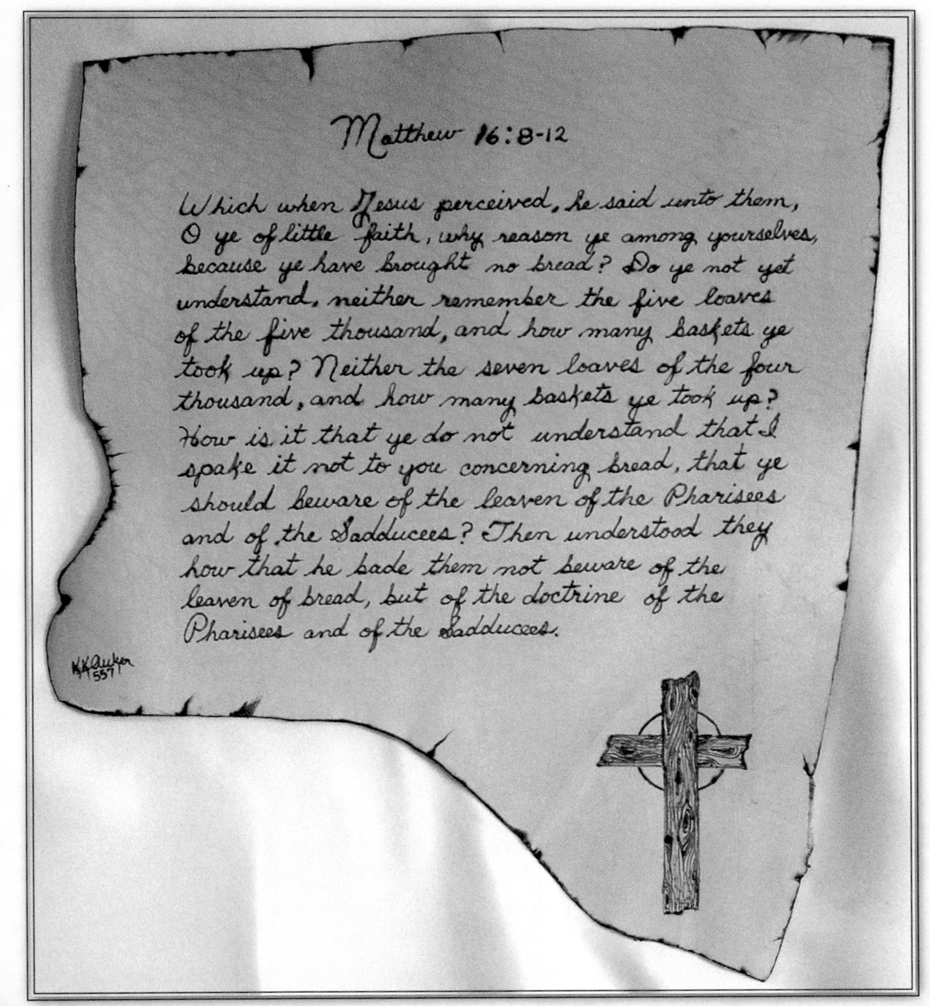
Matthew 16:8-12
Which when Jesus perceived, he said unto them,
O ye of little faith, why reason ye among yourselves,
because ye have brought no bread? Do ye not yet
understand, neither remember the five loaves
of the five thousand, and how many baskets ye
took up? Neither the seven loaves of the four
thousand, and how many baskets ye took up?
How is it that ye do not understand that I
spake it not to you concerning bread, that ye
should beware of the leaven of the Pharisees
and of the Sadducees? Then understood they
how that he bade them not beware of the
leaven of bread, but of the doctrine of the
Pharisees and of the Sadducees.
KKAuker
557

Matthew 16:13-16
When Jesus came into the coasts
of Caesarea Philippi, he asked
his disciples, saying, Whom do
men say that I the Son of man
am? And they said, Some say
that thou art John the Baptist:
some Elias: and others, Jeremias
or one of the prophets. He saith
unto them, But whom say ye
that I am? And Simon Peter
answer and said, Thou art the
Christ, the Son of the living
God.

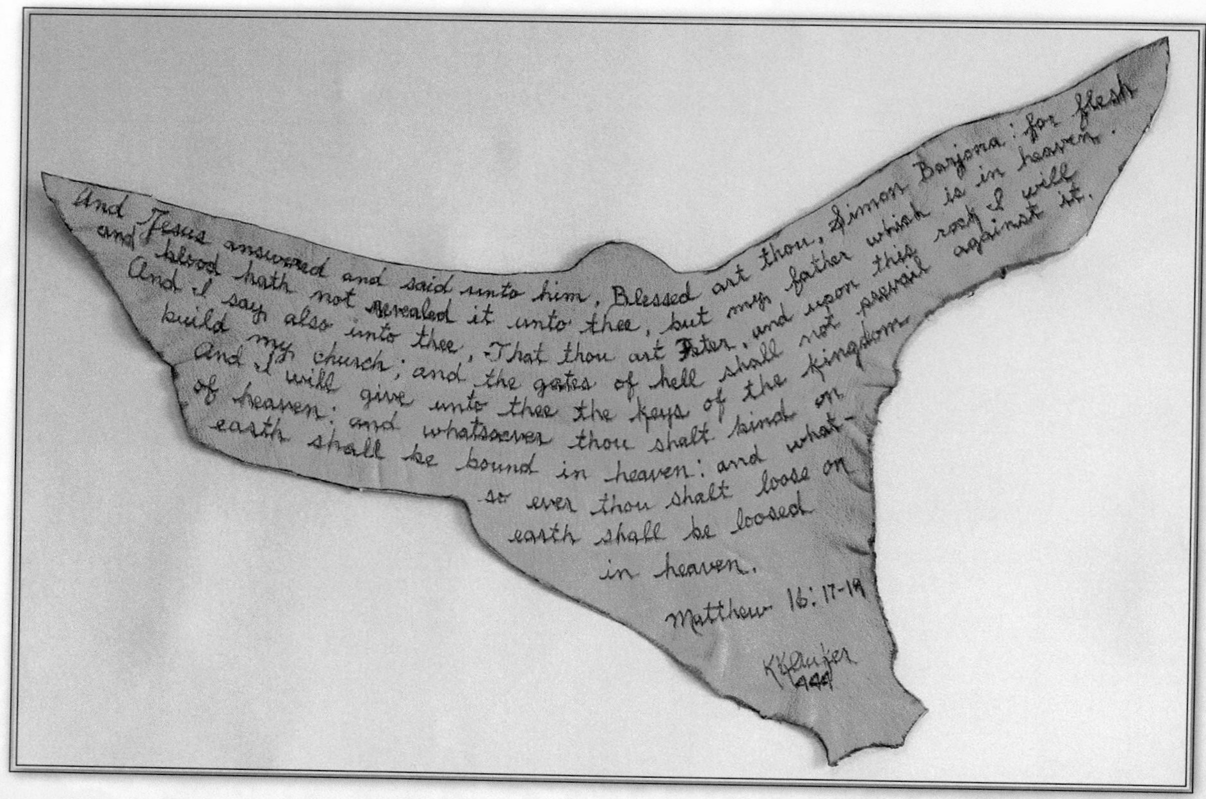

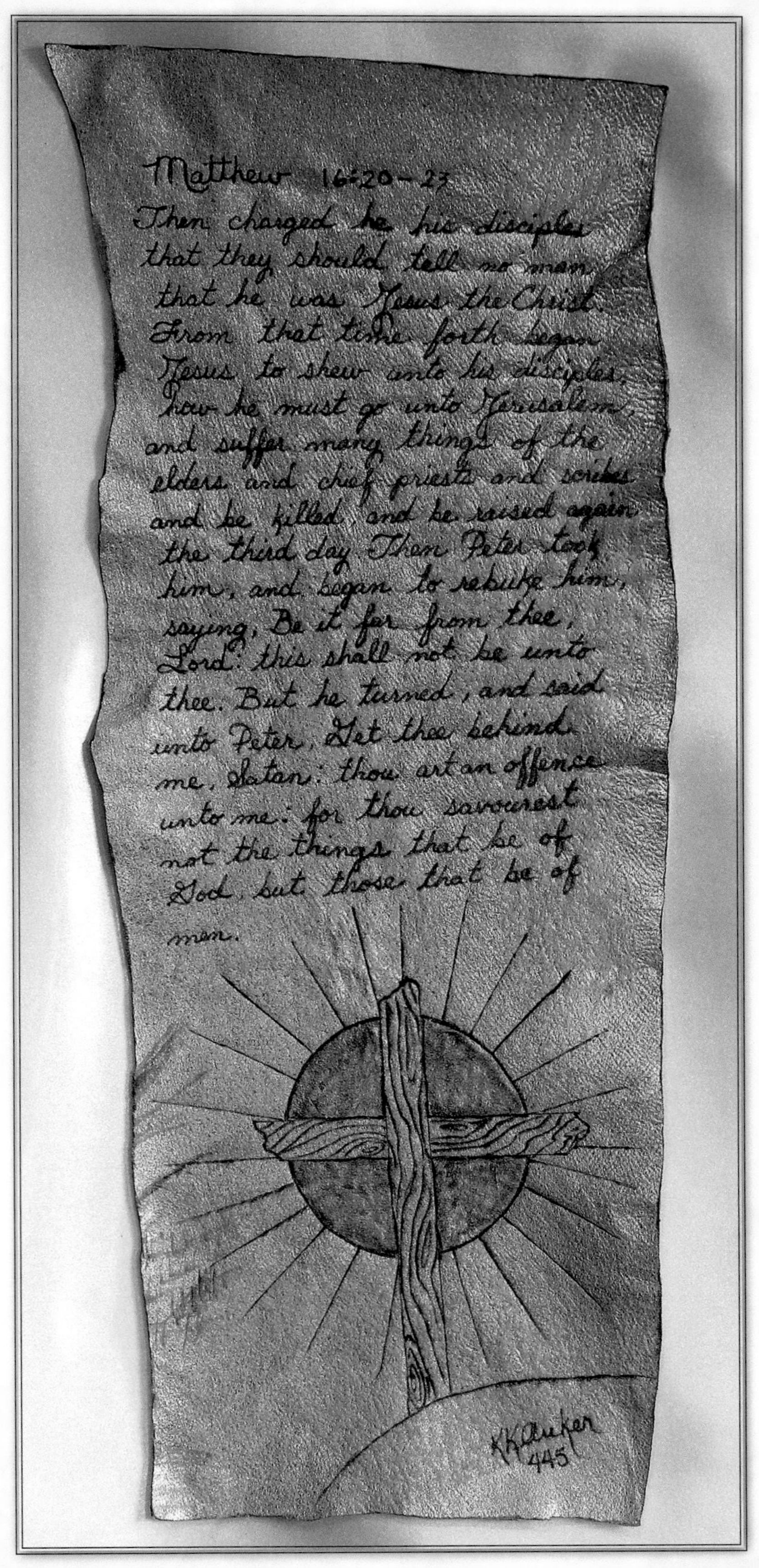
Matthew 16:20-23
Then charged he his disciples
that they should tell no man
that he was Jesus the Christ.
From that time forth began
Jesus to shew unto his disciples,
how he must go unto Jerusalem,
and suffer many things of the
elders and chief priests and scribes
and be killed and be raised again
the third day Then Peter took
him, and began to rebuke him,
saying, Be it far from thee,
Lord: this shall not be unto
thee. But he turned, and said
unto Peter, Get thee behind
me, Satan: thou art an offence
unto me: for thou savourest
not the things that be of
God, but those that be of
men.
KKlecker
445

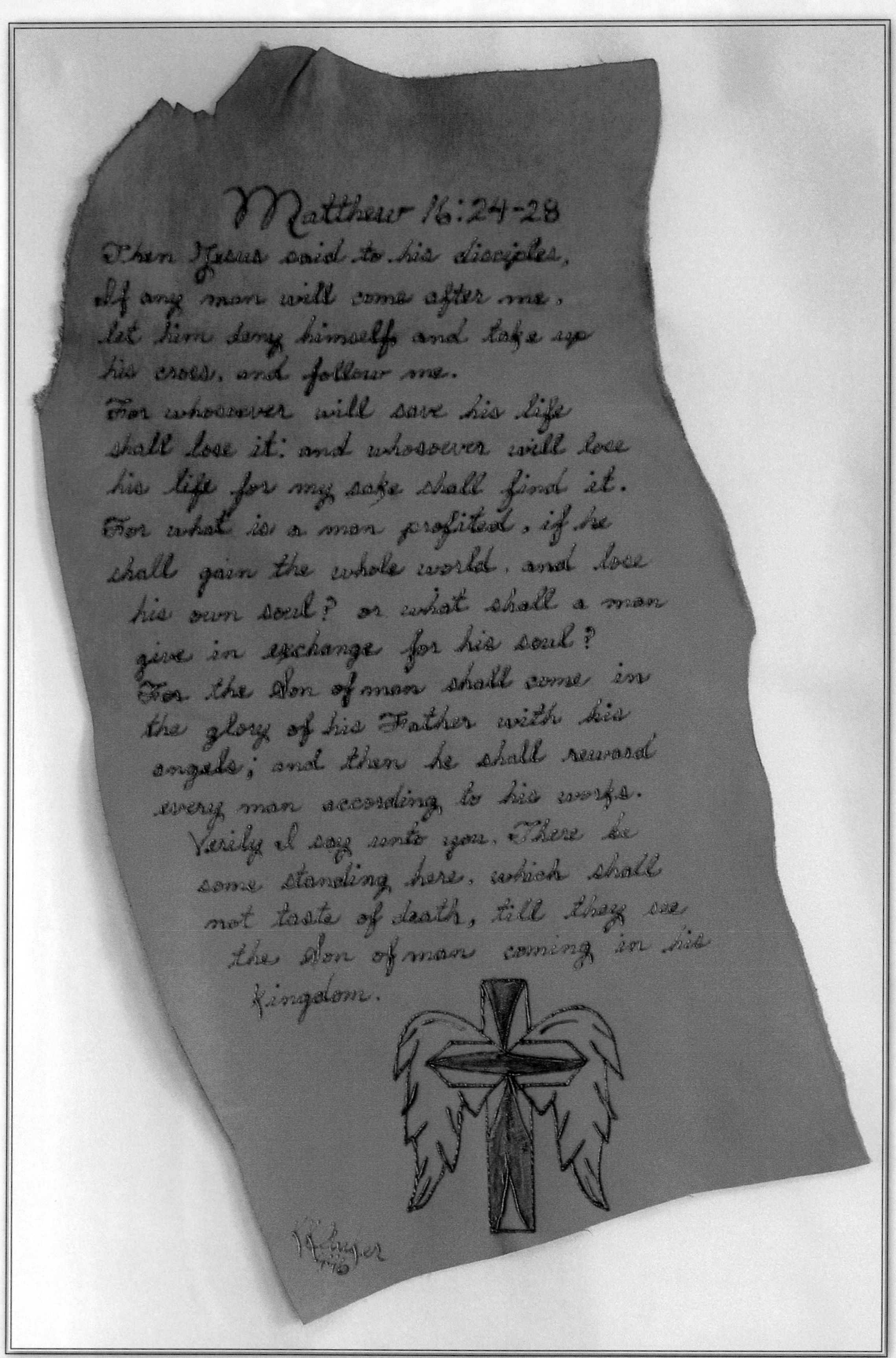
Matthew 16:24-28
Then Jesus said to his disciples,
If any man will come after me,
let him deny himself and take up
his cross, and follow me.
For whosoever will save his life
shall lose it: and whosoever will lose
his life for my sake shall find it.
For what is a man profited, if he
shall gain the whole world, and lose
his own soul? or what shall a man
give in exchange for his soul?
For the Son of man shall come in
the glory of his Father with his
angels; and then he shall reward
every man according to his works.
Verily I say unto you, There be
some standing here, which shall
not taste of death, till they see
the Son of man coming in his
kingdom.

Matthew 17:1-4 And after six days Jesus taketh Peter, James, and John his brother, and bringeth them up into an high mountain apart, And was transfigured before them: and his face did shine as the sun, and his raiment was white as the light. And, behold, there appeared unto them Moses and Elias talking with him. Then answered Peter, and said unto Jesus, Lord it is good for us to be here: if thou wilt, let us make here three tabernacles; one for thee, and one for Moses, and one for Elias.

KKDuyker 447

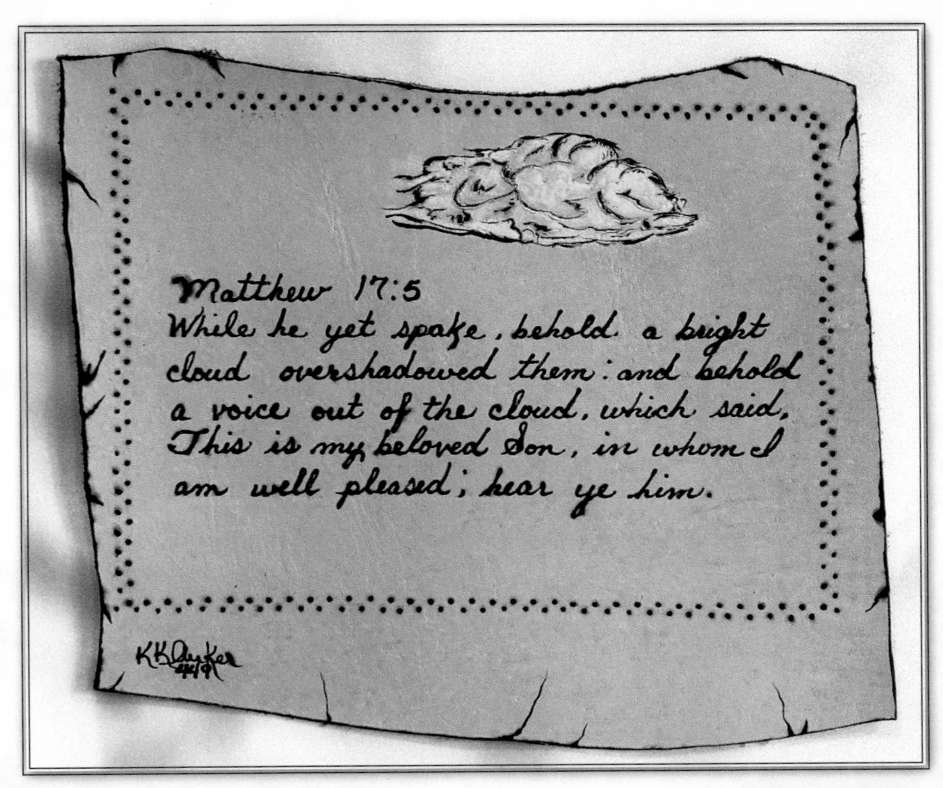

Matthew 17:5
While he yet spake, behold a bright cloud overshadowed them: and behold a voice out of the cloud, which said, This is my beloved Son, in whom I am well pleased; hear ye him.

KKDuyker 449

Matthew 17:6-9 And when the disciples heard it, they fell on their face, and were sore afraid. And Jesus came and touched them, and said Arise, and be not afraid. And when they had lifted up their eyes, they saw no man, save Jesus only. And as they came down from the mountain, Jesus charged them, saying, Tell the vision to no man, until the Son of man be risen again from the dead.

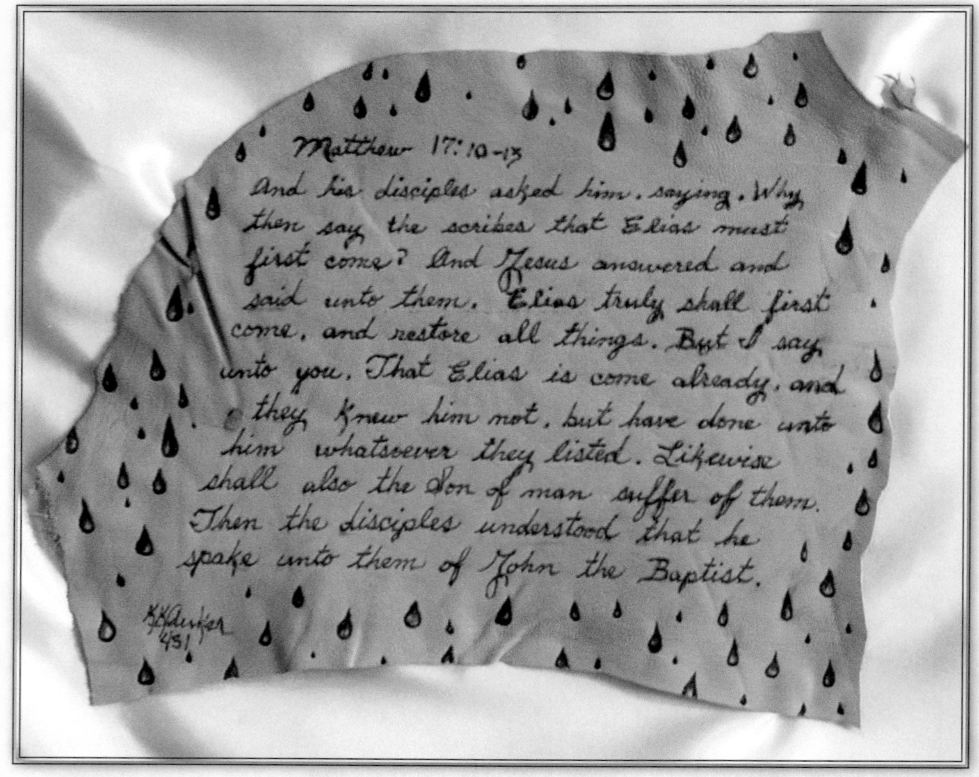

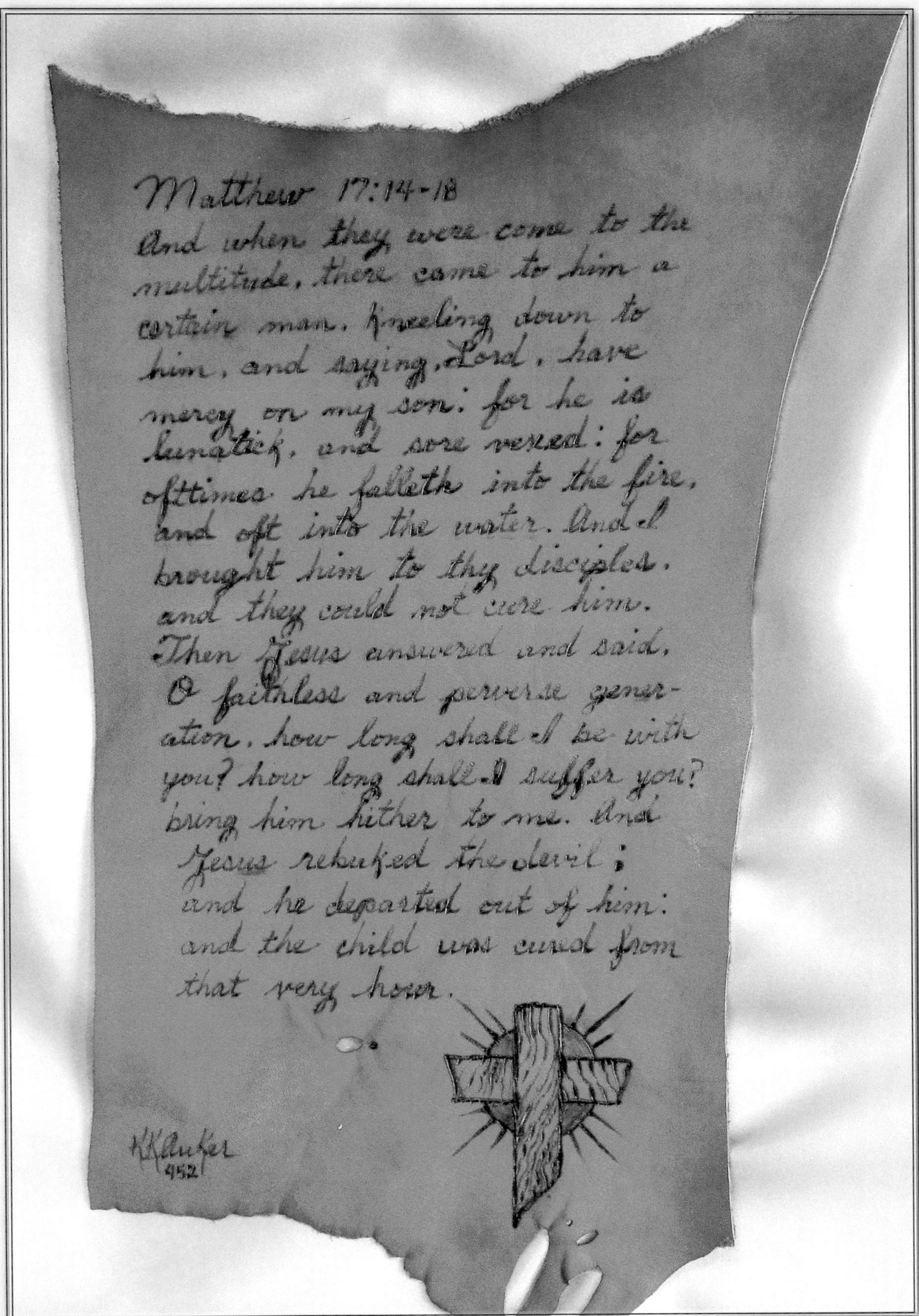

Matthew 17:14-18
And when they were come to the
multitude, there came to him a
certain man, kneeling down to
him, and saying, Lord, have
mercy on my son: for he is
lunatick, and sore vexed: for
ofttimes he falleth into the fire,
and oft into the water. And I
brought him to thy disciples,
and they could not cure him.
Then Jesus answered and said,
O faithless and perverse generation, how long shall I be with
you? how long shall I suffer you?
bring him hither to me. And
Jesus rebuked the devil;
and he departed out of him:
and the child was cured from
that very hour.
KKlauker
452

Matthew 17:19-21
Then came the disciples
to Jesus apart, and said,
Why could not we cast him
out? And Jesus said unto
them, Because of your unbelief:
for verily I say unto you, If ye
have faith as grain of mustard
seed, ye shall say unto this mountain, Remove hence to yonder place;
and it shall remove: and nothing
shall be impossible unto you.
Howbeit this kind goeth not out but
by prayer and fasting.

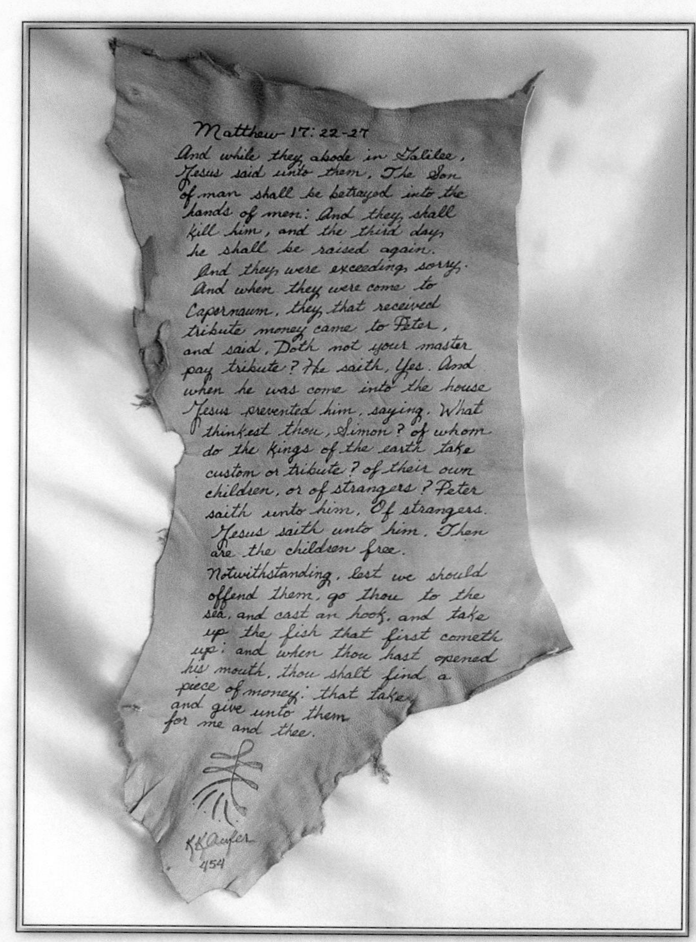
Matthew 17:22-27
And while they abode in Galilee,
Jesus said unto them, The Son
of man shall be betrayed into the
hands of men: And they shall
kill him, and the third day
he shall be raised again.
And they were exceeding sorry.
And when they were come to
Capernaum, they that received
tribute money came to Peter,
and said, Doth not your master
pay tribute? He saith, Yes. And
when he was come into the house
Jesus prevented him, saying, What
thinkest thou, Simon? of whom
do the kings of the earth take
custom or tribute? of their own
children, or of strangers? Peter
saith unto him, Of strangers.
Jesus saith unto him, Then
are the children free.
Notwithstanding, lest we should
offend them, go thou to the
sea, and cast an hook, and take
up the fish that first cometh
up; and when thou hast opened
his mouth, thou shalt find a
piece of money: that take,
and give unto them
for me and thee.

Matthew 18:1-6 At the same time came the disciples unto Jesus, saying, Who is the greatest in the kingdom of heaven? And Jesus called a little child unto him, and set him in the midst of them, And said, Verily I say unto you, Except ye be converted, and become as little children, ye shall not enter into the kingdom of heaven. Whosoever therefore shall humble himself as this little child, the same is greatest in the kingdom of heaven. And whoso shall receive one such little child in my name receiveth me. But whoso shall offend one of these little ones which believe in me, it were better for him that a millstone were hanged about his neck and that he were drowned in the depth of the sea.

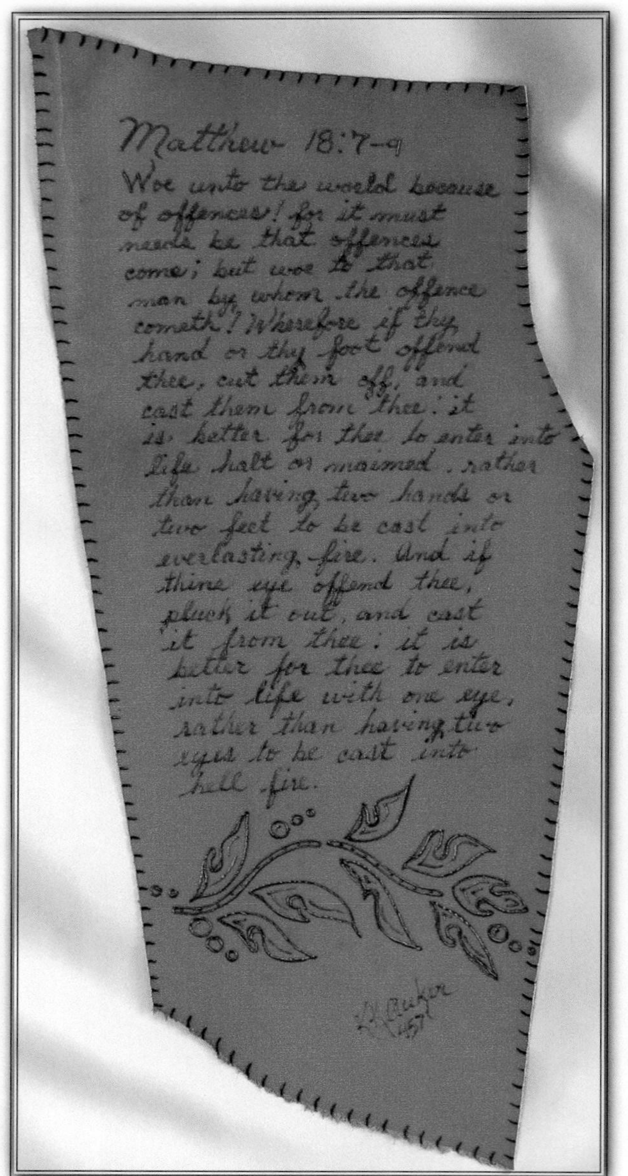
Matthew 18:7-9
Woe unto the world because of offences! for it must needs be that offences come; but woe to that man by whom the offence cometh! Wherefore if thy hand or thy foot offend thee, cut them off, and cast them from thee: it is better for thee to enter into life halt or maimed, rather than having two hands or two feet to be cast into everlasting fire. And if thine eye offend thee, pluck it out, and cast it from thee: it is better for thee to enter into life with one eye, rather than having two eyes to be cast into hell fire.
KKauker

Matthew 18:10-11
Take heed that ye despise not one of these little ones; for I say unto you, That in heaven their angels do always behold the face of my Father which is in heaven.
For the Son of man is come to save that which was lost.
KKauker
331

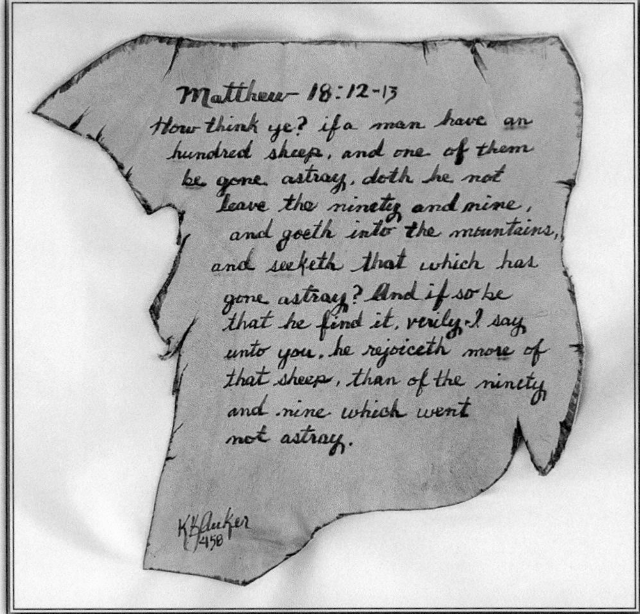
Matthew 18:12-13
How think ye? if a man have an
hundred sheep, and one of them
be gone astray, doth he not
leave the ninety and nine,
and goeth into the mountains,
and seeketh that which has
gone astray? And if so be
that he find it, verily I say
unto you, he rejoiceth more of
that sheep, than of the ninety
and nine which went
not astray.
KKAuker
458

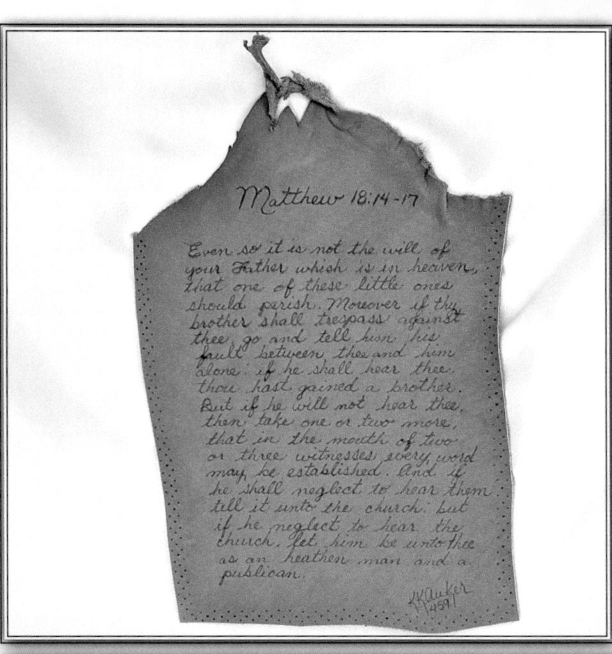
Matthew 18:14-17
Even so it is not the will of
your Father which is in heaven,
that one of these little ones
should perish. Moreover if thy
brother shall trespass against
thee, go and tell him his
fault between thee and him
alone: if he shall hear thee,
thou hast gained a brother.
But if he will not hear thee,
then take one or two more,
that in the mouth of two
or three witnesses every word
may be established. And if
he shall neglect to hear them
tell it unto the church: but
if he neglect to hear the
church, let him be unto thee
as an heathen man and a
publican.
KKAuker
459

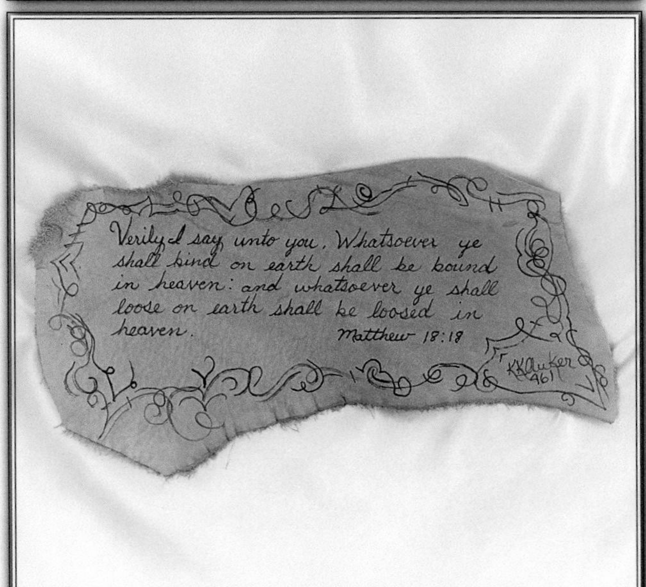
Verily I say unto you, Whatsoever ye
shall bind on earth shall be bound
in heaven: and whatsoever ye shall
loose on earth shall be loosed in
heaven. Matthew 18:18
KKAuker
461

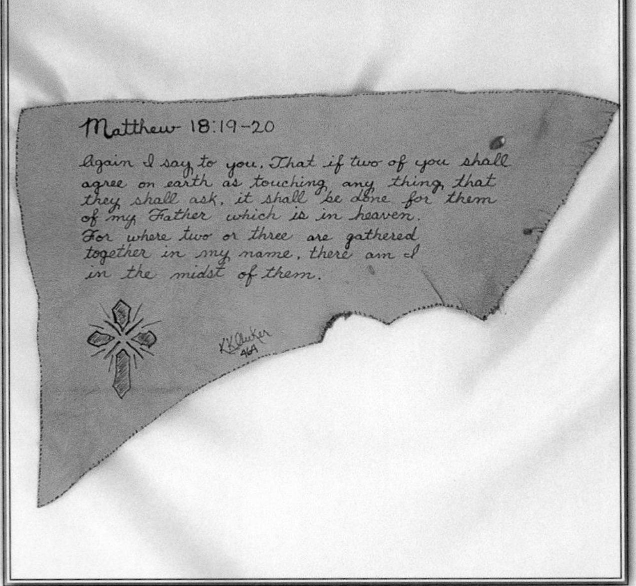
Matthew 18:19-20
Again I say to you, That if two of you shall
agree on earth as touching any thing that
they shall ask, it shall be done for them
of my Father which is in heaven.
For where two or three are gathered
together in my name, there am I
in the midst of them.
KKAuker

Matthew 18:21-35 Then came Peter to him, and said, Lord, how oft shall my brother sin against me, and I forgive him? till seven times? Jesus saith unto him, I say not unto thee, Until seven times? but, Until seventy times seven. Therefore is the kingdom of heaven likened unto a certain king, which would take account of his servants. And when he had begun to reckon, one was brought unto him, which owed him ten thousand talents. But forasmuch as he had not to pay, his lord commanded him to be sold, and his wife, and children, and all that he had, and payment to be made. The servant therefore fell down, and worshipped him, saying, Lord, have patience with me, and I will pay thee all. Then the lord of that servant was moved with compassion, and loosed him and forgave him the debt. But the same servant went out, and found one of his fellowservants, which owed him an hundred pence: and he laid hands on him, and took him by the throat, saying, Pay me that thou owest. And his fellowservant fell down at his feet, and besought him, saying, Have patience with me, and I will pay the all. And he would not: but went and cast him into prison, till he should pay the debt. So when his fellowservants saw what was done, they were very sorry, and came and told unto their lord all that was done. Then his lord, after that he had called him, said unto him, O thou wicked servant, I forgave thee all that debt, because thou desiredst me: Shouldest not thou also have had compassion on thy fellowservant, even as I had pity on thee? And his lord was wroth, and delivered him to the tormentors, till he should pay all that was due unto him. So likewise shall my heavenly Father do also unto you, if ye from your hearts forgive not every one his brother their trespasses.

Matthew 19:1-3
And it came to pass, that
when Jesus had finished
these Sayings, he departed
from Galilee, and came into
the coasts of Judaea beyond
Jordan;
And great mulitudes followed
him; and he healed them
there.
The Pharisees also came unto
him, tempting him, and
saying unto him, Is it
lawful for a man to put
away his wife for every
cause?

Matthew 19:4-6
And he answered and said unto
them, Have ye not read, that he
which made them at the beginning made them male and
female, And said, For this
cause shall a man leave
father and mother, and shall
cleave to his wife: and they
twain shall be one flesh?
Wherefore they are no more
twain, but one flesh. What
therefore God hath joined
together, let not man put
asunder.

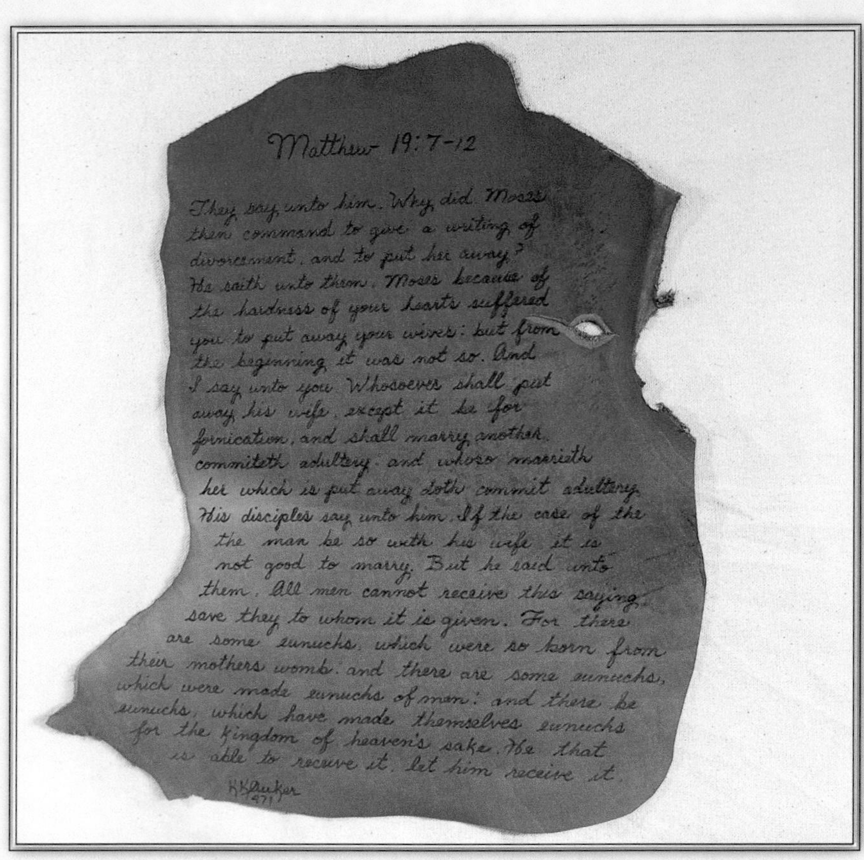
Matthew 19:7-12
They say unto him, Why did Moses
then command to give a writing of
divorcement, and to put her away?
He saith unto them, Moses because of
the hardness of your hearts suffered
you to put away your wives: but from
the beginning it was not so. And
I say unto you, Whosoever shall put
away his wife, except it be for
fornication, and shall marry another,
committeth adultery: and whoso marrieth
her which is put away doth commit adultery.
His disciples say unto him, If the case of the
the man be so with his wife, it is
not good to marry. But he said unto
them, All men cannot receive this saying,
save they to whom it is given. For there
are some eunuchs, which were so born from
their mothers womb: and there are some eunuchs,
which were made eunuchs of men: and there be
eunuchs, which have made themselves eunuchs
for the kingdom of heaven's sake. He that
is able to receive it, let him receive it.
KKlauker
471

Matthew 19:13-15
Then were there brought unto him
little children, that he should put
his hands on them, and pray: and
the disciples rebuked them. But
Jesus said, Suffer little children,
and forbid them not, to come unto
me: for of such is the kingdom
of heaven. And he laid his hands
on them, and departed thense.
KKlauker
474

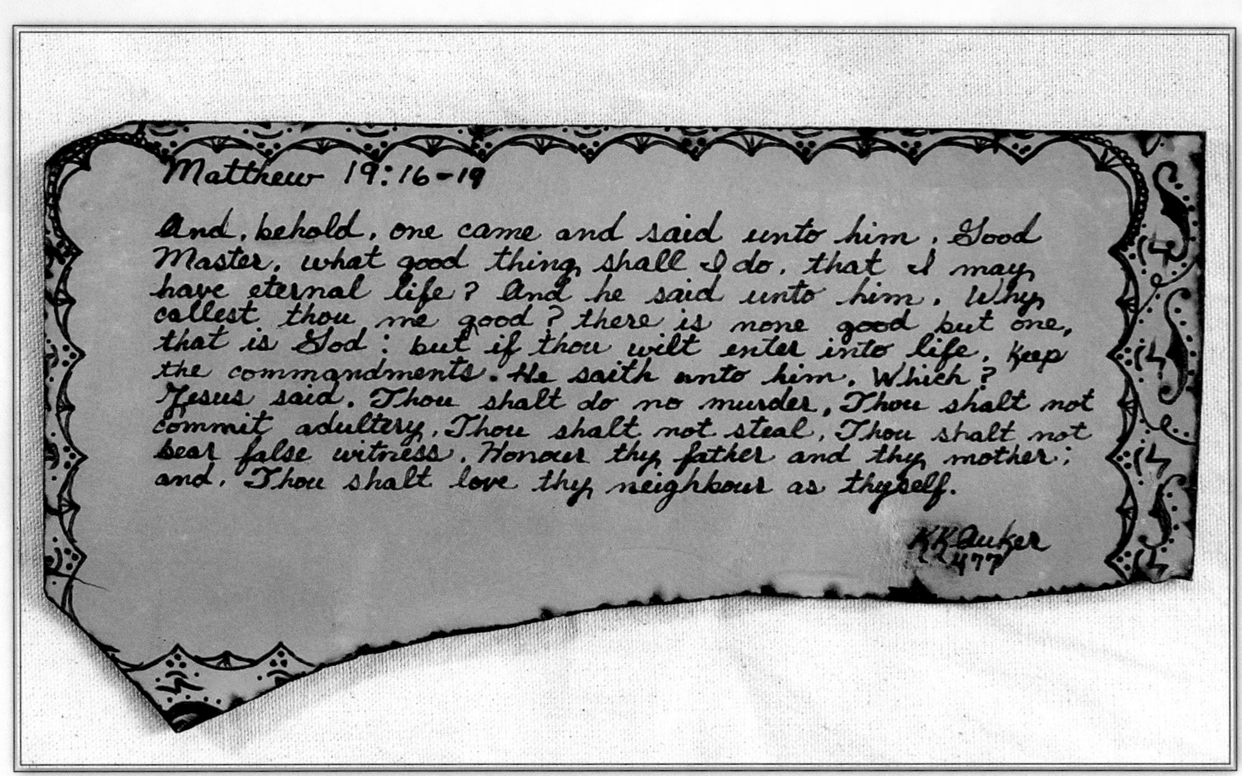
Matthew 19:16-19

And, behold, one came and said unto him, Good Master, what good thing shall I do, that I may have eternal life? And he said unto him, Why callest thou me good? there is none good but one, that is God: but if thou wilt enter into life, keep the commandments. He saith unto him, Which? Jesus said, Thou shalt do no murder, Thou shalt not commit adultery, Thou shalt not steal, Thou shalt not bear false witness, Honour thy father and thy mother: and, Thou shalt love thy neighbour as thyself.

KKAuker
477

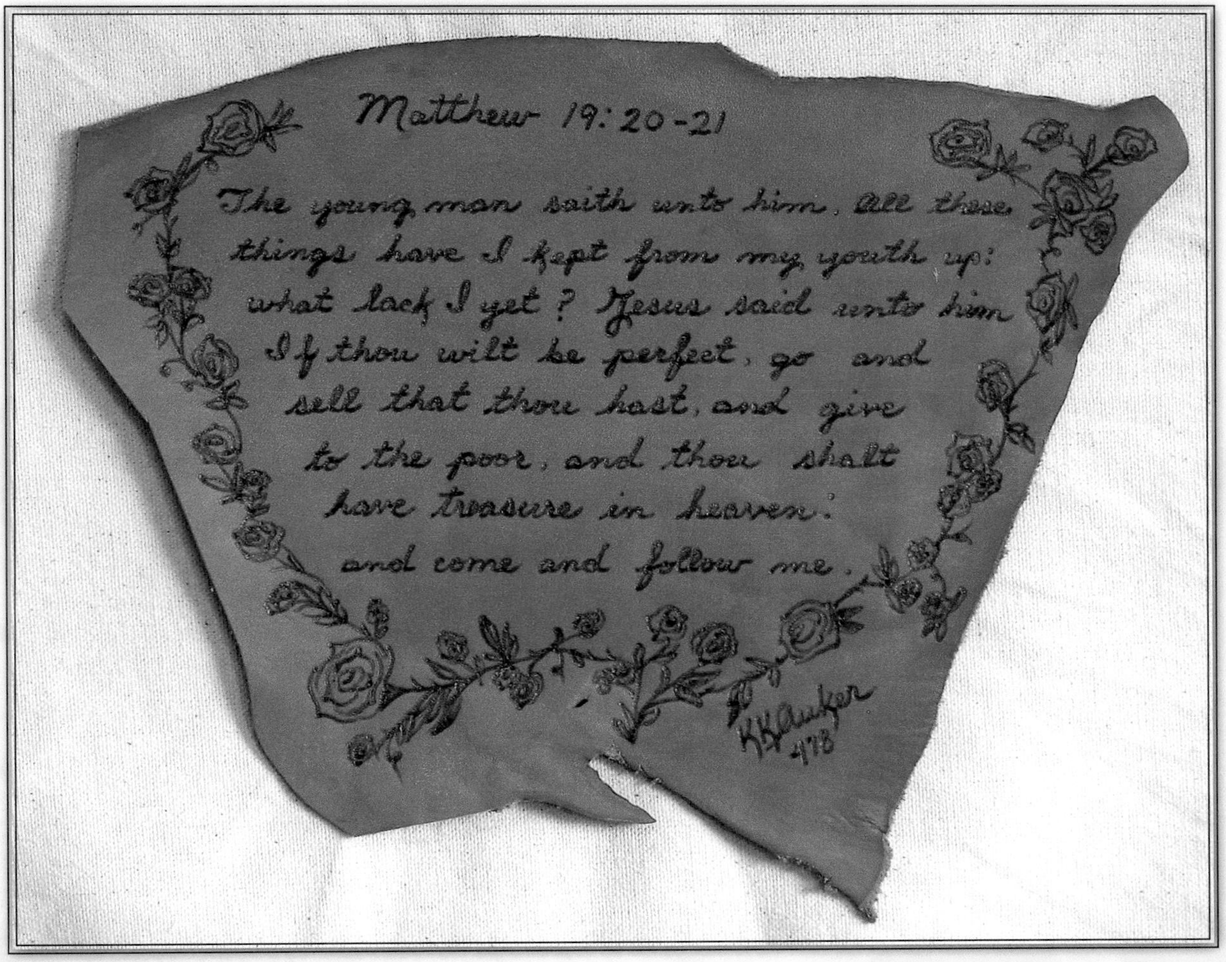

Matthew 19:20-21

The young man saith unto him, All these things have I kept from my youth up: what lack I yet? Jesus said unto him If thou wilt be perfect, go and sell that thou hast, and give to the poor, and thou shalt have treasure in heaven: and come and follow me.

KKAuker
478

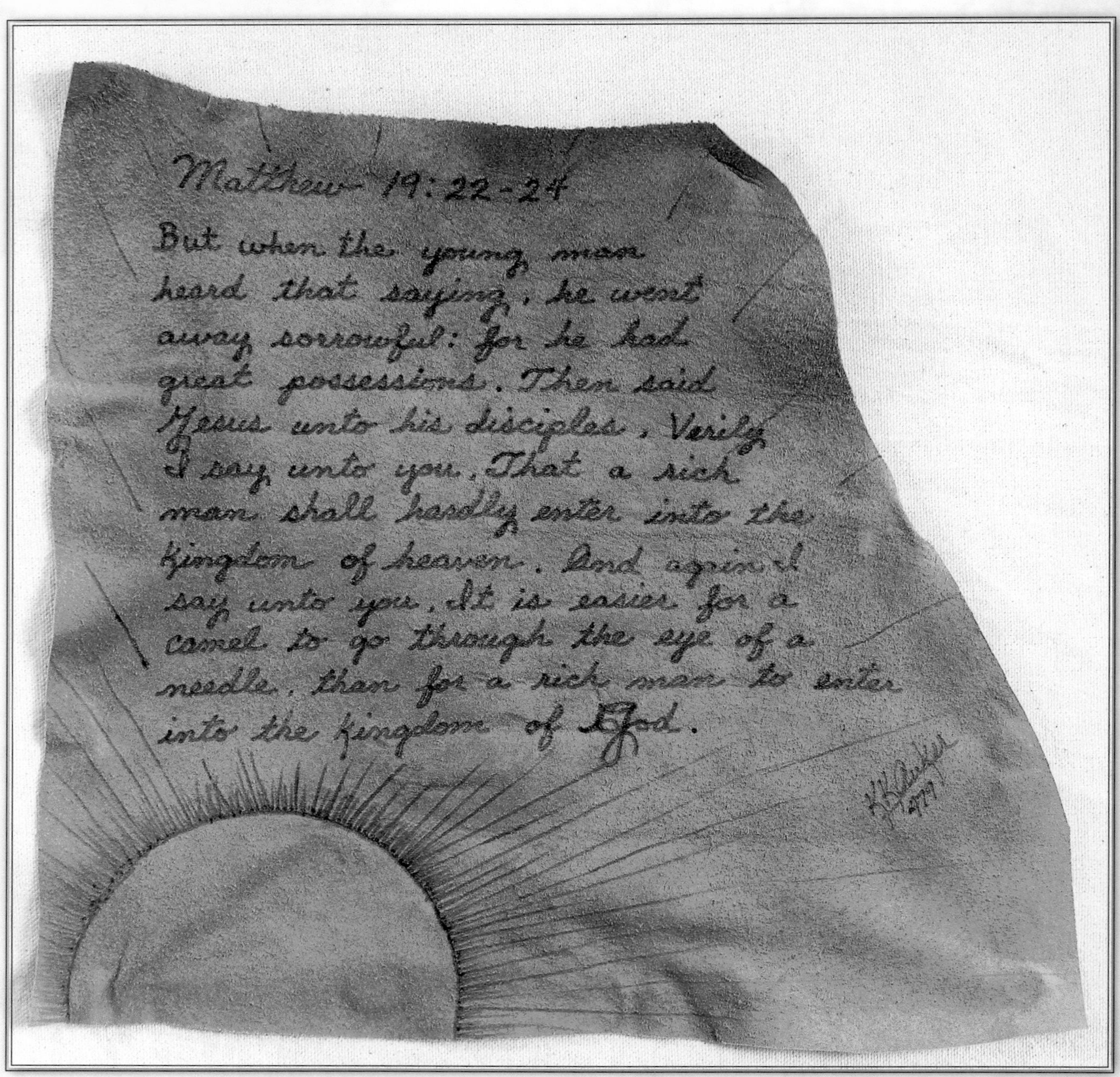
Matthew 19:22-24
But when the young man
heard that saying, he went
away sorrowful: for he had
great possessions. Then said
Jesus unto his disciples, Verily
I say unto you, That a rich
man shall hardly enter into the
kingdom of heaven. And again I
say unto you, It is easier for a
camel to go through the eye of a
needle, than for a rich man to enter
into the kingdom of God.

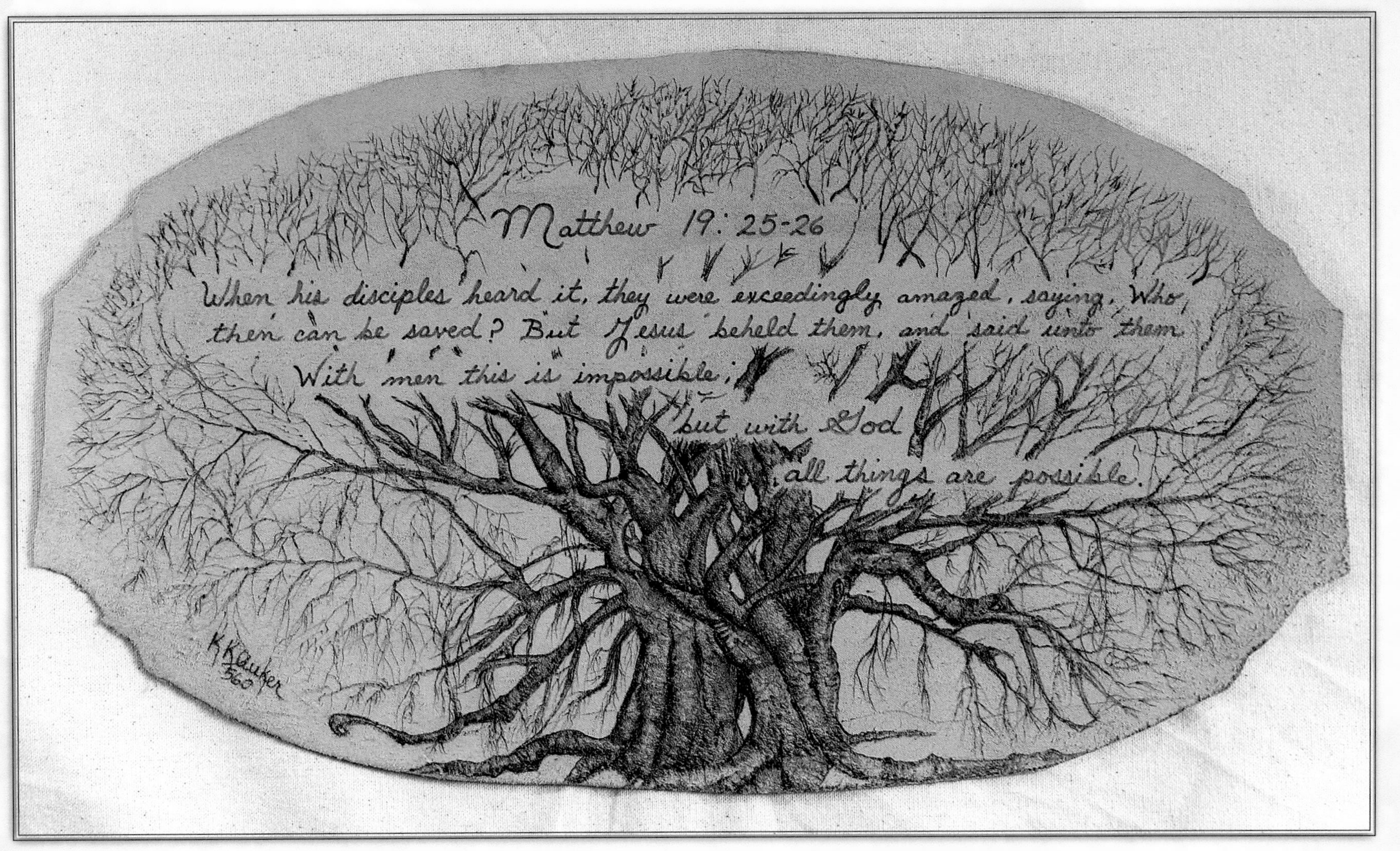
Matthew 19: 25-26
When his disciples heard it, they were exceedingly amazed, saying, Who
then can be saved? But Jesus beheld them, and said unto them
With men this is impossible;
but with God
all things are possible.

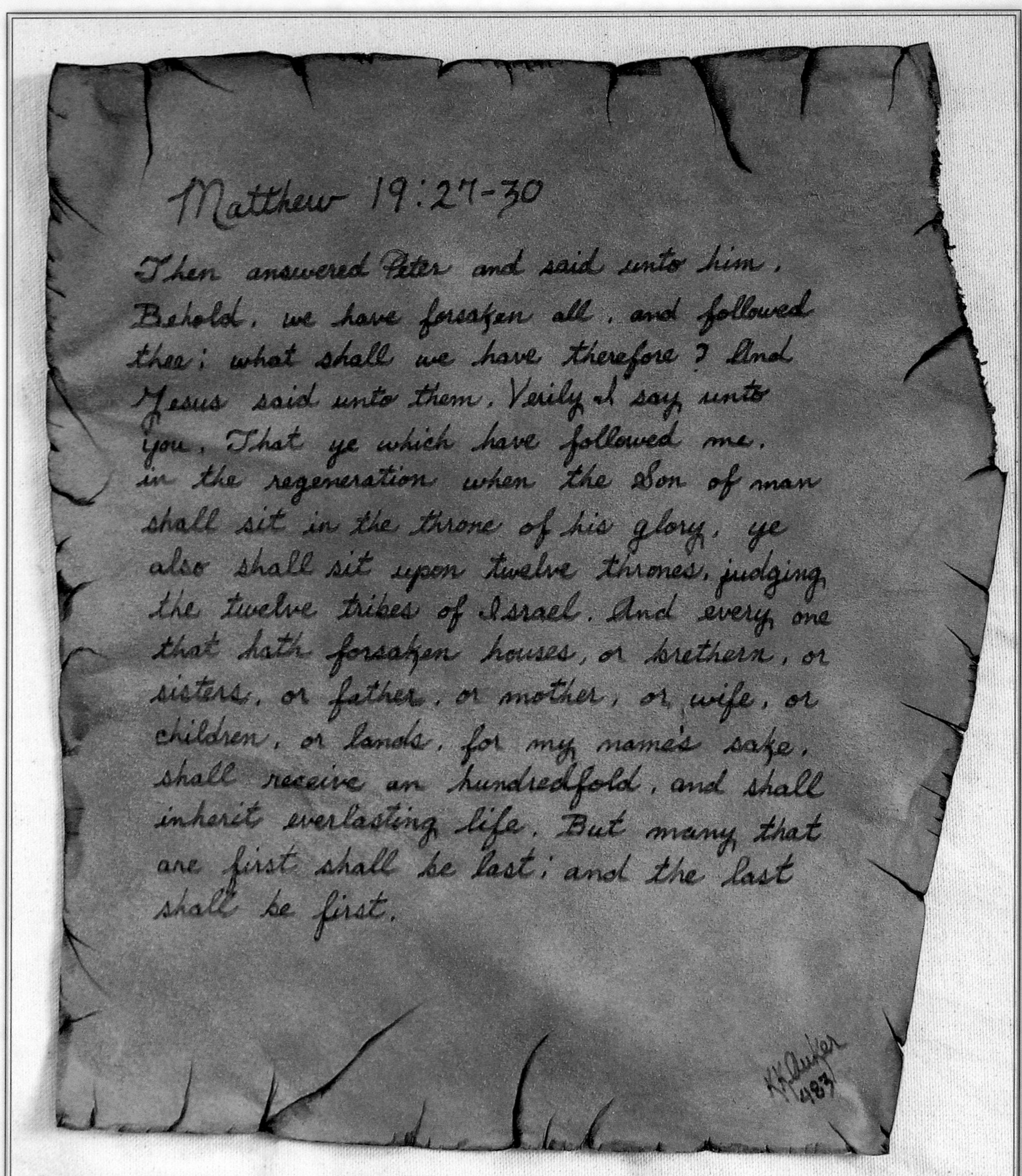
Matthew 19:27-30

Then answered Peter and said unto him, Behold, we have forsaken all, and followed thee; what shall we have therefore? And Jesus said unto them, Verily I say unto you, That ye which have followed me, in the regeneration when the Son of man shall sit in the throne of his glory, ye also shall sit upon twelve thrones, judging the twelve tribes of Israel. And every one that hath forsaken houses, or brethern, or sisters, or father, or mother, or wife, or children, or lands, for my name's sake, shall receive an hundredfold, and shall inherit everlasting life. But many that are first shall be last; and the last shall be first.

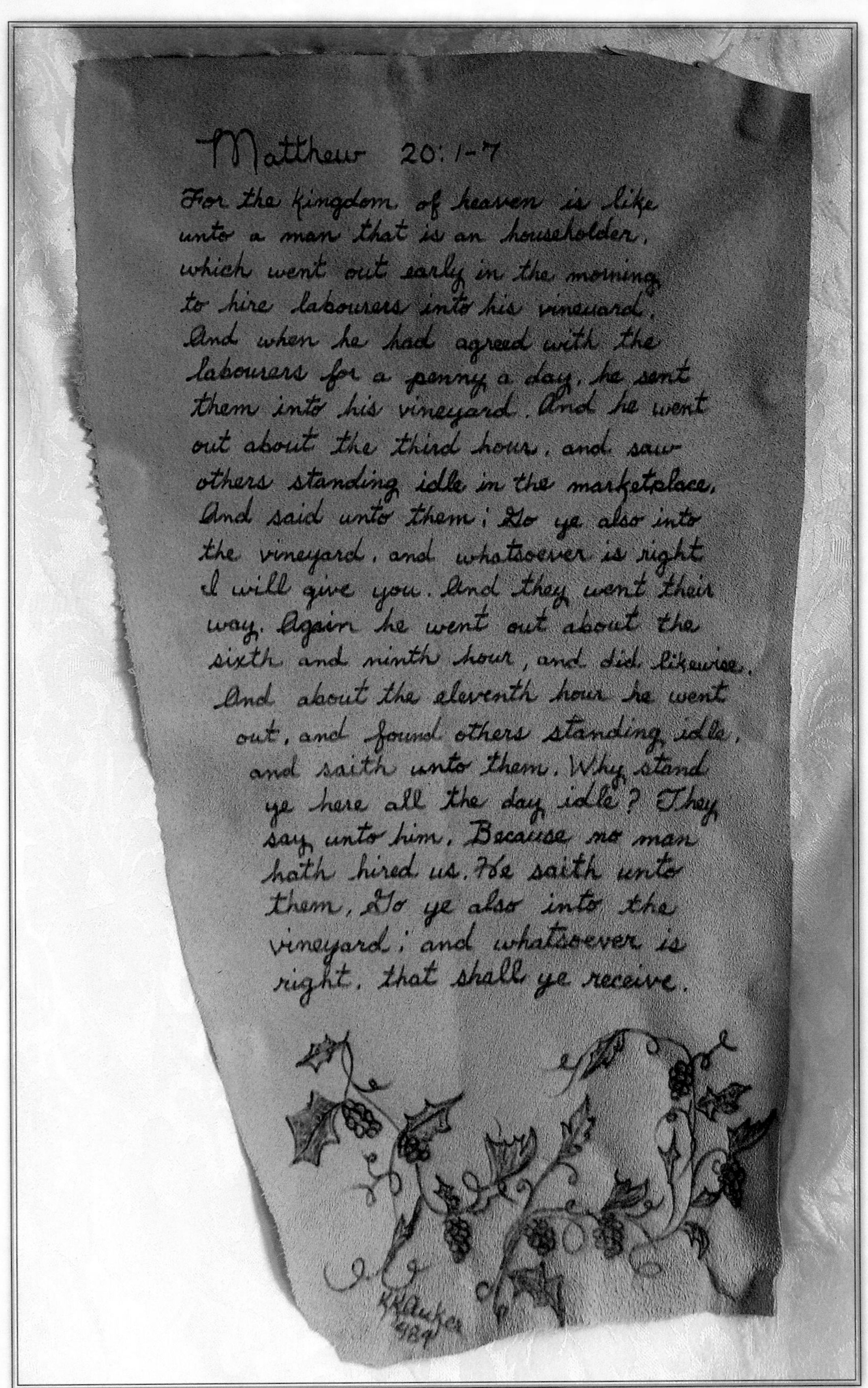
Matthew 20:1-7
For the kingdom of heaven is like
unto a man that is an householder,
which went out early in the morning
to hire labourers into his vineyard.
And when he had agreed with the
labourers for a penny a day, he sent
them into his vineyard. And he went
out about the third hour, and saw
others standing idle in the marketplace,
And said unto them; Go ye also into
the vineyard, and whatsoever is right
I will give you. And they went their
way. Again he went out about the
sixth and ninth hour, and did likewise.
And about the eleventh hour he went
out, and found others standing idle,
and saith unto them, Why stand
ye here all the day idle? They
say unto him, Because no man
hath hired us. He saith unto
them, Go ye also into the
vineyard; and whatsoever is
right, that shall ye receive.

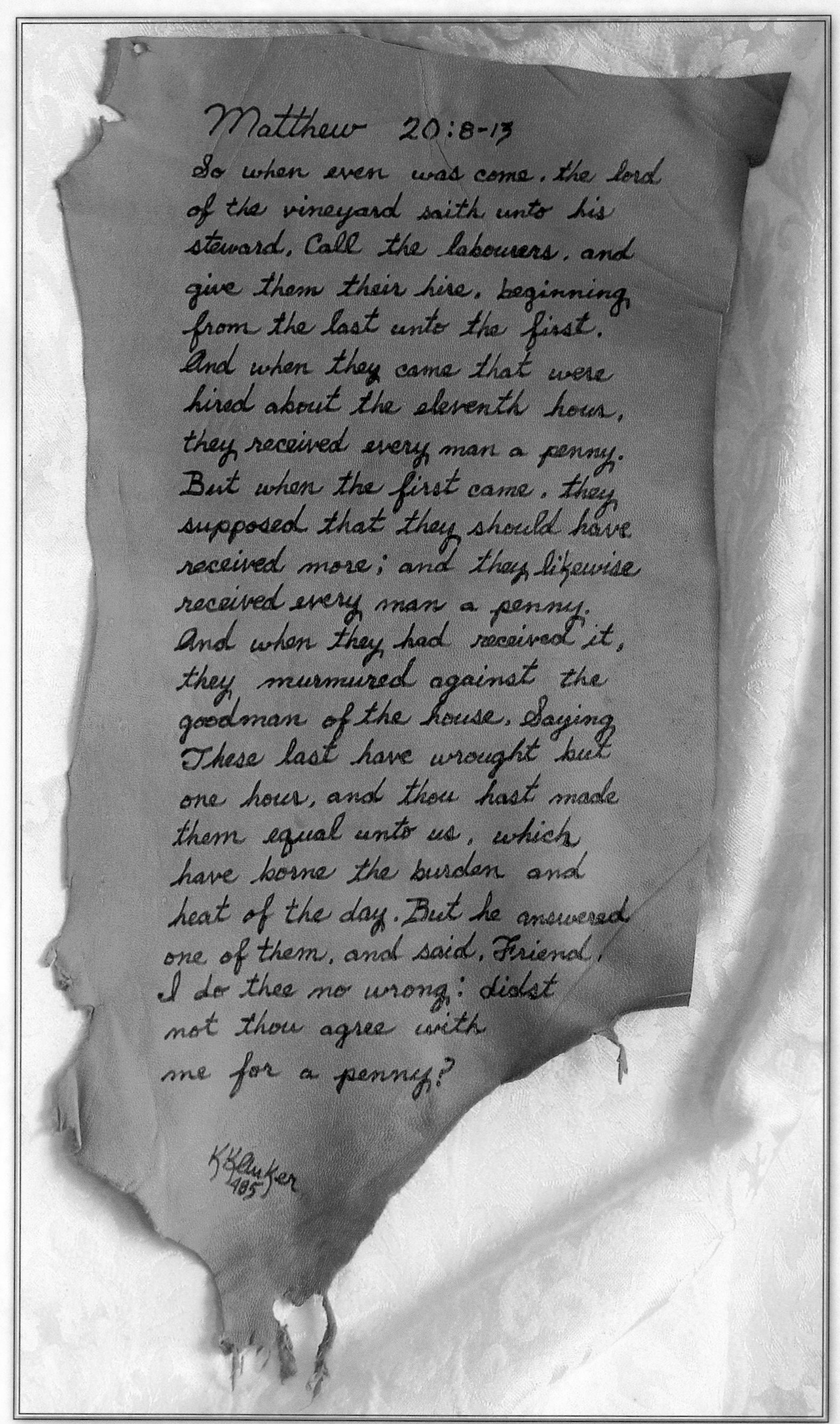
Matthew 20:8-13
So when even was come, the lord
of the vineyard saith unto his
steward, Call the labourers, and
give them their hire, beginning
from the last unto the first.
And when they came that were
hired about the eleventh hour,
they received every man a penny.
But when the first came, they
supposed that they should have
received more; and they likewise
received every man a penny.
And when they had received it,
they murmured against the
goodman of the house, Saying
These last have wrought but
one hour, and thou hast made
them equal unto us, which
have borne the burden and
heat of the day. But he answered
one of them, and said, Friend,
I do thee no wrong: didst
not thou agree with
me for a penny?
K Kluker
'85

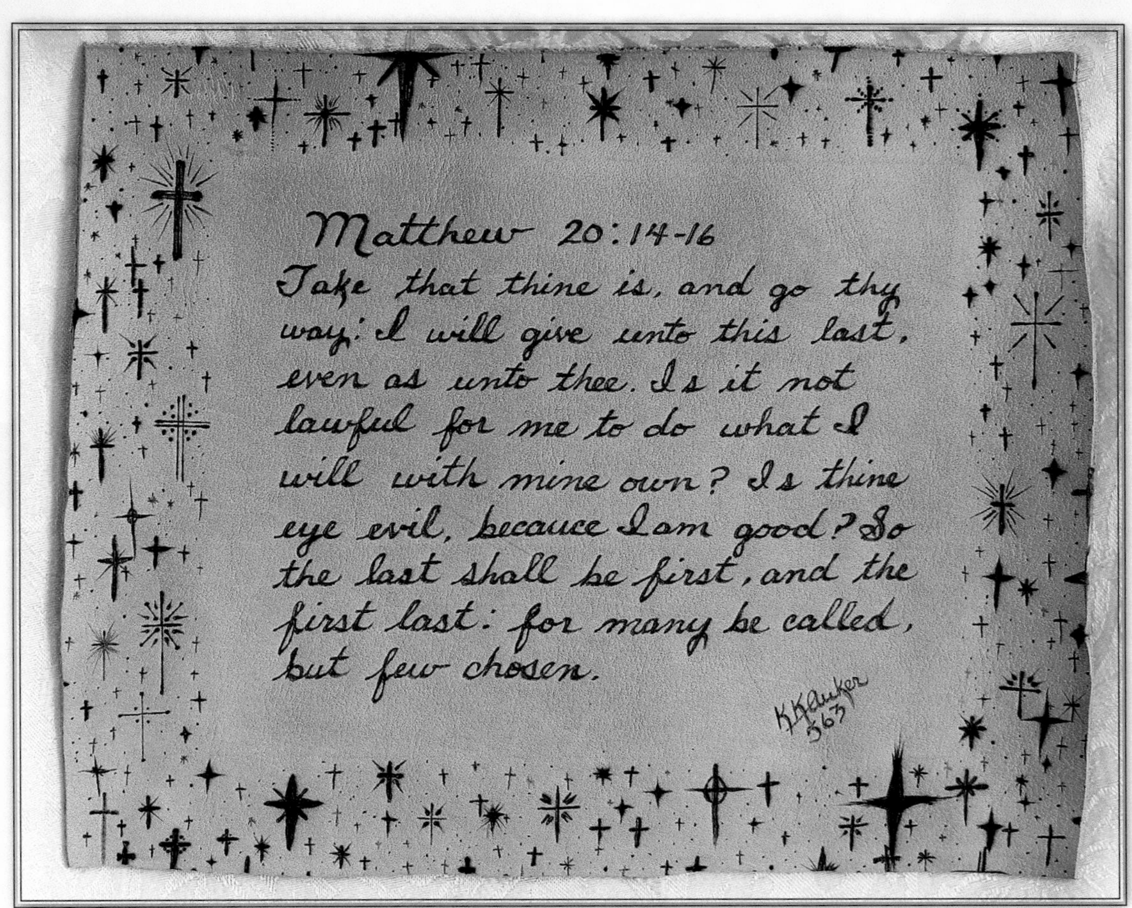
Matthew 20:14-16
Take that thine is, and go thy way: I will give unto this last, even as unto thee. Is it not lawful for me to do what I will with mine own? Is thine eye evil, because I am good? So the last shall be first, and the first last: for many be called, but few chosen.
KKCluker 563

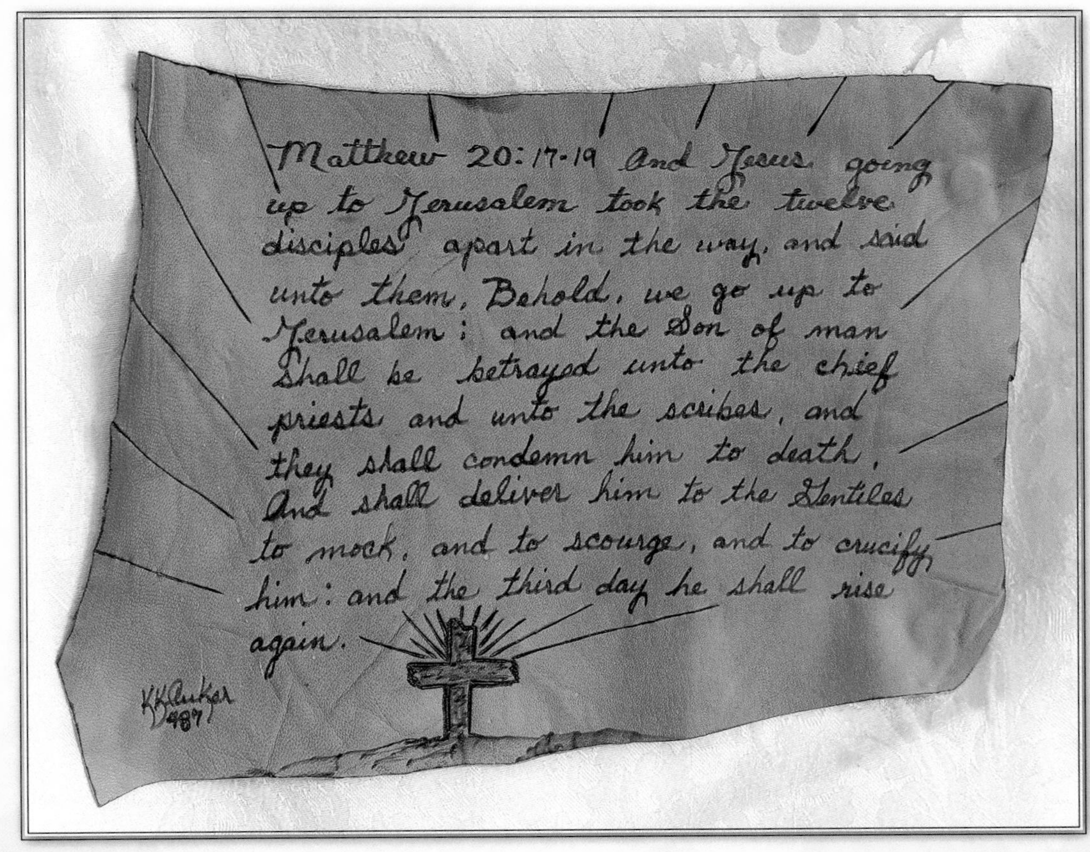
Matthew 20:17-19 And Jesus going up to Jerusalem took the twelve disciples apart in the way, and said unto them, Behold, we go up to Jerusalem; and the Son of man shall be betrayed unto the chief priests and unto the scribes, and they shall condemn him to death, And shall deliver him to the Gentiles to mock, and to scourge, and to crucify him: and the third day he shall rise again.
KKCluker 487

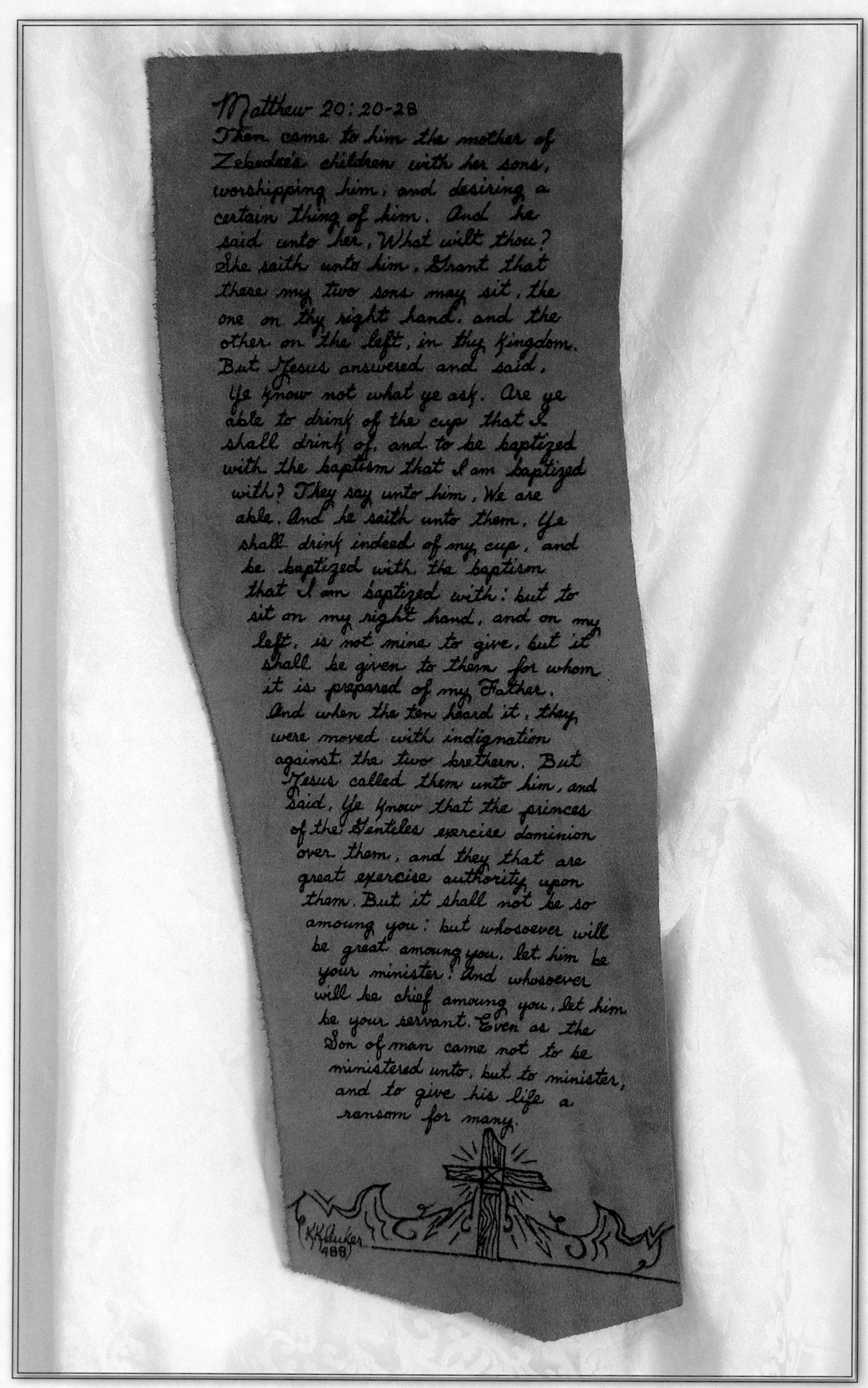
Matthew 20:20-28
Then came to him the mother of
Zebedee's children with her sons,
worshipping him, and desiring a
certain thing of him. And he
said unto her, What wilt thou?
She saith unto him, Grant that
these my two sons may sit, the
one on thy right hand, and the
other on the left, in thy kingdom.
But Jesus answered and said,
Ye know not what ye ask. Are ye
able to drink of the cup that I
shall drink of, and to be baptized
with the baptism that I am baptized
with? They say unto him, We are
able. And he saith unto them, Ye
shall drink indeed of my cup, and
be baptized with the baptism
that I am baptized with: but to
sit on my right hand, and on my
left, is not mine to give, but it
shall be given to them for whom
it is prepared of my Father.
And when the ten heard it, they
were moved with indignation
against the two bretheren. But
Jesus called them unto him, and
said, Ye know that the princes
of the Gentiles exercise dominion
over them, and they that are
great exercise authority upon
them. But it shall not be so
amoung you: but whosoever will
be great amoung you, let him be
your minister; And whosoever
will be chief amoung you, let him
be your servant. Even as the
Son of man came not to be
ministered unto, but to minister,
and to give his life a
ransom for many.

Matthew 20: 29-34 And as they departed from Jericho, a great multitude followed him. And,
behold, two blind men sitting by the way side, when they heard that Jesus passed by, cried out, saying,
Have mercy on us, O Lord, thou son of David. And the multitude rebuked them, because they should hold
their peace: but they cried the more, saying, Have mercy on us, O Lord, thou son of David. And Jesus
stood still, and called them, and said, What will ye that I shall do unto you? They say unto him,
Lord, that our eyes may be opened. So Jesus had compassion on them, and touched their eyes:
and immediately their eyes received sight, and they followed him.

Matthew 21:1-8
And when they drew nigh unto Jerusalem, and were
come to Bethphage, unto the mount of Olives, then
sent Jesus two disciples, Saying unto them, Go into
the village over against you, and straightway ye
shall find an ass tied, and a colt with her:
loose them, and bring them unto me. And if
any man say ought unto you, ye shall say,
The Lord hath need of them; and straightway he will send them.
All this was done, that it might be fulfilled, which was spoken
by the prophet, saying, Tell ye the daughter of Sion, Behold, thy King
cometh unto thee, meek, and sitting upon an ass, and a colt the foal of an ass.
And the disciples went, and did as Jesus commanded them, And brought the
ass, and the colt, and put on them their clothes, and they set him thereon.
And a very great multitude spread their garments in the way; others cut
down branches from the trees, and strawed them in the way.

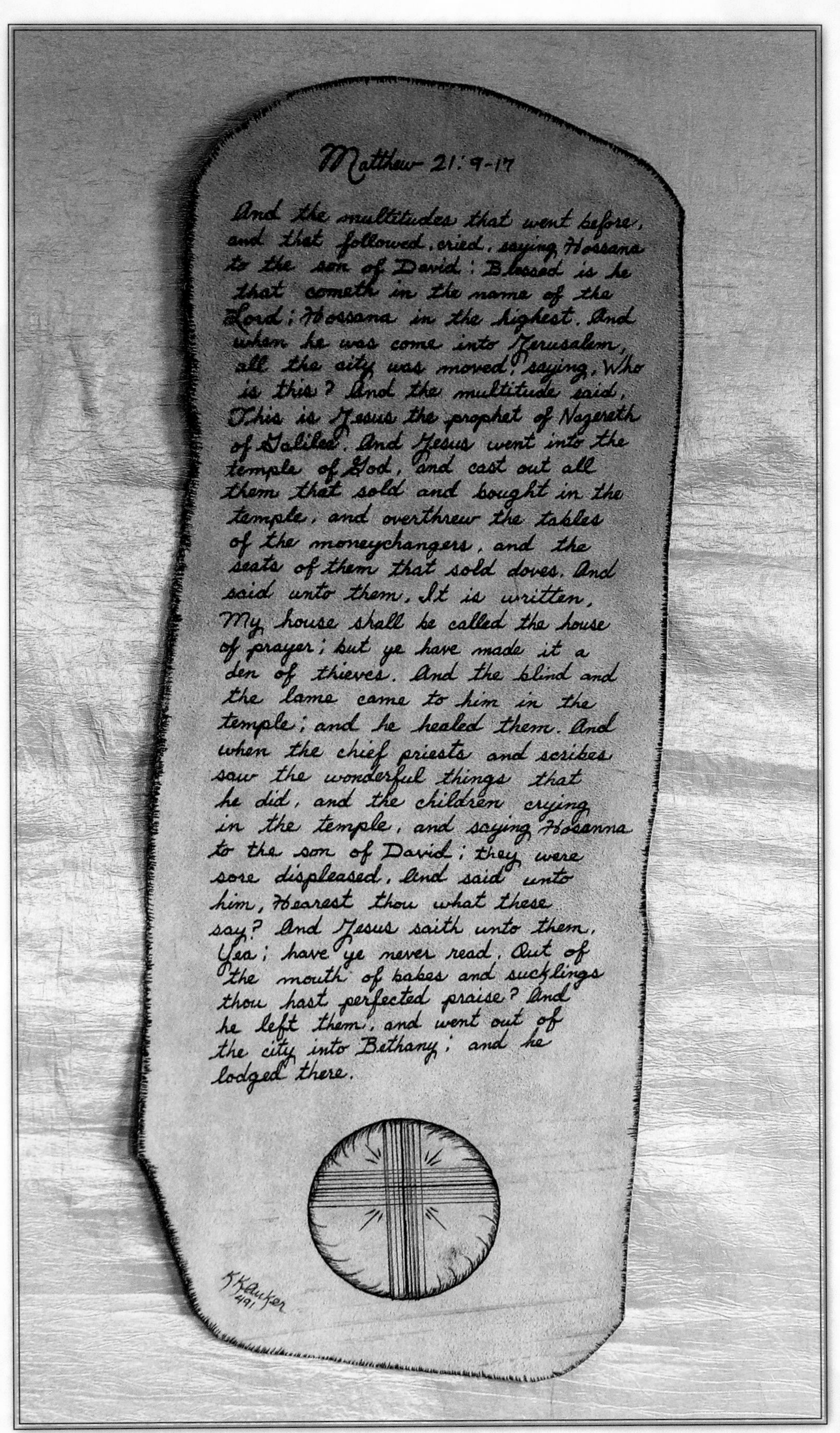
Matthew 21:9-17
And the multitudes that went before,
and that followed, cried, saying, Hossana
to the son of David: Blessed is he
that cometh in the name of the
Lord; Hossana in the highest. And
when he was come into Jerusalem,
all the city was moved, saying, Who
is this? And the multitude said,
This is Jesus the prophet of Nazereth
of Galilee. And Jesus went into the
temple of God, and cast out all
them that sold and bought in the
temple, and overthrew the tables
of the moneychangers, and the
seats of them that sold doves. And
said unto them, It is written,
My house shall be called the house
of prayer; but ye have made it a
den of thieves. And the blind and
the lame came to him in the
temple; and he healed them. And
when the chief priests and scribes
saw the wonderful things that
he did, and the children crying
in the temple, and saying Hosanna
to the son of David; they were
sore displeased, And said unto
him, Hearest thou what these
say? And Jesus saith unto them,
Yea; have ye never read, Out of
the mouth of babes and sucklings
thou hast perfected praise? And
he left them, and went out of
the city into Bethany; and he
lodged there.
KKauker
4/91

Matthew 21:18-20
Now in the morning as
he returned into the city
he hungered. And when
he saw a fig tree in the
way, he came to it, and
found nothing thereon,
but leaves only, and said
unto it, Let no fruit
grow on thee henceforward
for ever. And presently
the fig tree withered
away!
KKClucker
'92

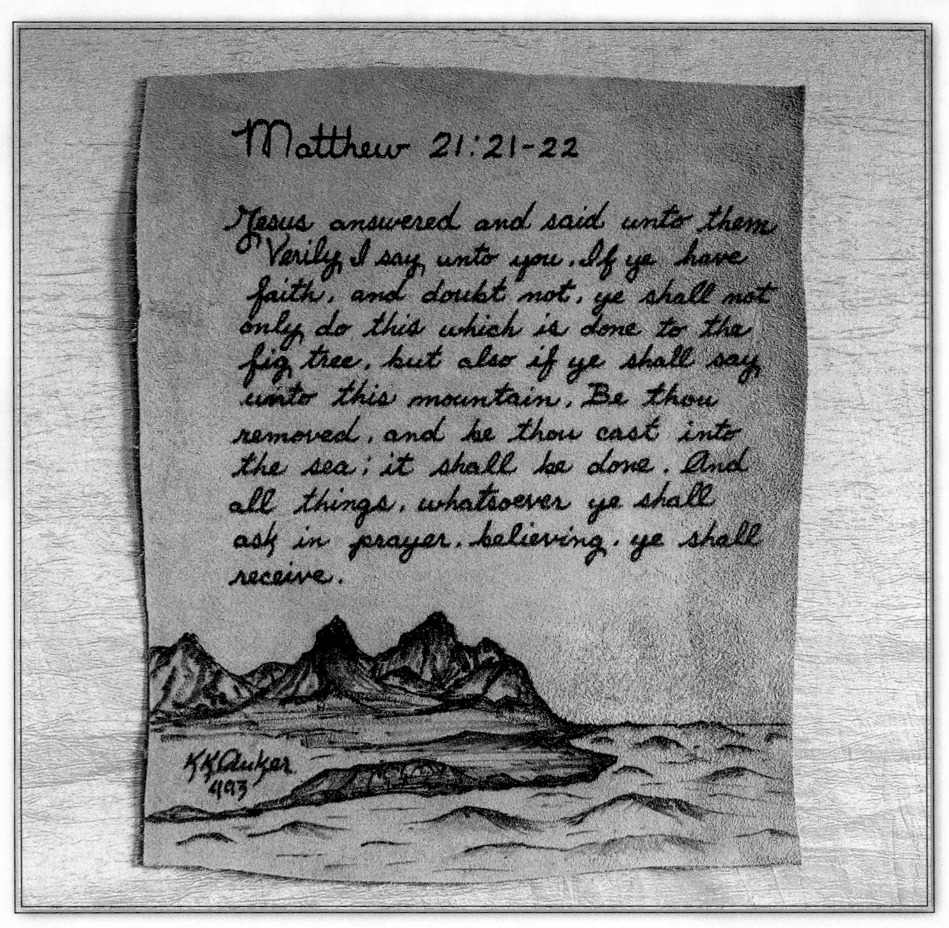
Matthew 21:21-22
Jesus answered and said unto them
Verily I say unto you, If ye have
faith, and doubt not, ye shall not
only do this which is done to the
fig tree, but also if ye shall say
unto this mountain, Be thou
removed, and be thou cast into
the sea; it shall be done. And
all things, whatsoever ye shall
ask in prayer, believing, ye shall
receive.
KKAuker
493

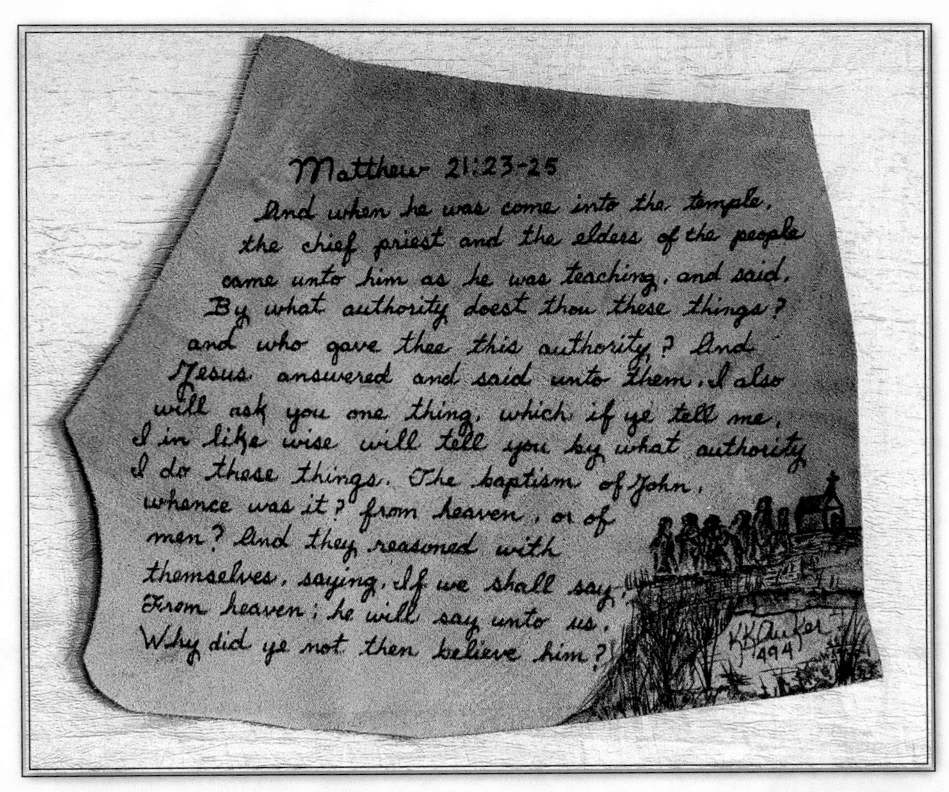
Matthew 21:23-25
And when he was come into the temple,
the chief priest and the elders of the people
came unto him as he was teaching, and said,
By what authority doest thou these things?
and who gave thee this authority? And
Jesus answered and said unto them, I also
will ask you one thing, which if ye tell me,
I in like wise will tell you by what authority
I do these things. The baptism of John,
whence was it? from heaven, or of
men? And they reasoned with
themselves, saying, If we shall say,
From heaven; he will say unto us,
Why did ye not then believe him?
KKAuker
494

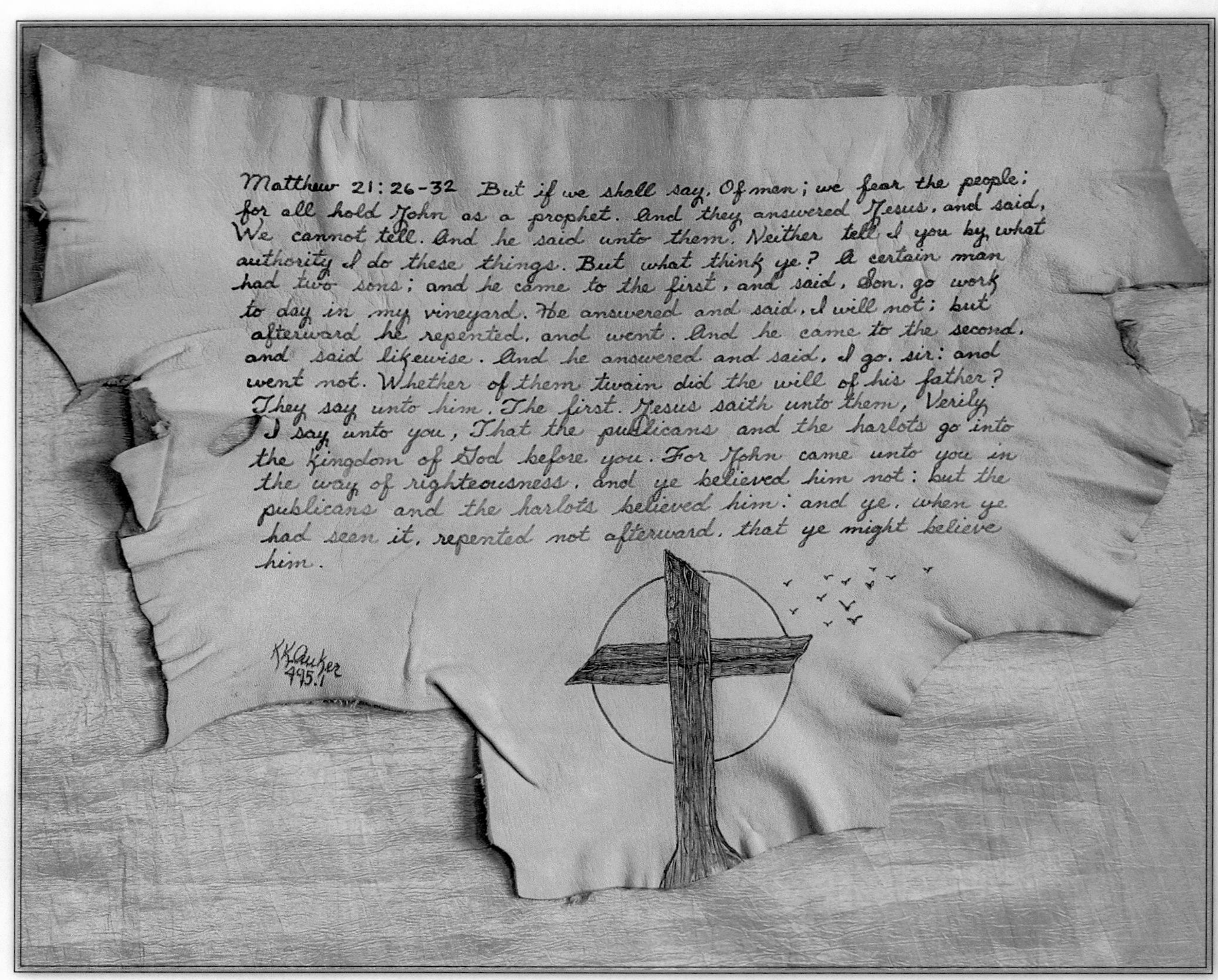
Matthew 21:26-32 But if we shall say, Of men; we fear the people;
for all hold John as a prophet. And they answered Jesus, and said,
We cannot tell. And he said unto them, Neither tell I you by what
authority I do these things. But what think ye? A certain man
had two sons; and he came to the first, and said, Son, go work
to day in my vineyard. He answered and said, I will not: but
afterward he repented, and went. And he came to the second,
and said likewise. And he answered and said, I go, sir: and
went not. Whether of them twain did the will of his father?
They say unto him, The first. Jesus saith unto them, Verily
I say unto you, That the publicans and the harlots go into
the kingdom of God before you. For John came unto you in
the way of righteousness, and ye believed him not: but the
publicans and the harlots believed him: and ye, when ye
had seen it, repented not afterward, that ye might believe
him.

Matthew 21:33-46 Hear another parable: There was a
certain householder, which planted a vineyard, and hedged
it round about, and digged a wine press in it, and
built a tower, and let it out to husbandmen, and went
went into a far country: And when the time of the fruit
drew near, he sent his servants to the husbandmen, that
they might receive the fruits of it. And the husbandmen took
his servants, and beat one, and killed another, and stoned
another. Again, he sent other servants more than the first;
and they did unto them likewise. But last of all he sent
unto them his son, saying, They will reverence my son.
But when the husbandmen saw the son, they said among
themselves, This is the heir; come, let us kill him, and
let us seize on his inheritance. And they caught him,
and cast him out of the vineyard, and slew him. When
the lord therefore of the vineyard cometh, what will he
do unto those husbandmen? They say unto him, He will
miserably destroy those wicked men, and will let out his
vineyard unto other husbandmen, which shall render him
the fruits in their seasons. Jesus saith unto them, Did
ye never read in the scriptures, The stone which the builders
rejected, the same is become the head of the corner: this
is the Lord's doing, and it is marvellous in our eyes?
Therefore say I unto you, The kingdom of God shall be
taken from you, and given to a nation bringing forth
the fruits thereof. And whosoever shall fall on this stone
shall be broken: but on whomsoever it shall fall, it will
grind him to powder. And when the chief priests and Pharisees
had heard his parables, they perceived that he spake of them.
But when they sought to lay hands on him, they feared the
multitude, because they took him for a prophet.

KKlucker
495

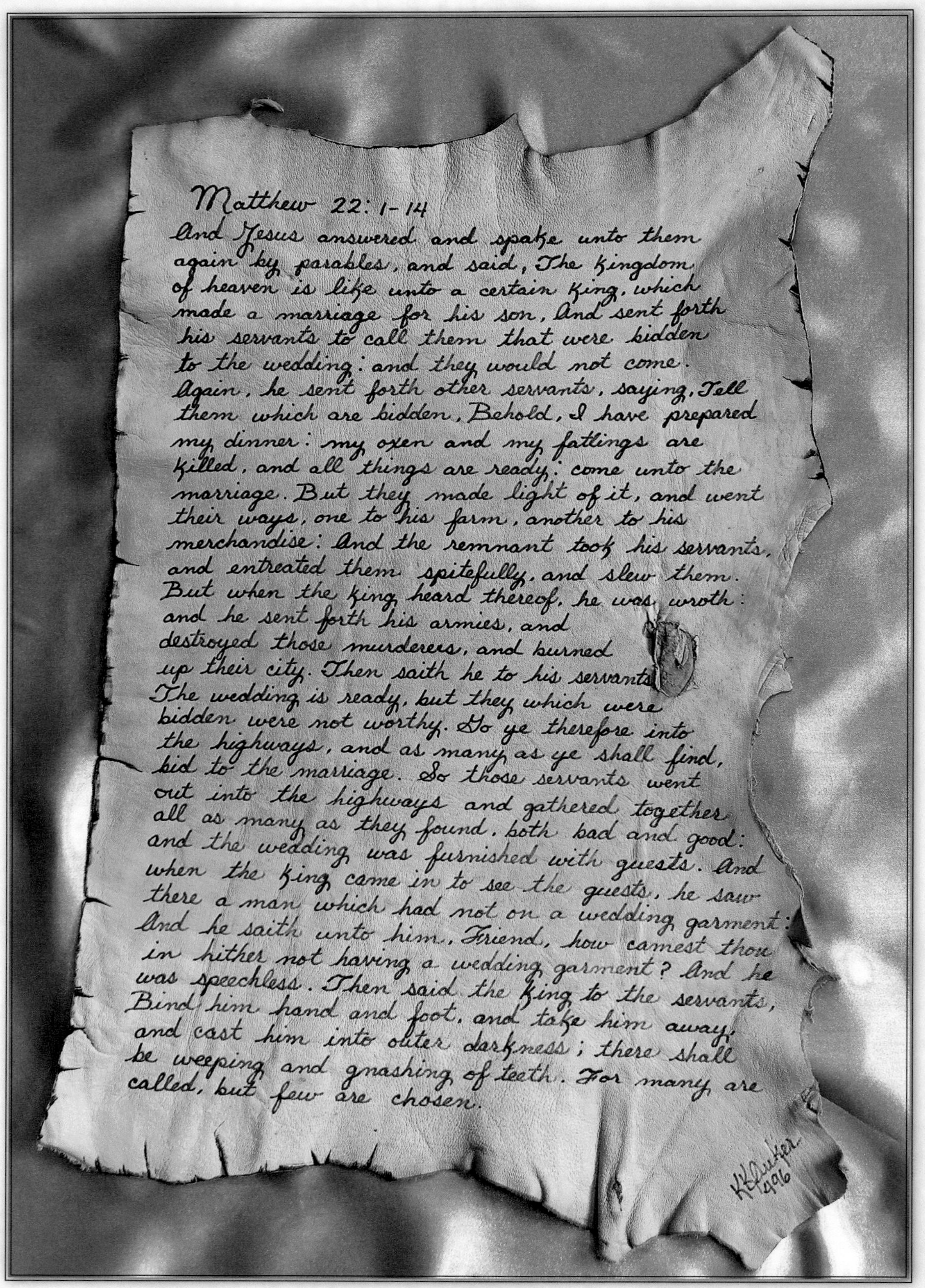

Matthew 22: 1-14

And Jesus answered and spake unto them again by parables, and said, The kingdom of heaven is like unto a certain king, which made a marriage for his son, And sent forth his servants to call them that were bidden to the wedding: and they would not come. Again, he sent forth other servants, saying, Tell them which are bidden, Behold, I have prepared my dinner: my oxen and my fatlings are killed, and all things are ready: come unto the marriage. But they made light of it, and went their ways, one to his farm, another to his merchandise: And the remnant took his servants, and entreated them spitefully, and slew them. But when the king heard thereof, he was wroth: and he sent forth his armies, and destroyed those murderers, and burned up their city. Then saith he to his servants, The wedding is ready, but they which were bidden were not worthy. Go ye therefore into the highways, and as many as ye shall find, bid to the marriage. So those servants went out into the highways and gathered together all as many as they found, both bad and good: and the wedding was furnished with guests. And when the king came in to see the guests, he saw there a man which had not on a wedding garment: And he saith unto him, Friend, how camest thou in hither not having a wedding garment? And he was speechless. Then said the king to the servants, Bind him hand and foot, and take him away, and cast him into outer darkness; there shall be weeping and gnashing of teeth. For many are called, but few are chosen.

K Fluker
1996

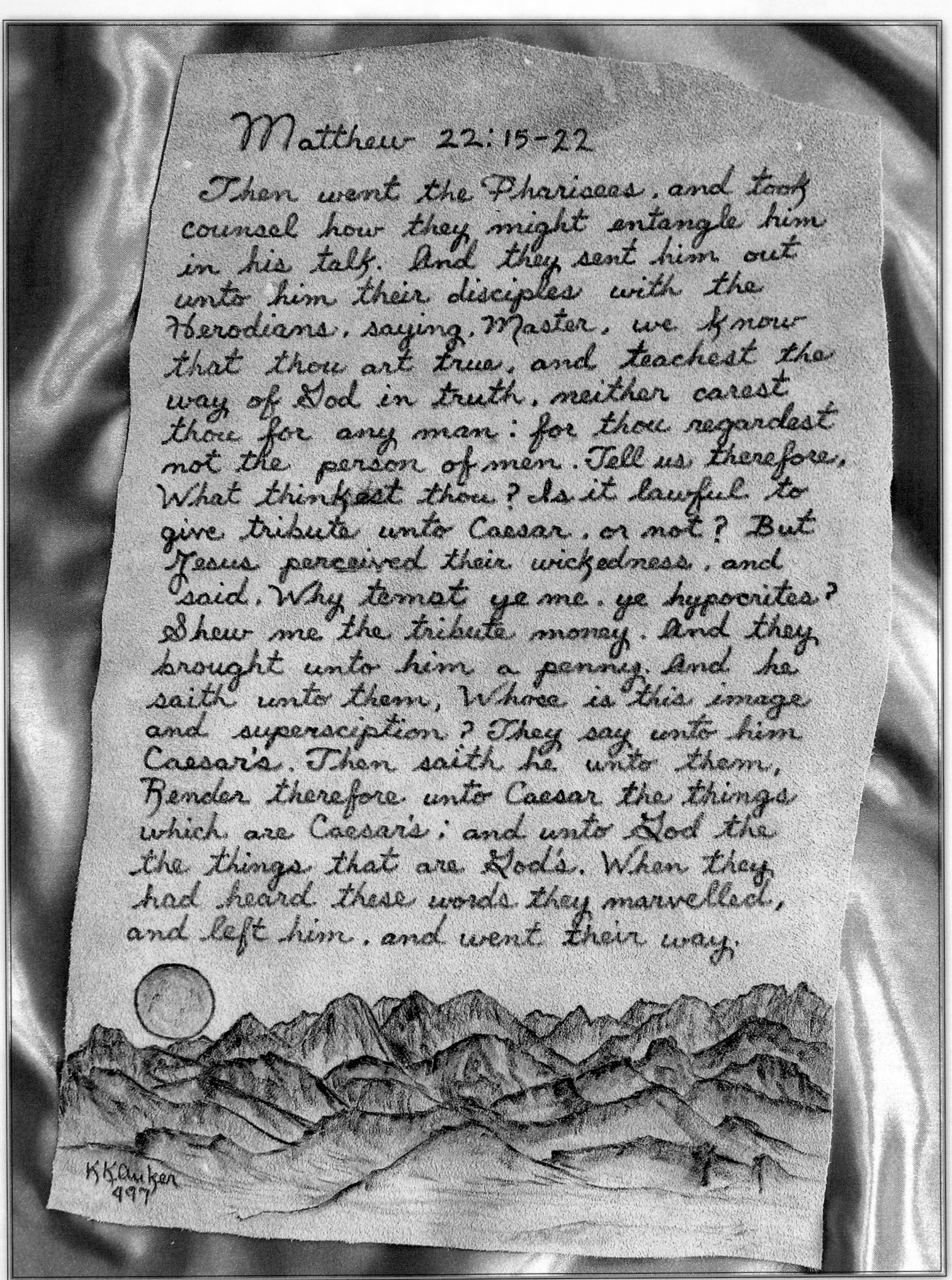

Matthew 22:15-22

Then went the Pharisees, and took counsel how they might entangle him in his talk. And they sent him out unto him their disciples with the Herodians, saying, Master, we know that thou art true, and teachest the way of God in truth, neither carest thou for any man: for thou regardest not the person of men. Tell us therefore, What thinkest thou? Is it lawful to give tribute unto Caesar, or not? But Jesus perceived their wickedness, and said, Why temst ye me, ye hypocrites? Shew me the tribute money. And they brought unto him a penny. And he saith unto them, Whose is this image and supersciption? They say unto him Caesar's. Then saith he unto them, Render therefore unto Caesar the things which are Caesar's; and unto God the the things that are God's. When they had heard these words they marvelled, and left him, and went their way.

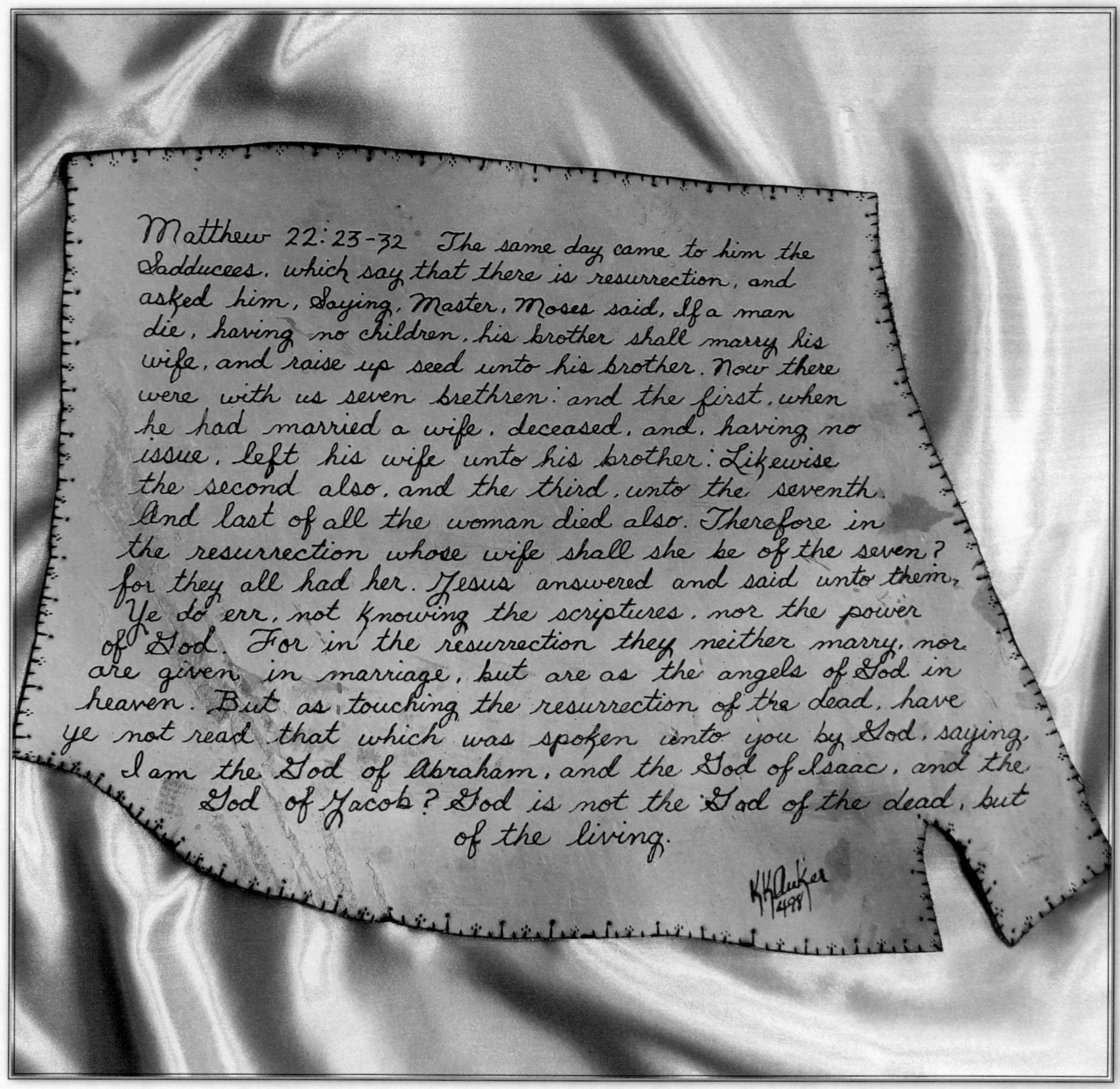

Matthew 22:23-32 The same day came to him the
Sadducees, which say that there is resurrection, and
asked him, Saying, Master, Moses said, If a man
die, having no children, his brother shall marry his
wife, and raise up seed unto his brother. Now there
were with us seven brethren: and the first, when
he had married a wife, deceased, and, having no
issue, left his wife unto his brother: Likewise
the second also, and the third, unto the seventh.
And last of all the woman died also. Therefore in
the resurrection whose wife shall she be of the seven?
for they all had her. Jesus answered and said unto them,
Ye do err, not knowing the scriptures, nor the power
of God. For in the resurrection they neither marry, nor
are given in marriage, but are as the angels of God in
heaven. But as touching the resurrection of the dead, have
ye not read that which was spoken unto you by God, saying,
I am the God of Abraham, and the God of Isaac, and the
God of Jacob? God is not the God of the dead, but
of the living.

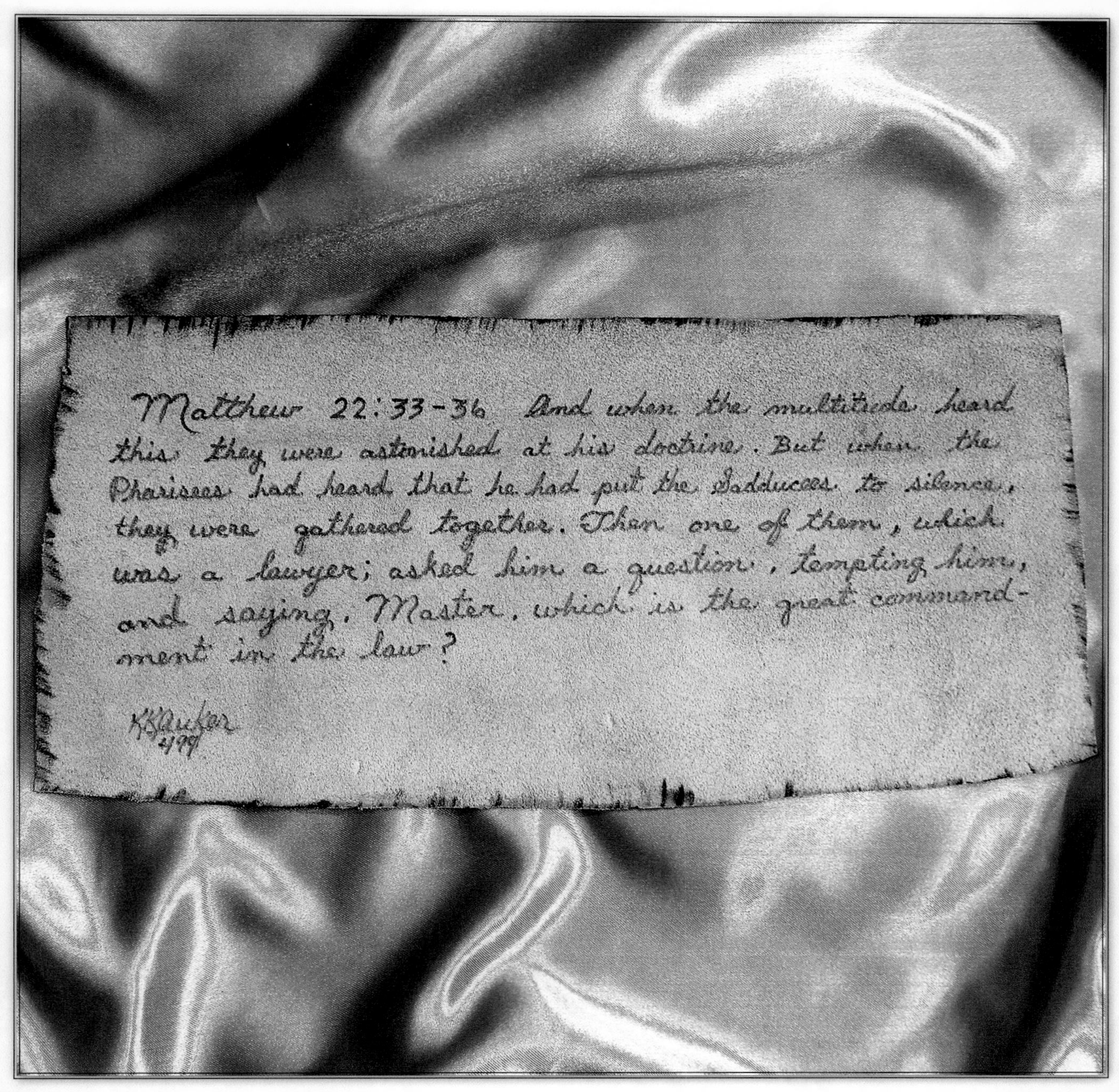
Matthew 22:33-36 And when the multitude heard
this they were astonished at his doctrine. But when the
Pharisees had heard that he had put the Sadducees to silence,
they were gathered together. Then one of them, which
was a lawyer, asked him a question, tempting him,
and saying, Master, which is the great commandment in the law?

Matthew 22:37-40
Jesus said unto him, Thou shalt love the Lord thy God with all thy heart, and with all thy soul, and with all thy mind. This is the first and great commandment. And the second is like unto it, Thou shalt love thy neighbour as thyself. On these two commandments hang all the law and the prophets.
KKlauker
500

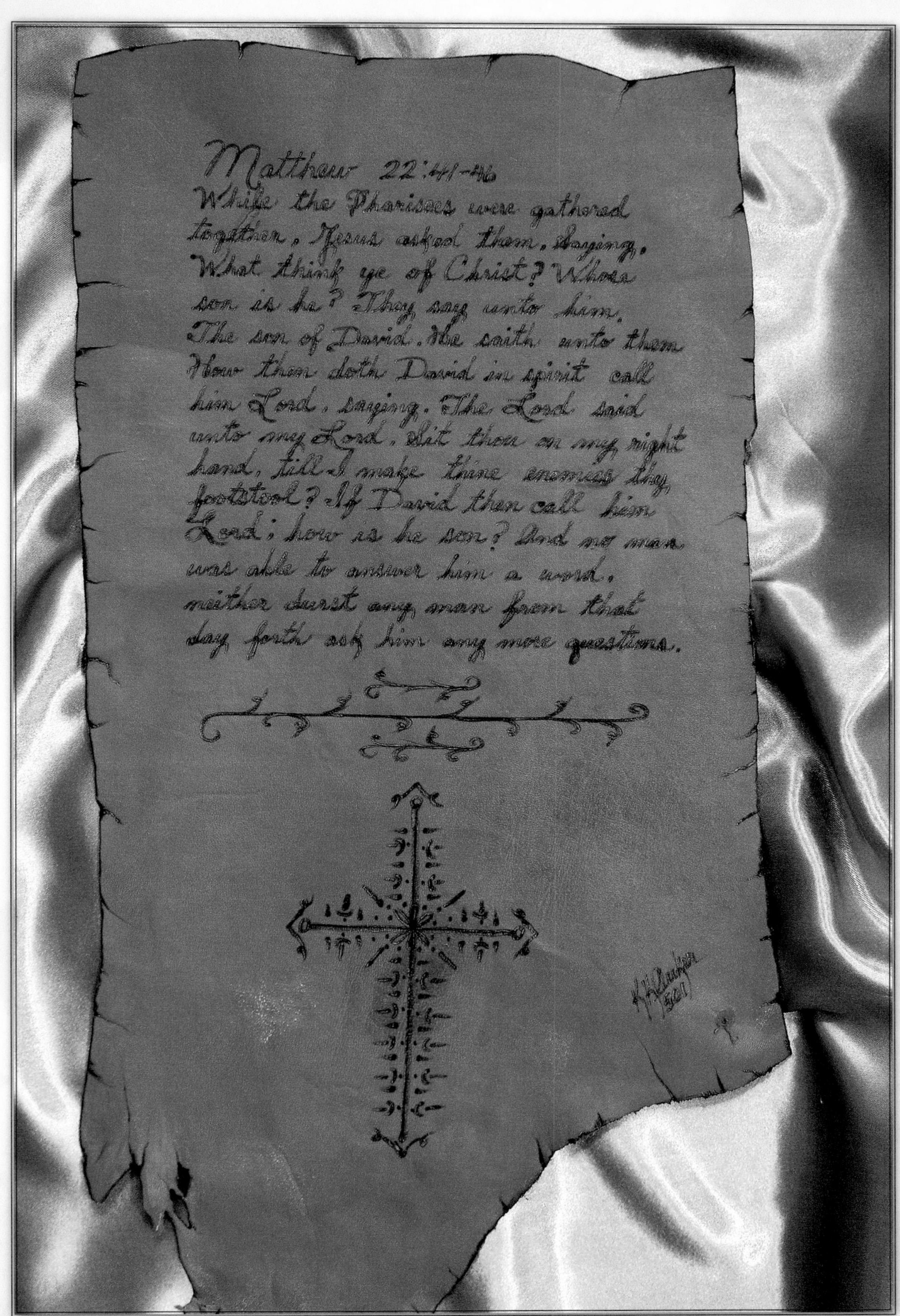
Matthew 22:41-46
While the Pharisees were gathered
together, Jesus asked them, Saying,
What think ye of Christ? Whose
son is he? They say unto him,
The son of David. He saith unto them
How then doth David in spirit call
him Lord, saying, The Lord said
unto my Lord, Sit thou on my right
hand, till I make thine enemies thy
footstool? If David then call him
Lord; how is he son? And no man
was able to answer him a word,
neither durst any man from that
day forth ask him any more questions.

Matthew 23:1-39

Matthew 23:13
But woe unto you, scribes and
Pharisees, hypocrites! for ye shut up the
kingdom of heaven against men:
for ye neither go in yourselves, neither
suffer ye them that are entering to go in.

Matthew 24:1-2
And Jesus went out, and departed from the temple: and his disciples
came to him for to shew him the buildings of the temple. And
Jesus said unto them, See ye not all these things? verily, I say unto
you, There shall not be left here one stone upon another, that shall
not be thrown down.

Matthew 24:3-8
And as he sat upon the mount of Olives, the disciples came
unto him privately, saying, Tell us, when shall these things be? and what shall be the sign
of thy coming, and of the end of the world? And Jesus answered and said unto them,
Take heed that no man deceive you. For many shall come in my name, saying,
I am Christ; and shall deceive many. And ye shall hear of wars and rumours of wars;
see that ye be not troubled: for all these things must come to pass, but the end is
not yet. For nation shall rise against nation, and kingdom against kingdom: and
there shall be famines, and pestilences, and earthquakes, in divers places. All these
are the beginning of sorrow.

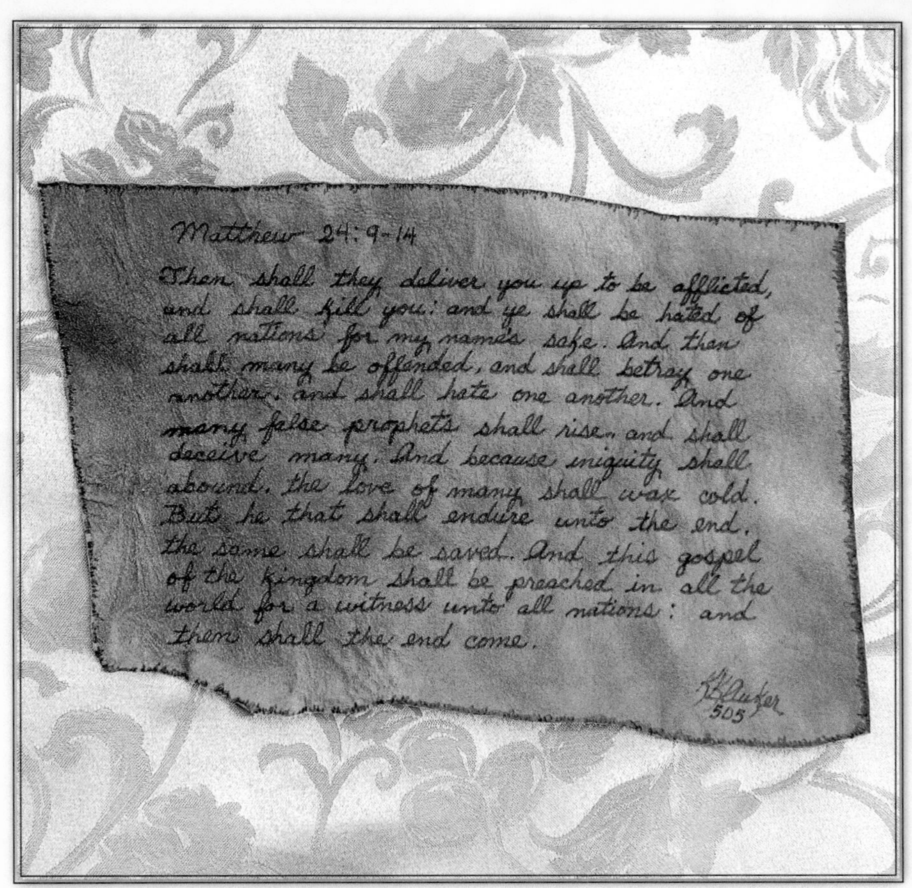
Matthew 24:9-14
Then shall they deliver you up to be afflicted,
and shall kill you: and ye shall be hated of
all nations for my name's sake. And then
shall many be offended, and shall betray one
another, and shall hate one another. And
many false prophets shall rise, and shall
deceive many. And because iniquity shall
abound, the love of many shall wax cold.
But he that shall endure unto the end,
the same shall be saved. And this gospel
of the kingdom shall be preached in all the
world for a witness unto all nations: and
then shall the end come.
505

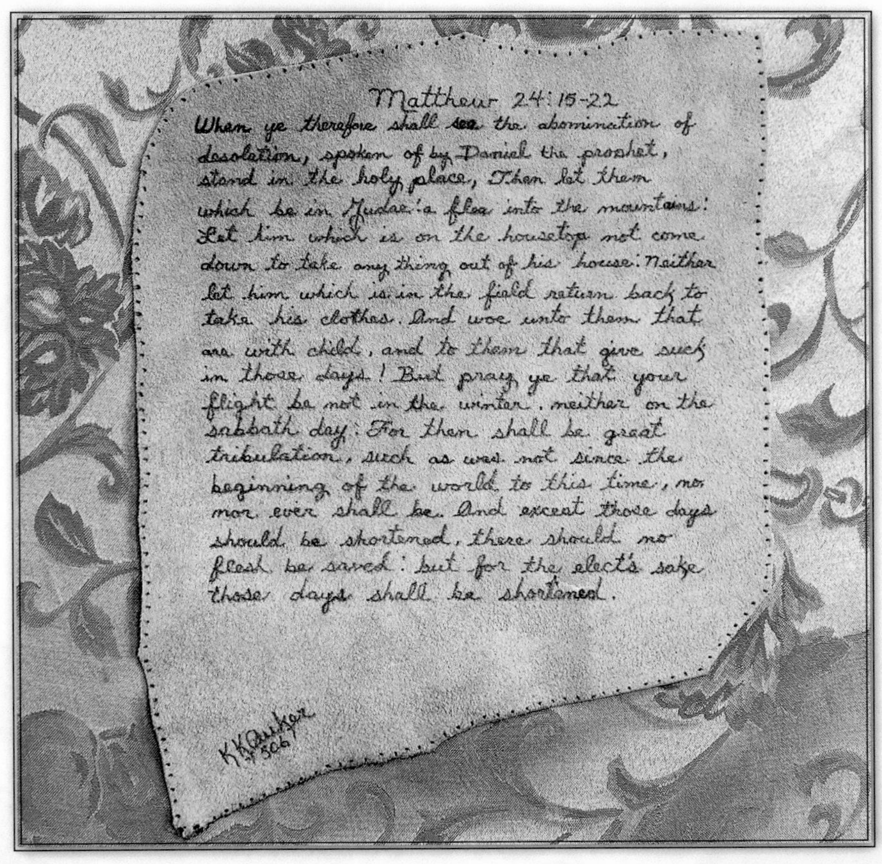
Matthew 24:15-22
When ye therefore shall see the abomination of
desolation, spoken of by Daniel the prophet,
stand in the holy place, Then let them
which be in Judae'a flee into the mountains:
Let him which is on the housetop not come
down to take any thing out of his house: Neither
let him which is in the field return back to
take his clothes. And woe unto them that
are with child, and to them that give suck
in those days! But pray ye that your
flight be not in the winter, neither on the
sabbath day: For then shall be great
tribulation, such as was not since the
beginning of the world to this time, no,
nor ever shall be. And except those days
should be shortened, there should no
flesh be saved: but for the elect's sake
those days shall be shortened.
506

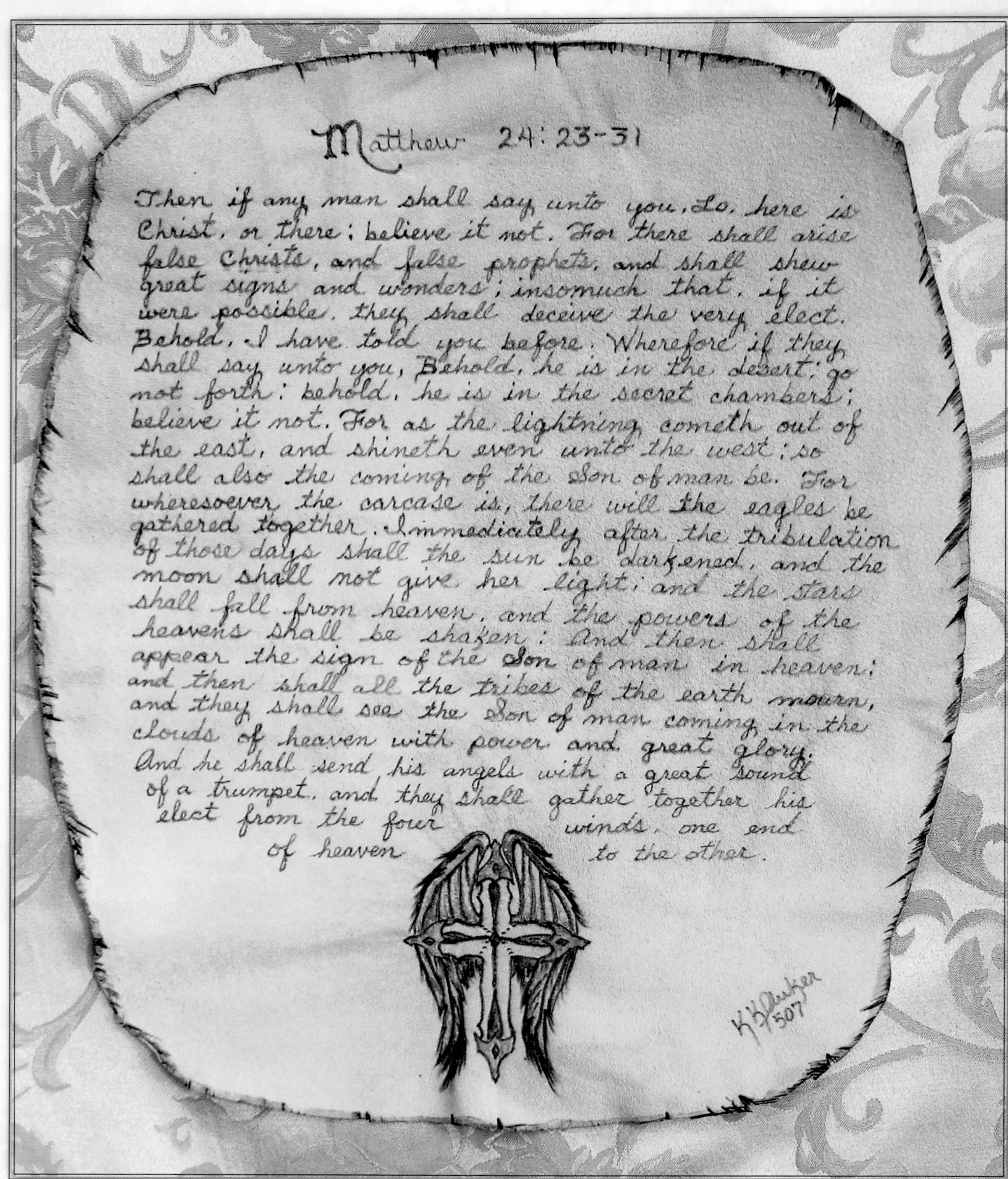
Matthew 24:23-31
Then if any man shall say unto you, Lo, here is
Christ, or there; believe it not. For there shall arise
false Christs, and false prophets, and shall shew
great signs and wonders; insomuch that, if it
were possible, they shall deceive the very elect.
Behold, I have told you before. Wherefore if they
shall say unto you, Behold, he is in the desert; go
not forth: behold, he is in the secret chambers;
believe it not. For as the lightning cometh out of
the east, and shineth even unto the west; so
shall also the coming of the Son of man be. For
wheresoever the carcase is, there will the eagles be
gathered together. Immediately after the tribulation
of those days shall the sun be darkened, and the
moon shall not give her light, and the stars
shall fall from heaven, and the powers of the
heavens shall be shaken: And then shall
appear the sign of the Son of man in heaven:
and then shall all the tribes of the earth mourn,
and they shall see the Son of man coming in the
clouds of heaven with power and great glory.
And he shall send his angels with a great sound
of a trumpet, and they shall gather together his
elect from the four winds, one end
of heaven to the other.
K Parker 507

Matthew 24:32-51
Now learn a parable of the fig tree: When his branch is yet tender
and putteth forth leaves, ye know that summer is nigh: So
likewise ye, when ye shall see all these things, know that it is
near, even at the doors. Verily I say unto you, This generation shall
not pass, till all these things be fulfilled. Heaven and earth
shall pass away, but my words shall not pass away. But of that
day and hour knoweth no man, no, not the angels of heaven,
but my Father only. But as the days of No-e were, so shall
also the coming of the Son of man be. For as in the days that
were before the flood they were eating and drinking, marrying and
giving in marriage, until the day that No-e entered into the ark,
And knew not until the flood came, and took them all away; so shall
also the coming of the Son of man be. Then shall two be in the field;
the one shall be taken, and the other left. Two women shall be grinding
at the mill; the one shall be taken, and the other left. Watch therefore: for
ye know not what hour your Lord doth come. But know this, that if
the goodman of the house had known in what watch the thief would come
he would have watched, and would not have suffered his house to be broken up.
Therefore be ye also ready: for in such an hour as ye think not the Son of man
cometh. Who then is a faithful and wise servant, whom his lord hath made
ruler over his household, to give them meat in due season? Blessed is that
servant, whom his lord when he cometh shall find so doing. Verily I say unto you,
That he shall make him ruler over all his goods. But and if that evil servant
shall say in his heart, My lord delayeth his coming; And shall begin to smite
his fellowservants, and to eat and drink with the drunken; the lord of that
servant shall come in a day when he looketh not for him, and in an hour
that he is not aware of, And shall cut him asunder, and appoint him
his portion with the hypocrites: there shall be weeping and gnashing
of teeth.

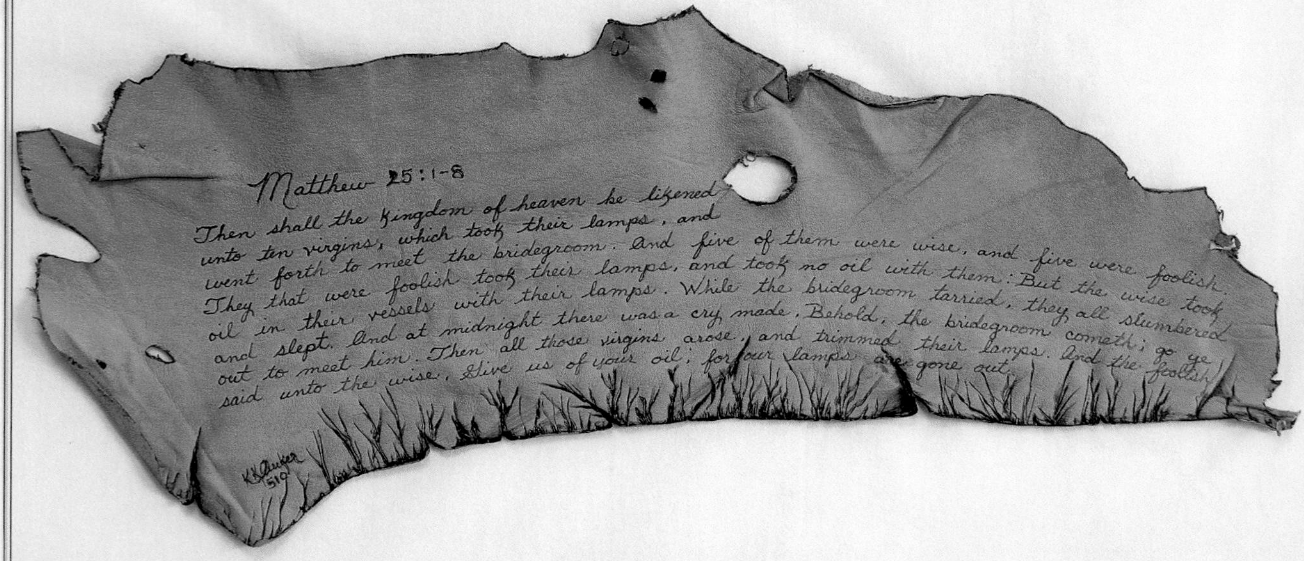

Matthew 25:1-8
Then shall the kingdom of heaven be likened
unto ten virgins, which took their lamps, and
went forth to meet the bridegroom. And five of them were wise, and five were foolish.
They that were foolish took their lamps, and took no oil with them: But the wise took
oil in their vessels with their lamps. While the bridegroom tarried, they all slumbered
and slept. And at midnight there was a cry made, Behold, the bridegroom cometh; go ye
out to meet him. Then all those virgins arose, and trimmed their lamps. And the foolish
said unto the wise, Give us of your oil; for our lamps are gone out.

Matthew 25:9-10
But the wise answered, saying, Not so; lest
there be not enough for us and you: but
go ye rather to them that sell, and buy
for yourselves. And while they went to buy
the bridegroom came; and they that were
ready went in with him to the marriage:
and the door was shut.

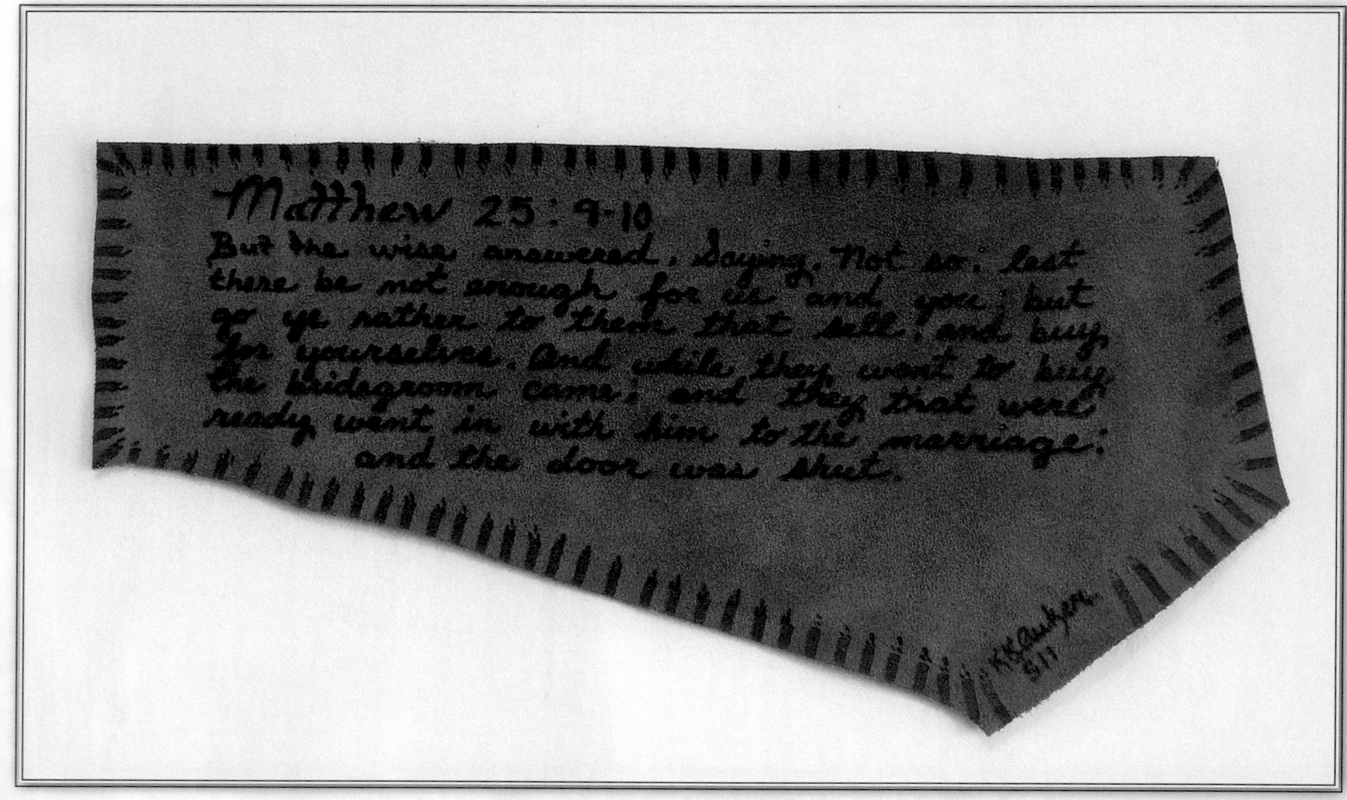

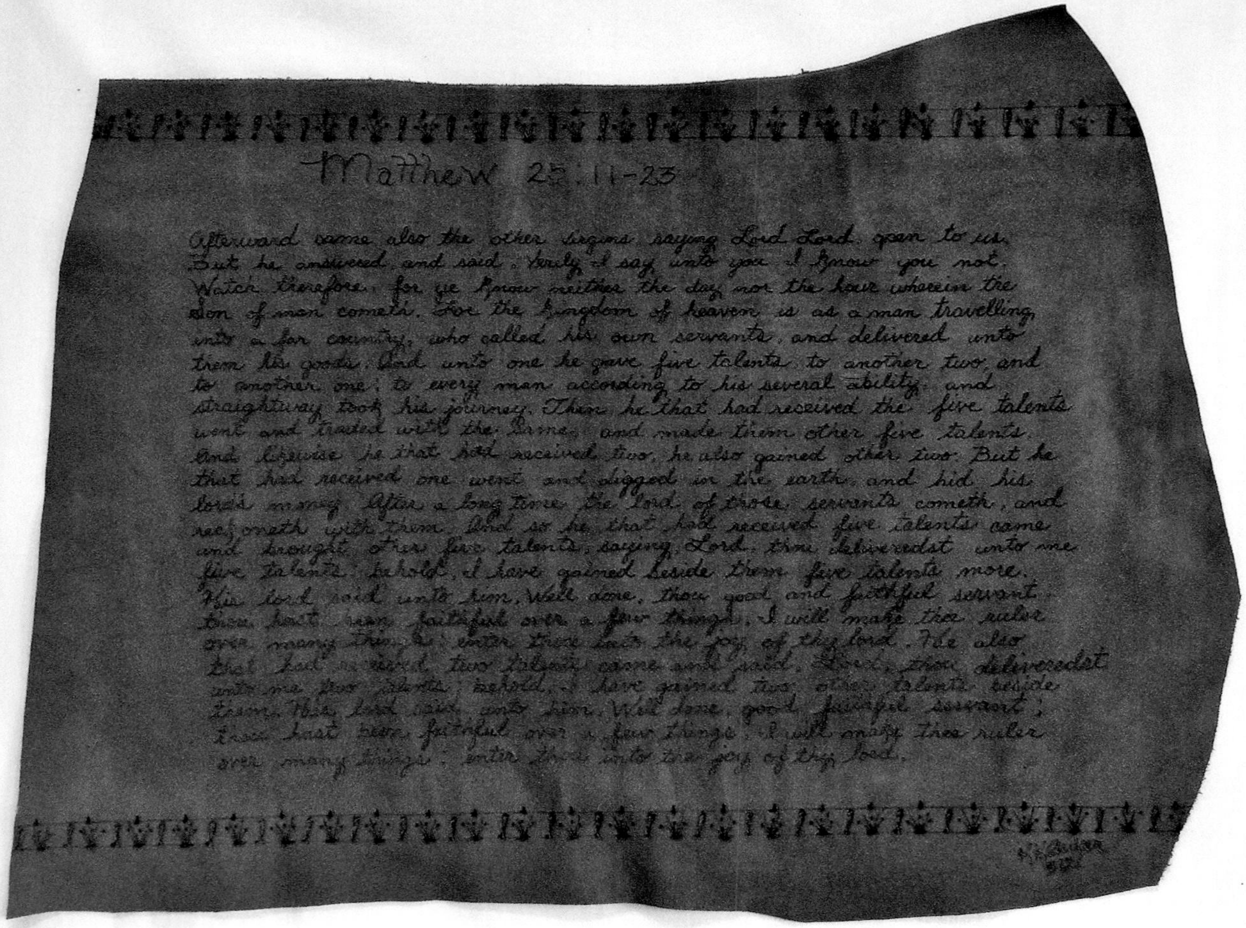

Matthew 25:11-23

Afterward came also the other virgins, saying Lord, Lord, open to us.
But he answered and said, Verily I say unto you, I know you not.
Watch therefore, for ye know neither the day nor the hour wherein the
Son of man cometh. For the kingdom of heaven is as a man travelling
into a far country, who called his own servants, and delivered unto
them his goods. And unto one he gave five talents, to another two, and
to another one; to every man according to his several ability; and
straightway took his journey. Then he that had received the five talents
went and traded with the same, and made them other five talents.
And likewise he that had received two, he also gained other two. But he
that had received one went and digged in the earth, and hid his
lord's money. After a long time the lord of those servants cometh, and
reckoneth with them. And so he that had received five talents came
and brought other five talents, saying, Lord, thou deliveredst unto me
five talents: behold, I have gained beside them five talents more.
His lord said unto him, Well done, thou good and faithful servant:
thou hast been faithful over a few things, I will make thee ruler
over many things: enter thou into the joy of thy lord. He also
that had received two talents came and said, Lord, thou deliveredst
unto me two talents: behold, I have gained two other talents beside
them. His lord said unto him, Well done, good faithful servant;
thou hast been faithful over a few things, I will make thee ruler
over many things: enter thou into the joy of thy lord.

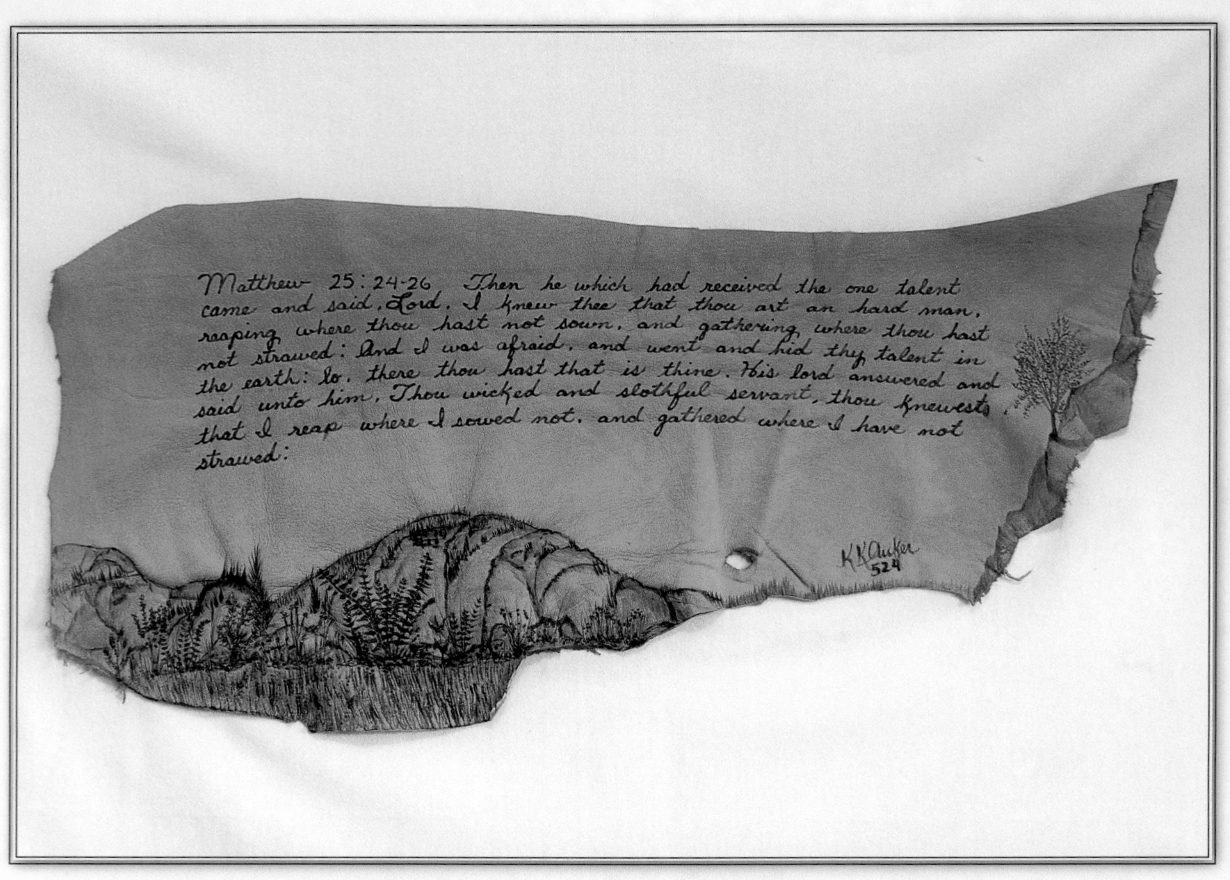
Matthew 25:24-26 Then he which had received the one talent
came and said, Lord, I knew thee that thou art an hard man,
reaping where thou hast not sown, and gathering where thou hast
not strawed: And I was afraid, and went and hid thy talent in
the earth: lo, there thou hast that is thine. His lord answered and
said unto him, Thou wicked and slothful servant, thou knewest
that I reap where I sowed not, and gathered where I have not
strawed:
K.K.Anker
524

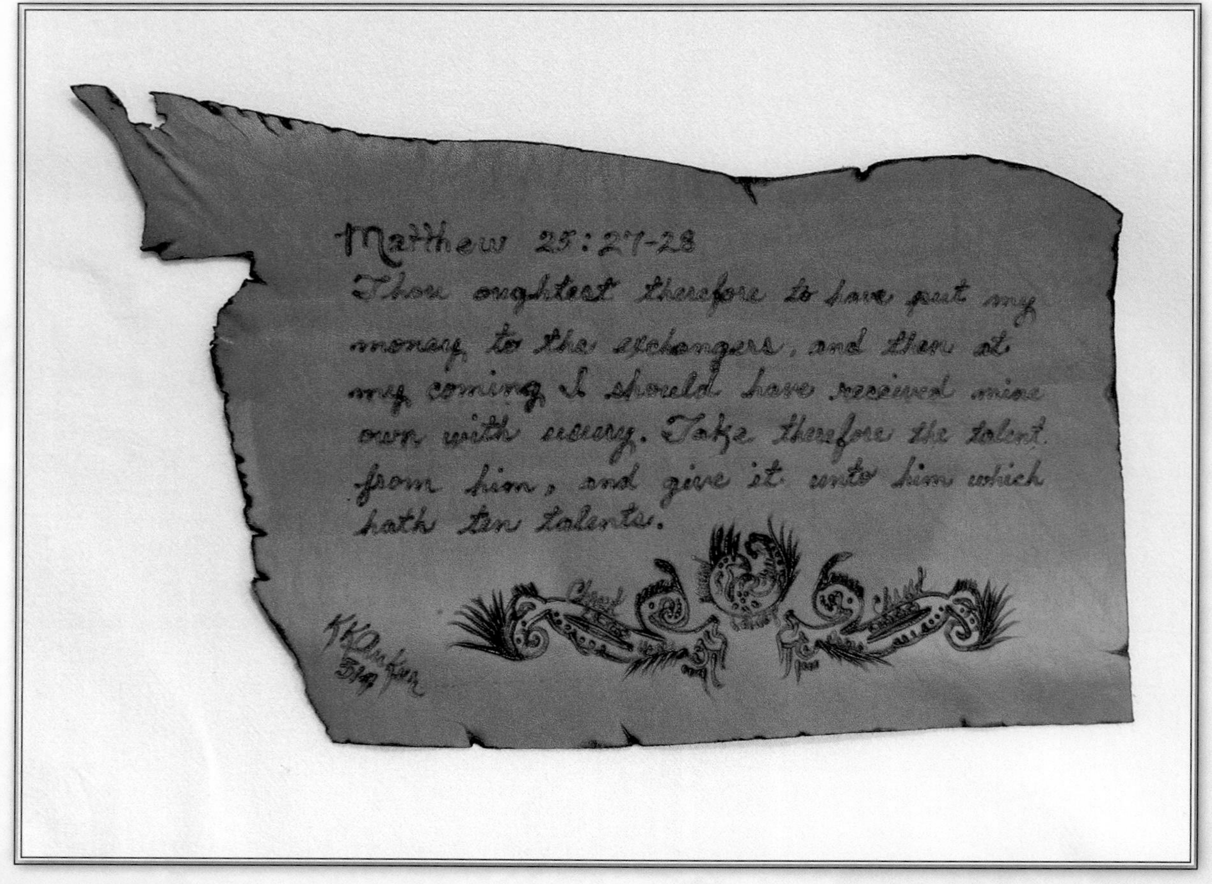
Matthew 25:27-28
Thou oughtest therefore to have put my
money to the exchangers, and then at
my coming I should have received mine
own with usury. Take therefore the talent
from him, and give it unto him which
hath ten talents.

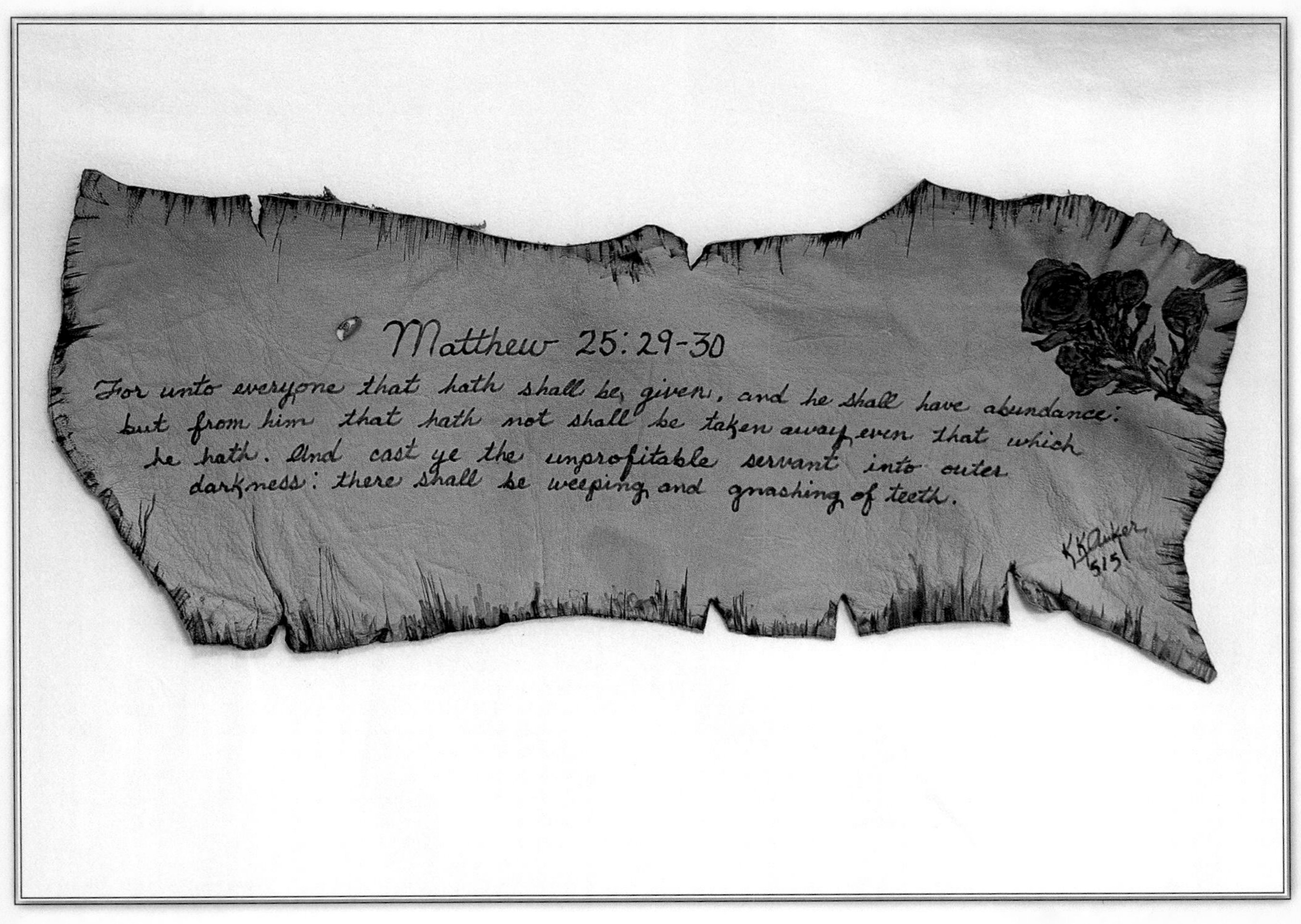
Matthew 25:29-30
For unto everyone that hath shall be given, and he shall have abundance:
but from him that hath not shall be taken away even that which
he hath. And cast ye the unprofitable servant into outer
darkness: there shall be weeping and gnashing of teeth.
515

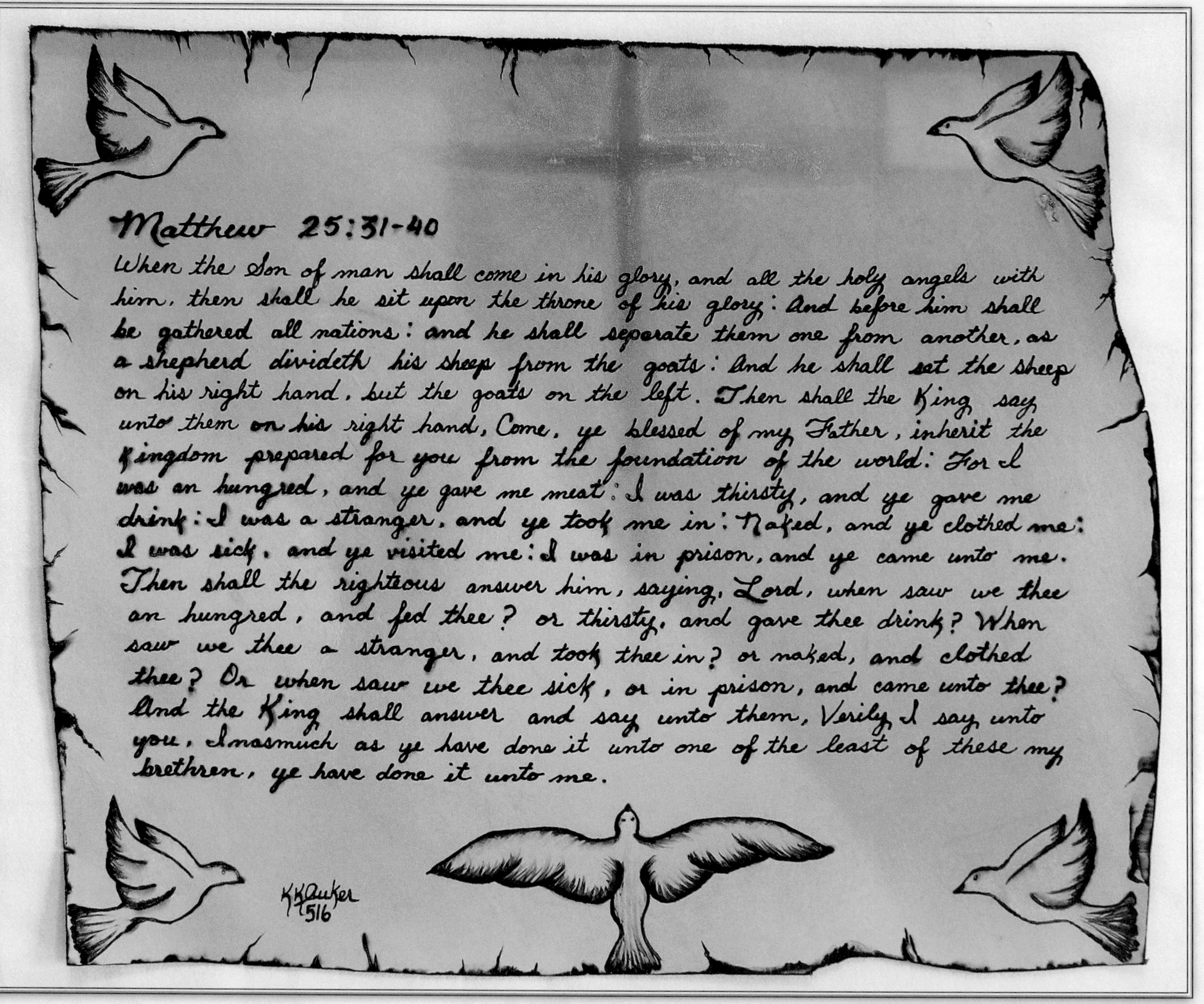

Matthew 25:31-40

When the Son of man shall come in his glory, and all the holy angels with
him, then shall he sit upon the throne of his glory: And before him shall
be gathered all nations: and he shall seperate them one from another, as
a shepherd divideth his sheep from the goats: And he shall set the sheep
on his right hand, but the goats on the left. Then shall the King say
unto them on his right hand, Come, ye blessed of my Father, inherit the
kingdom prepared for you from the foundation of the world: For I
was an hungred, and ye gave me meat: I was thirsty, and ye gave me
drink: I was a stranger, and ye took me in: Naked, and ye clothed me:
I was sick, and ye visited me: I was in prison, and ye came unto me.
Then shall the righteous answer him, saying, Lord, when saw we thee
an hungred, and fed thee? or thirsty, and gave thee drink? When
saw we thee a stranger, and took thee in? or naked, and clothed
thee? Or when saw we thee sick, or in prison, and came unto thee?
And the King shall answer and say unto them, Verily I say unto
you, Inasmuch as ye have done it unto one of the least of these my
brethren, ye have done it unto me.

KKAuker
516

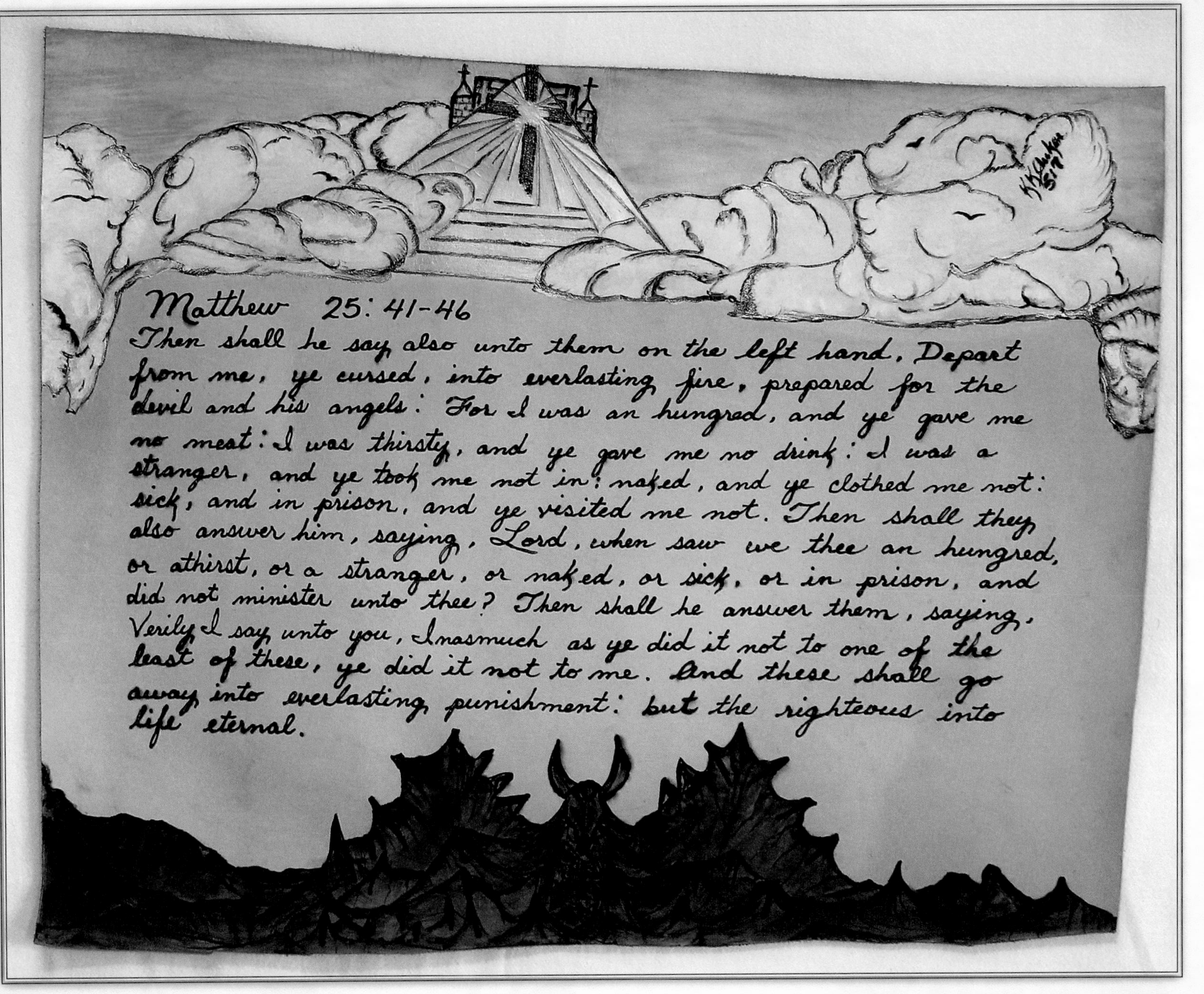
Matthew 25: 41-46
Then shall he say also unto them on the left hand, Depart
from me, ye cursed, into everlasting fire, prepared for the
devil and his angels: For I was an hungred, and ye gave me
no meat: I was thirsty, and ye gave me no drink: I was a
stranger, and ye took me not in: naked, and ye clothed me not:
sick, and in prison, and ye visited me not. Then shall they
also answer him, saying, Lord, when saw we thee an hungred,
or athirst, or a stranger, or naked, or sick, or in prison, and
did not minister unto thee? Then shall he answer them, saying,
Verily I say unto you, Inasmuch as ye did it not to one of the
least of these, ye did it not to me. And these shall go
away into everlasting punishment: but the righteous into
life eternal.

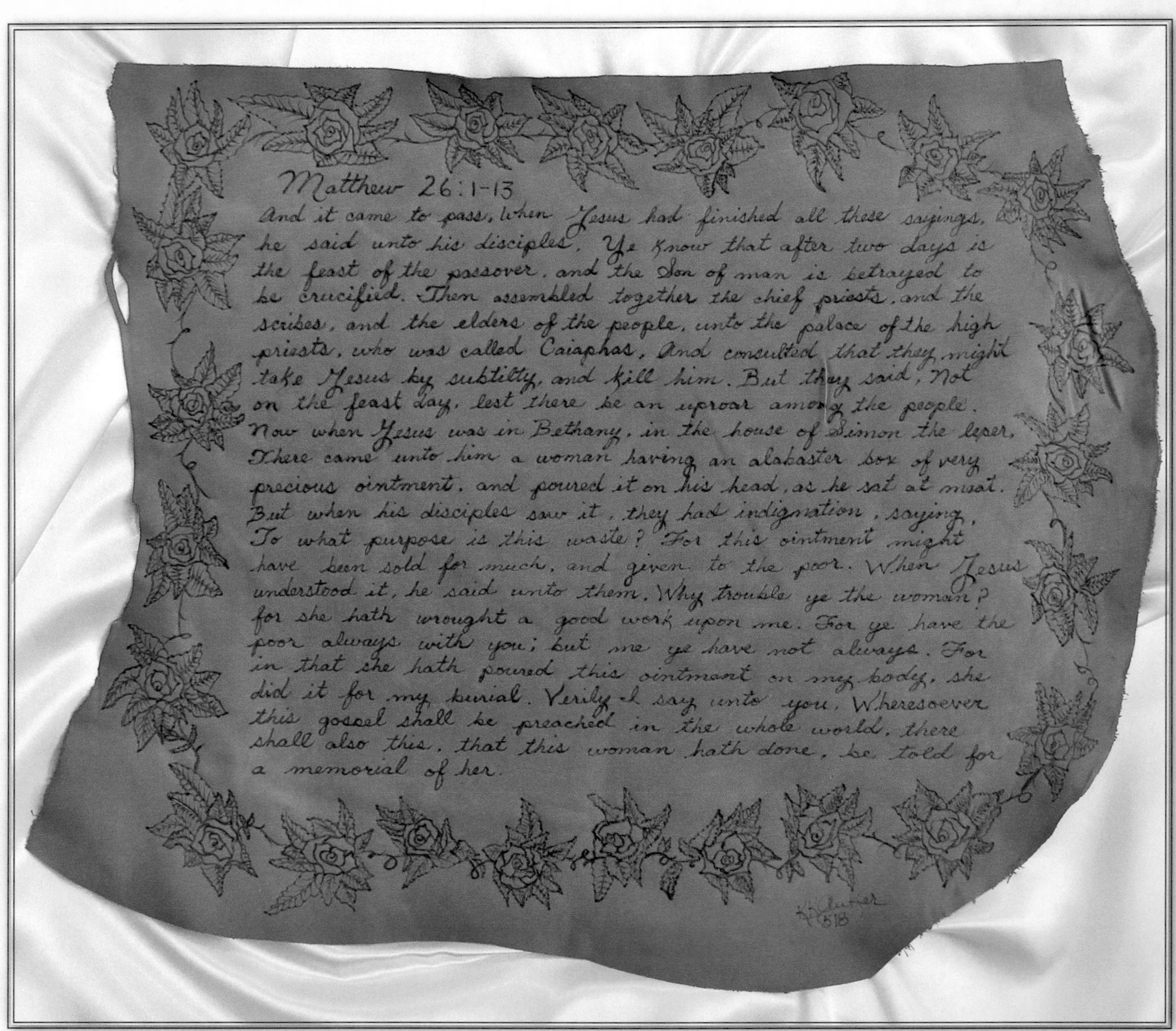
Matthew 26:1-13
And it came to pass, when Jesus had finished all these sayings,
he said unto his disciples, Ye know that after two days is
the feast of the passover, and the Son of man is betrayed to
be crucified. Then assembled together the chief priests, and the
scribes, and the elders of the people, unto the palace of the high
priests, who was called Caiaphas, And consulted that they might
take Jesus by subtilty, and kill him. But they said, Not
on the feast day, lest there be an uproar among the people.
Now when Jesus was in Bethany, in the house of Simon the leper,
There came unto him a woman having an alabaster box of very
precious ointment, and poured it on his head, as he sat at meat.
But when his disciples saw it, they had indignation, saying,
To what purpose is this waste? For this ointment might
have been sold for much, and given to the poor. When Jesus
understood it, he said unto them, Why trouble ye the woman?
for she hath wrought a good work upon me. For ye have the
poor always with you; but me ye have not always. For
in that she hath poured this ointment on my body, she
did it for my burial. Verily I say unto you, Wheresoever
this gospel shall be preached in the whole world, there
shall also this, that this woman hath done, be told for
a memorial of her.

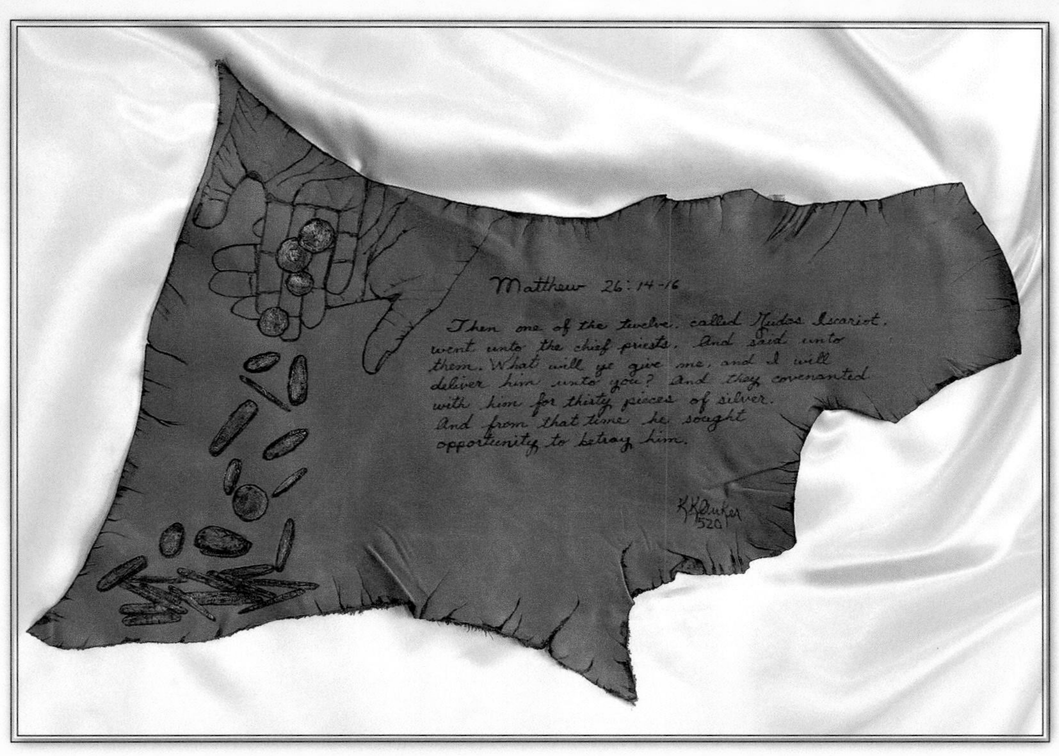
Matthew 26:14-16
Then one of the twelve, called Judas Iscariot,
went unto the chief priests, And said unto
them, What will ye give me, and I will
deliver him unto you? And they covenanted
with him for thirty pieces of silver.
And from that time he sought
opportunity to betray him.

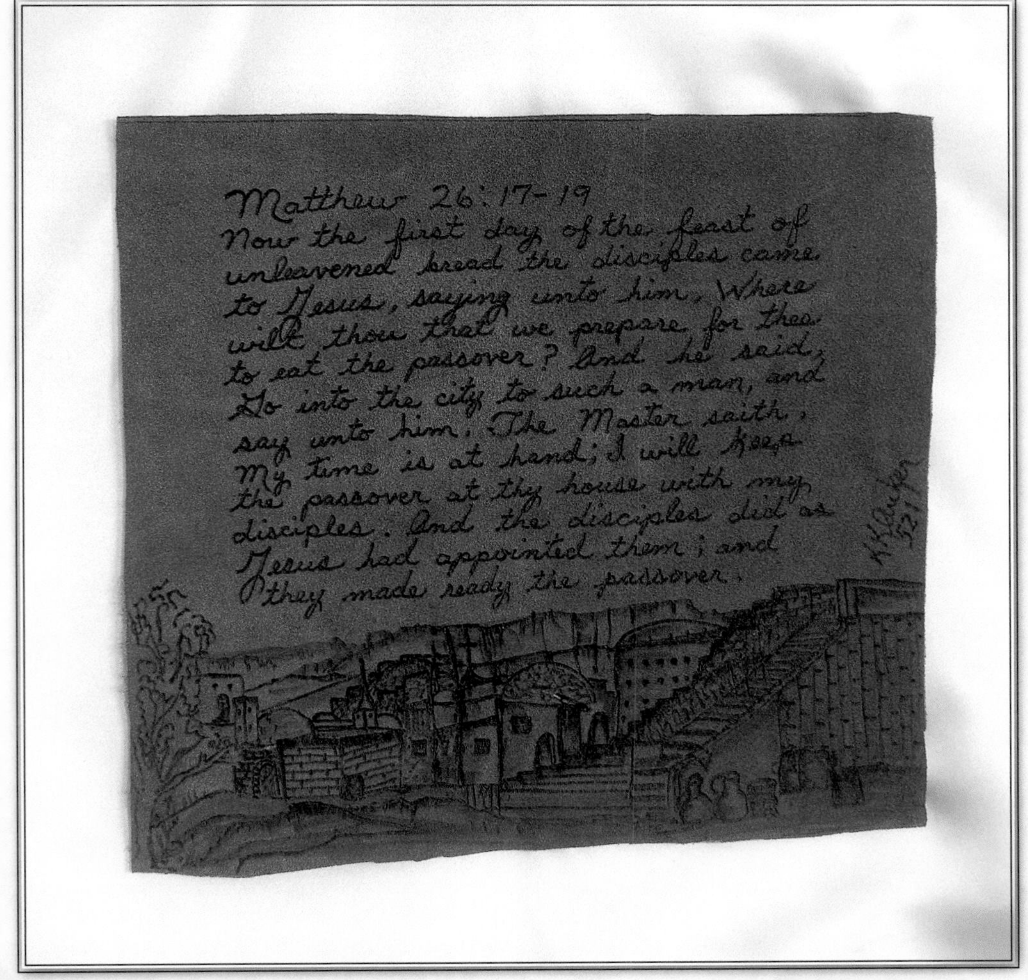
Matthew 26:17-19
Now the first day of the feast of
unleavened bread the disciples came
to Jesus, saying unto him, Where
wilt thou that we prepare for thee
to eat the passover? And he said,
Go into the city to such a man, and
say unto him, The Master saith,
My time is at hand; I will keep
the passover at thy house with my
disciples. And the disciples did as
Jesus had appointed them; and
they made ready the passover.

Matthew 26:20-29
Now when the even was come, he sat down with
the twelve. And as they did eat, he said, Verily, I
say unto you, that one of you shall betray me. And
they were exceeding sorrowful, and began every one of
them to say unto him, Lord is it I? And he answered
and said, He that dippeth his hand with me in the dish,
the same shall betray me. The Son of man goeth as it
is written of him: but woe unto that man by whom the
Son of man is betrayed! it had been good for that man
if he had not been born. Then Judas, which betrayed him,
answered and said, Master is it I? He said unto him, Thou hast
said. And as they were eating, Jesus took bread, and blessed it,
and break it, and gave it to the disciples, and said, Take eat;
this is my body. And he took the cup, and gave thanks,
and gave it to them, saying, Drink ye all of it; For this
is my blood of the new testament, which is shed for
many for the remission of sins. But I say unto you,
I will not drink henceforth of this fruit of the
vine, until that day when I drink it new
with you in my Fathers Kingdom.

Matthew 26:30-35
And when they had sung an hymn,
they went out into the mount
of Olives. Then saith Jesus unto
them, All ye shall be offended because of me this night: for it is
written, I will smite the shepherd, and
the sheep of the flock shall be scattered
abroad. But after I am risen again, I will
go before you into Galilee. Peter answered
and said unto him, Though all men shall
be offended because of thee, yet will I never
be offended. Jesus said unto him, Verily I
say unto thee, That this night, before the cock
crow, thou shalt deny me thrice. Peter said unto
him, Though I should die with thee, yet will I not
deny thee. Likewise also said all the disciples.
KK Aiken
523

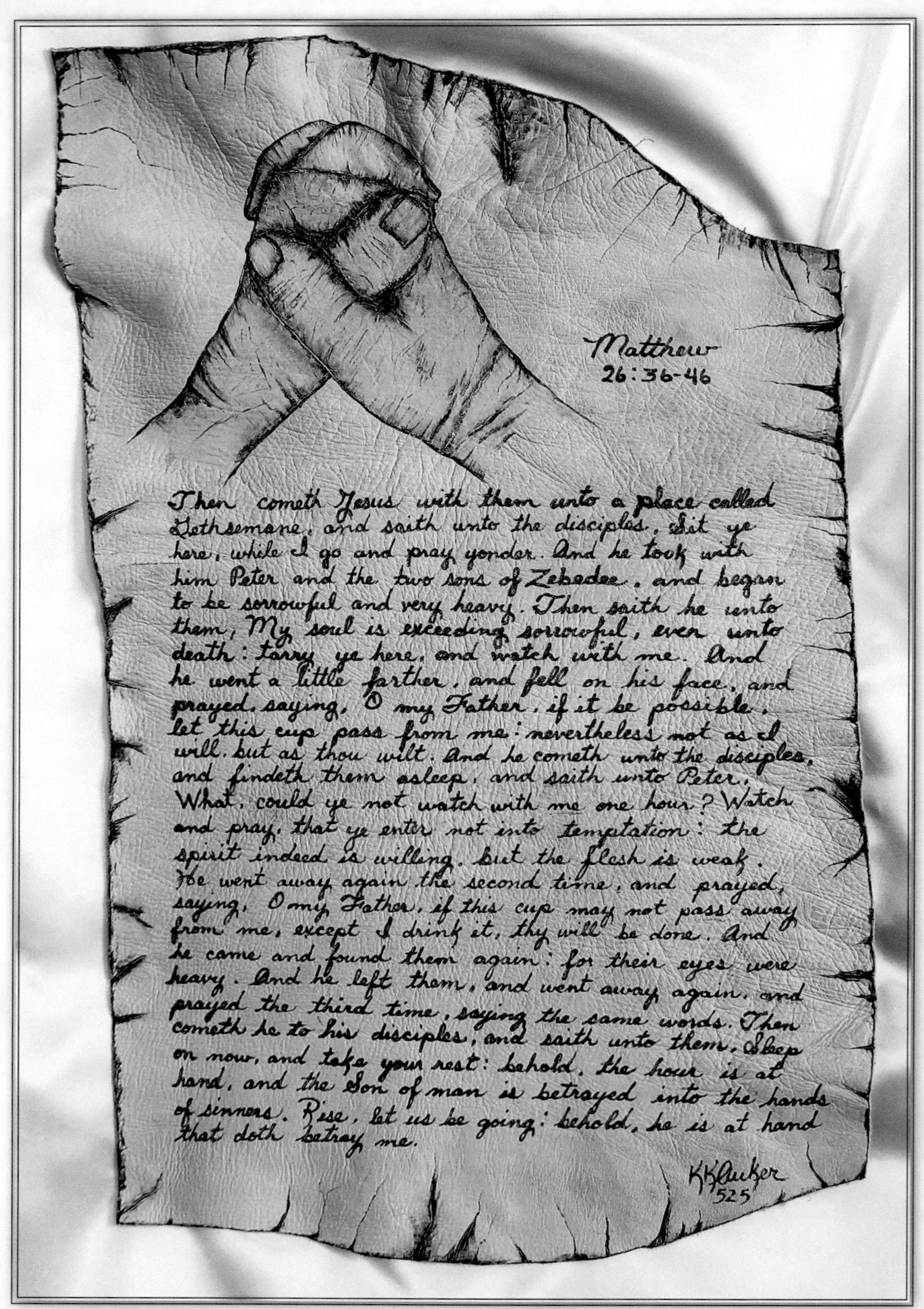
Matthew
26:36-46
Then cometh Jesus with them unto a place called
Gethsemane, and saith unto the disciples, Sit ye
here, while I go and pray yonder. And he took with
him Peter and the two sons of Zebedee, and began
to be sorrowful and very heavy. Then saith he unto
them, My soul is exceeding sorrowful, even unto
death: tarry ye here, and watch with me. And
he went a little farther, and fell on his face, and
prayed, saying, O my Father, if it be possible,
let this cup pass from me: nevertheless not as I
will, but as thou wilt. And he cometh unto the disciples,
and findeth them asleep, and saith unto Peter,
What, could ye not watch with me one hour? Watch
and pray, that ye enter not into temptation: the
spirit indeed is willing, but the flesh is weak.
He went away again the second time, and prayed,
saying, O my Father, if this cup may not pass away
from me, except I drink it, thy will be done. And
he came and found them again: for their eyes were
heavy. And he left them, and went away again, and
prayed the third time, saying the same words. Then
cometh he to his disciples, and saith unto them, Sleep
on now, and take your rest: behold, the hour is at
hand, and the Son of man is betrayed into the hands
of sinners. Rise, let us be going: behold, he is at hand
that doth betray me.

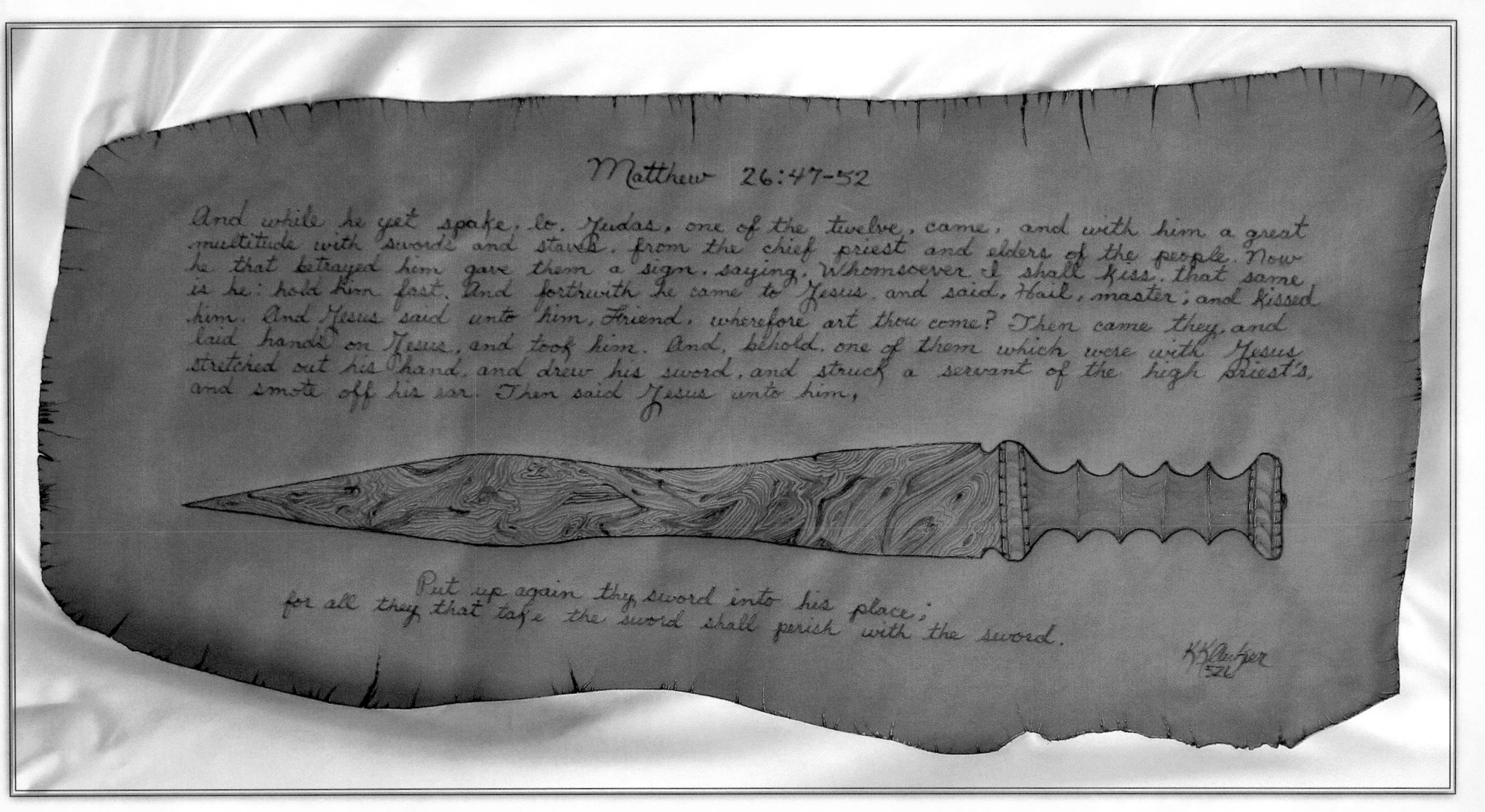
Matthew 26:47-52
And while he yet spake, lo, Judas, one of the twelve, came, and with him a great
multitude with swords and staves, from the chief priest and elders of the people. Now
he that betrayed him gave them a sign, saying, Whomsoever I shall kiss, that same
is he: hold him fast. And forthwith he came to Jesus, and said, Hail, master; and kissed
him. And Jesus said unto him, Friend, wherefore art thou come? Then came they, and
laid hands on Jesus, and took him. And, behold, one of them which were with Jesus
stretched out his hand, and drew his sword, and struck a servant of the high priest's,
and smote off his ear. Then said Jesus unto him,
Put up again thy sword into his place;
for all they that take the sword shall perish with the sword.

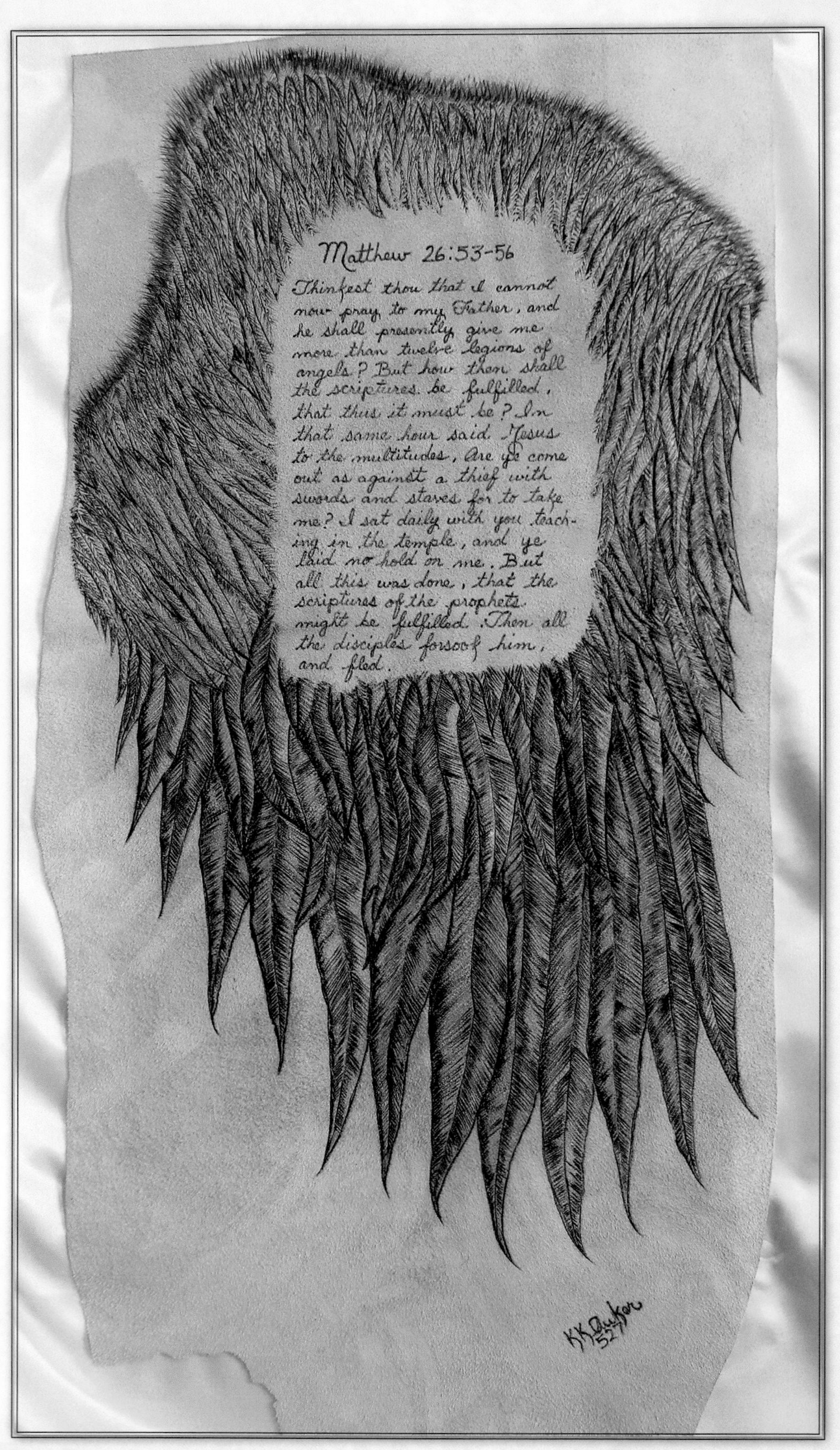
Matthew 26:53-56
Thinkest thou that I cannot
now pray to my Father, and
he shall presently give me
more than twelve legions of
angels? But how then shall
the scriptures be fulfilled,
that thus it must be? In
that same hour said Jesus
to the multitudes, Are ye come
out as against a thief with
swords and staves for to take
me? I sat daily with you teaching in the temple, and ye
laid no hold on me. But
all this was done, that the
scriptures of the prophets
might be fulfilled. Then all
the disciples forsook him,
and fled.

Matthew 26:57-64
And they that had
laid hold on Jesus led
him away to Caiaphas the
high priest, where the scribes
and the elders were assembled. But
Peter followed him afar off unto the
high priests palace, and went in,
and sat with the servants, to see the
end. Now the chief priests, and elders,
and all the council, sought false witness
against Jesus, to put him to death; But
found none: yea, though many false witnesses came,
yet found they none. At the last came two false
witnesses, And said, This fellow said, I am able to destroy
the temple of God, and build it in three days. And the high
priest arose, and said unto him, Answerest thou nothing? what is it which
these witness against thee? But Jesus held his peace. And the high priest
answered and said unto him, I adjure thee by the living God, that thou
tell us whether thou be the Christ, the Son of God. Jesus saith unto him,
Thou hast said: nevertheless I say unto you, Hereafter shall ye see the
Son of man sitting on the right hand of power, and coming in the
clouds of heaven.
KKAuker
528

Matthew 26:65-75

Then the high priest rent his clothes, saying, He hath spoken blasphemy; what further need have we of witnesses? behold, now ye have heard his blasphemy. What think ye? They answered and said, He is guilty of death. Then did they spit in his face, and buffeted him; and others smote him with the palms of their hands, Saying, Prophesy unto us, thou Christ, Who is he that smote thee? Now Peter sat without in the palace: and a damsel came unto him, saying, Thou also wast with Jesus of Galilee. But he denied before them all, saying, I know not what thou sayest. And when he was gone out into the porch, another maid saw him, and said unto them that were there, This fellow was also with Jesus of Nazareth. And again he denied with an oath, I do not know the man. And after a while came unto him they that stood by, and said to Peter, Surely thou also art one of them; for thy speech bewrayeth thee. Then began he to curse and to swear, saying, I know not the man. And immediately the cock crew. And Peter remembered the word of Jesus, which said unto him, Before the cock crow, thou shalt deny me thrice. And he went out, and wept bitterly.

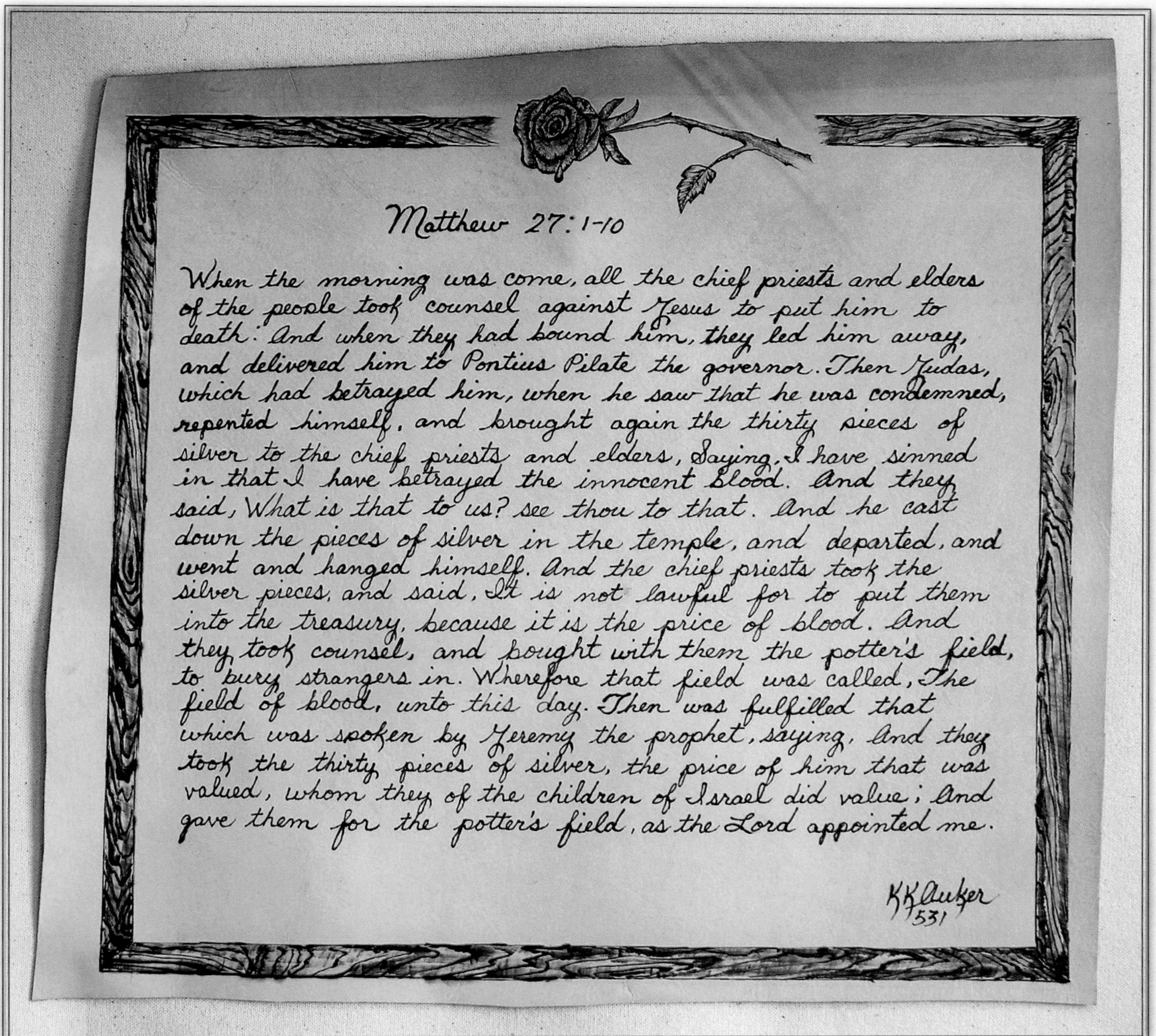
Matthew 27:1-10

When the morning was come, all the chief priests and elders of the people took counsel against Jesus to put him to death: And when they had bound him, they led him away, and delivered him to Pontius Pilate the governor. Then Judas, which had betrayed him, when he saw that he was condemned, repented himself, and brought again the thirty pieces of silver to the chief priests and elders, Saying, I have sinned in that I have betrayed the innocent blood. And they said, What is that to us? see thou to that. And he cast down the pieces of silver in the temple, and departed, and went and hanged himself. And the chief priests took the silver pieces, and said, It is not lawful for to put them into the treasury, because it is the price of blood. And they took counsel, and bought with them the potter's field, to bury strangers in. Wherefore that field was called, The field of blood, unto this day. Then was fulfilled that which was spoken by Jeremy the prophet, saying, And they took the thirty pieces of silver, the price of him that was valued, whom they of the children of Israel did value; And gave them for the potter's field, as the Lord appointed me.

K.K. Auker
531

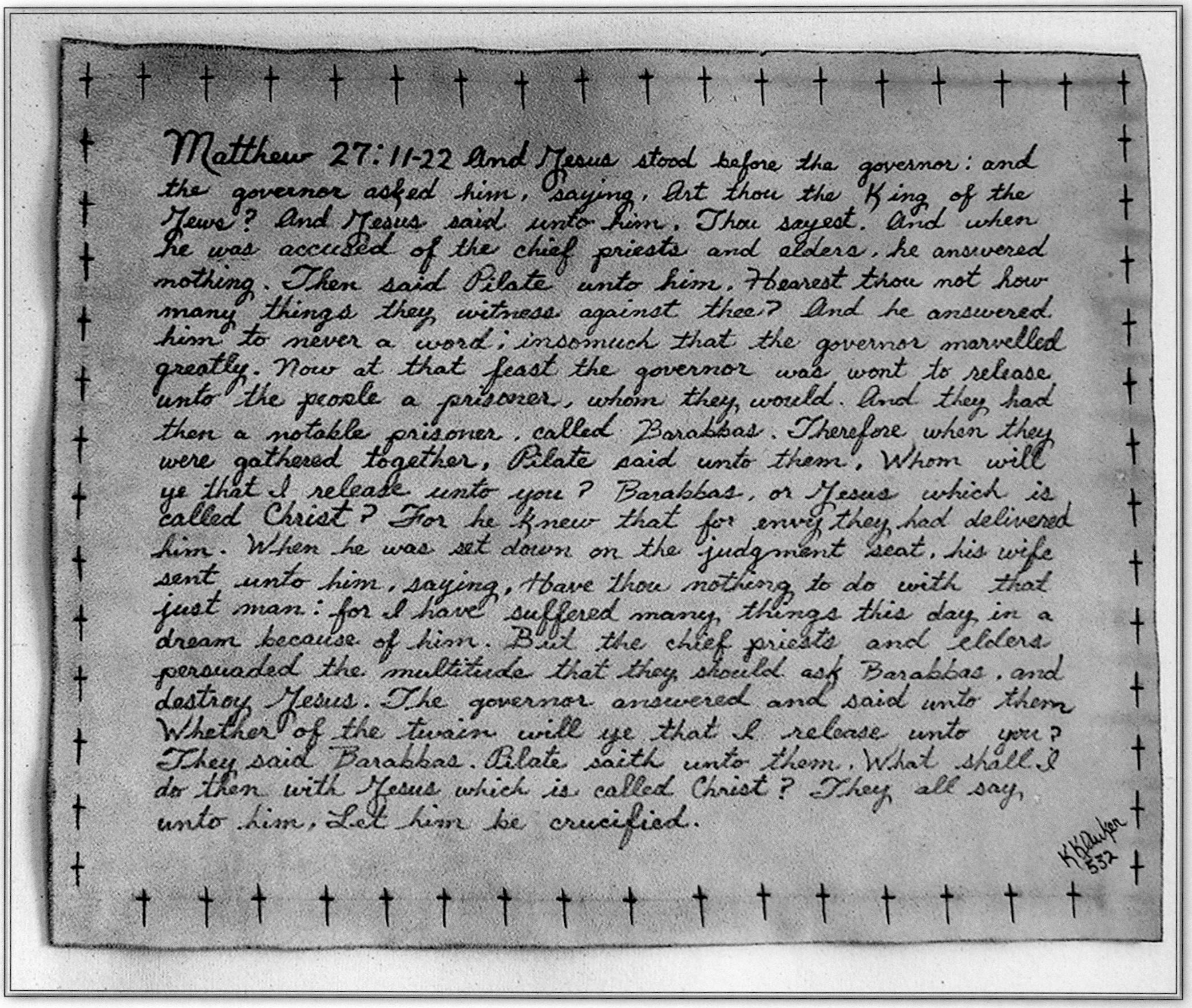
Matthew 27:11-22 And Jesus stood before the governor: and
the governor asked him, saying, Art thou the King of the
Jews? And Jesus said unto him, Thou sayest. And when
he was accused of the chief priests and elders, he answered
nothing. Then said Pilate unto him, Hearest thou not how
many things they witness against thee? And he answered
him to never a word; insomuch that the governor marvelled
greatly. Now at that feast the governor was wont to release
unto the people a prisoner, whom they would. And they had
then a notable prisoner, called Barabbas. Therefore when they
were gathered together, Pilate said unto them, Whom will
ye that I release unto you? Barabbas, or Jesus which is
called Christ? For he knew that for envy they had delivered
him. When he was set down on the judgment seat, his wife
sent unto him, saying, Have thou nothing to do with that
just man: for I have suffered many things this day in a
dream because of him. But the chief priests and elders
persuaded the multitude that they should ask Barabbas, and
destroy Jesus. The governor answered and said unto them
Whether of the twain will ye that I release unto you?
They said Barabbas. Pilate saith unto them, What shall I
do then with Jesus which is called Christ? They all say
unto him, Let him be crucified.
532

Matthew 27:23-66
This is Jesus the King of the Jews

Matthew 28:1-20
In the end of the sabbath, as it began to dawn
toward the first day of the week, came Mary Magdalene
and the other Mary to see the sepulchre. And, behold,
there was a great earthquake: for the angel of the
Lord descended from heaven, and came and rolled
back the stone from the door, and sat upon it. His
countenance was like lightening, and his raiment
white as snow: And for fear of him the keepers
did shake, and became as dead men. And the
angel answered and said unto the women, Fear
not ye: for I know that ye seek Jesus, which
was crucified. He is not here: for he is risen,
as he said. Come, see the place where the
Lord lay. And go quickly, and tell his disciples
that he is risen from the dead; and, behold,
he goeth before you into Galilee; there shall ye
see him: lo, I have told you. And they departed
quickly from the sepulchre with fear and great
joy; and did run to bring his disciples word.
And as they went to tell his disciples, behold,
Jesus met them, saying, All hail. And they
came and held him by the feet, and worshipped
him. Then said Jesus unto them, Be not afraid:
go tell my brethren that they go into Galilee,
and there shall they see me. Now when they
were going, behold, some of the watch came into
the city, and shewed unto the chief priests all the
things that were done. And when they were
assembled with the elders, and had taken counsel,
they gave large money unto the soldiers, Saying,
Say ye, His disciples came by night, and stole
him away while we slept. And if this come to
the governor's ears, we will persuade him, and
secure you. So they took the money, and did as
they were taught: and this saying is commonly
reported among the Jews until this day. Then
the eleven disciples went away into Galilee, into
a mountain where Jesus had appointed them.
And when they saw him, they worshipped him: but
some doubted. And Jesus came and spake unto them, saying,
All power is given unto me in heaven and in earth. Go ye therefore, and teach all nations, baptizing them in the
name of the Father, and of the Son, and of the Holy Ghost: Teaching them to observe all things whatsoever I have
commanded you: and, lo, I am with you alway, even unto the end of the world. Amen.